An Autumn Remembered

An Autumn Remembered

Bud Wilkinson's Legendary '56 Sooners

Gary T. King

Foreword by Barry Switzer

University of Oklahoma Press
Norman

Originally published as *An Autumn Remembered: The Legend of Bud Wilkinson's 1956 Sooners,* copyright © 1988 by Gary T. King. Revised edition published 2006 by the University of Oklahoma Press, Norman, Publishing Division of the University. All rights reserved. Manufactured in the U.S.A.

1 2 3 4 5 6 7 8 9 10

Library of Congress Cataloging-in-Publication Data
King, Gary T.
  An autumn remembered: Bud Wilkinson's Legendary '56 Sooners / by Gary King; foreword by Barry Switzer
      p. cm.
   Includes index.
   ISBN 0-8061-3786-X (pbk: alk. paper)
     1. University of Oklahoma—Football—History. 2. Oklahoma Sooners (Football team)—History. I. Title.

GV958.O4K5 2006
796.332'630976637—dc22
                                                    2005055946

Port Robertson (1956)

To the memory of Port Robertson, 1914–2003

Port was one of the biggest influences in all our lives.

—*Jimmy Harris*

Port's the one guy, along with Bud and Gomer, that I really had respect for. He was probably the best man of all that group.

—*Jerry Tubbs*

As a wrestler at the University of Oklahoma (OU), Port won Big Six Conference titles at 165 pounds in 1935 and 1937, earning All-American honors in 1935. He was the varsity wrestling coach at OU from 1947 to 1959 and again in 1962. He also coached the freshman football team from 1947 to 1961. Throughout all of his forty years of service at OU he was the sole scholastic guidance counselor overseeing the grades, class attendance, eligibility, and nightly study halls of three to four hundred student athletes, hiring and managing tutors, and maintaining liaison with faculty. And these were only a few of the duties he performed for the University of Oklahoma. No coach in the history of OU athletics was more respected by student-athletes than Port Robertson and that includes Bud Wilkinson.

Port Robertson did so much for so many for so long that his career at OU invites comparison with John 21:25: "And there are also many other things which Jesus did, the which if they should be written every one, I suppose that even all the world itself could not contain all the books that should be written."

One day there will surely be a book written about Port, and in this book (or books) there will be many stories about Port the coach, the counselor, the disciplinarian, and no doubt there will be this one.

The following is an excerpt from a eulogy for Port Robertson given by Ambassador (Ret.) Edwin Corr (one of Port's wrestlers in the mid-fifties), June 14, 2003.

Port the War Hero

When my brother Bert, others and I came to OU, we assumed that Port's flattened ear was from it having been cauliflowered on the mat. The first clue that there was more to that ear and to Port's life was when my wife's uncle, Wilson Everts, told me that Port had saved his and a number of other soldiers' lives at the Normandy invasion. In the confusion of battle, the landing craft let Port's unit off in deep water. With their heavy, wet 782 packs, and weapons, many fell to the bottom and could not get to their feet. Port went from man to man, lifting them and their gear up and heading them toward the beach.

About a month later the Germans counterattacked. As a forward artillery observer, Port remained in position, calling fire in on the enemy and on himself. Finally, a German round landed on or near him, slamming his radio into his ear and blowing him rotating into the air. He regained consciousness in a field hospital, and his mind did not stop spinning for a couple of years. It took will and determination to regain his balance and equilibrium. For the rest of his life, he sometimes had ringing in his ears. He was awarded the Purple Heart and the Bronze Star.

Wade Walker, an All-American tackle at OU in 1947 who later became the Sooners athletic director, told me that he once asked Port how it was that, in contrast to other people, Port never cursed or was ever profane. Port answered only, "Well, I made a deal with the Lord at Normandy, and I have tried to live up to that promise."

And I further dedicate this book to my mother, Dr. Charlyce King, professor emerita from the University of Oklahoma, who introduced me to many of these players when I was twelve years old.

Of course, there are those of us who grow out of sports. And there are others who are born with the wisdom to know that nothing lasts. These are the truly tough among us, the ones who can live without illusion, or without even the hope of illusion. I am not that grown up or up to date. I am a simple creature, tied to more primitive patterns and cycles, I need to think something lasts forever, and it might as well be that state of being that is a game; it might as well be that, in a green field in the sun.

—A. Bartlett Giamatti, former president of Yale University and former commissioner of Major League Baseball

CONTENTS

ACKNOWLEDGMENTS

Barry Switzer said many times, "Bud Wilkinson created this monster. I'm just feeding it." Now, seven decades after Wilkinson created the "monster" that is football at the University of Oklahoma, its care and feeding is in the capable hands of Bob Stoops, who has led the Sooners to a return to national prominence.

The OU tradition of football excellence began under the guidance of Wilkinson just after World War II, but Bud brought much more to the state of Oklahoma than just football victories. His winning teams and his winning personality helped to dispel the state's "Okie" image and drive away the dark dust-bowl clouds. No other football coach has meant so much to so many.

Wilkinson won national championships in 1950, 1955, and 1956. By far the best of these was the '56 squad. This was not just Bud's best team and not just OU's best team; it was the greatest team in the history of college football.

The year 2006 marks the fiftieth anniversary of this exceptional squad. To me, this seemed like a great opportunity to go back to the sources, conduct new interviews with the former players, and update and reprise *An Autumn Remembered,* which was first published in 1988. Fortunately, Charles Rankin, associate director /editor, of the University of Oklahoma Press, agreed, and the OU fans now have one final opportunity to relive this golden football autumn.

In addition to Mr. Rankin there are several other people I must acknowledge for their help in putting this book together. First, I must mention Volney Meece and Harold Keith. It would be impossible to write even a single paragraph about the University of Oklahoma's 1956 football team had it not been for the work of these two men. Volney Meece, sportswriter for the *Daily Oklahoman,* followed the Sooners through the '56 season. His lucid accounts of the games preserve this season forever.

Harold Keith was OU's sports information director (SID) for over forty years. He edited Bud Wilkinson's newsletters and wrote two excellent books on OU football, *Oklahoma Kickoff* and *Forty-Seven Straight.* Mr. Keith is to the position of SID, what Bud Wilkinson is to the position of football coach.

I never met Mr. Keith or Mr. Meece. I have only read their work. I grew up reading their articles, and I share their affection for this "Golden Era of OU Football." Although I am clearly not in their league as a writer, I hope this book can create some new fans for this "old" team.

Another person who must be cited is former OU president, Dr. George L. Cross, whose books, *Presidents Can't Punt* and *Blacks in White Colleges,* were very important to me in my research. I would also like to thank the former OU ticket manager Harold "Red" Reid for loaning me his collection of the Bud Wilkinson newsletters.

I am most grateful to the former coaches Bud Wilkinson and Port Robertson and to all the former players who graciously met with me to talk about this great season. This was the most enjoyable part of the whole process, talking to these former players, the very men who were my childhood heroes.

All of the above-mentioned gentlemen, Meece, Keith, Cross, Reid, Robertson, and Wilkinson, are now deceased, as are many of the players from that era. That is why it is so important for us to preserve an account of this great team for those who were born too late to remember this splendid autumn season.

I also want to thank Ms. Sally Pricer (who provided many of the pictures that appear in this book), Kirk Bjornsgaard of the University of Oklahoma Press, and my editor, Debbie Self. My wife, Pat, was my proofreader and also my chief photographer; many thanks to her as well.

I must warn the reader that this is a dull book. There is no sex, no drugs, and there are no murders. This is a story about a very simple uncomplicated game, college football, as it was played in a very simple uncomplicated time, the 1950s, and that is the whole point.

—Gary King, 2005

FOREWORD

I was fortunate to coach at an institution that has such great football tradition as the University of Oklahoma. I have learned a lot about the history of OU football since I first moved to Norman almost forty years ago. I know we had some great teams before World War II. Bennie Owen coached four undefeated squads in 1911, 1915, 1918, and 1920 and Tom Stidham's 1938 team (the first Sooner team to go to the Orange Bowl) may have been one of our best ever.

But, as I think most OU fans would acknowledge, it was Bud Wilkinson who built the University of Oklahoma into a national football power in the 1940s and 1950s. I was able to build on this tradition in the 1970s and 1980s. I am proud that I was able to carry on this tradition of football excellence. Now, the football fortunes at OU are in the capable hands of Coach Bob Stoops. Bud, Barry . . . and Bob. That sounds pretty good to me.

This book, *An Autumn Remembered: Bud Wilkinson's Legendary '56 Sooners,* tells the story of one of Wilkinson's greatest teams. Whether or not they were the greatest team in the history of college football or even OU's greatest team is really a moot point. It is meaningless to try to compare players and teams from different eras. I know Coach Stoops agrees with me on this point, and I'm sure that Coach Wilkinson would have as well.

However, I do believe that every Sooner football fan will enjoy reading this book. If you can remember sitting in Memorial Stadium and watching Tommy McDonald snag passes from Jimmy Harris and Billy Pricer opening big holes for Clendon Thomas to run through and Jerry Tubbs and Bob Harrison smashing ball carriers to the turf, then certainly you will enjoy reliving this memorable season once more. If you are too young to have seen the team in person, then I know you will definitely enjoy learning about them through the pages of this book. In fact, I do not think one has to be a football fan at all to appreciate *An Autumn Remembered.* The images and emotions evoked here and the inspiration that can be taken extend far beyond the boundaries of the gridiron.

Above all this is a story about a group of young men who grew up during the days of the Dust Bowl and the Great Depression. I know about this very well, because I am of the same era. I understand what it was like to grow up in a home that did not have electricity and indoor plumbing.

We "sons of the depression" wanted to go to college to make a better life for ourselves and for our children. We worked hard, studied hard, and (usually) graduated. It is almost incidental that many of us just happened to achieve great success in athletics as well . . . and the 1956 Sooners certainly did that.

—Barry Switzer

I live for autumn. All year long I have reveries of those cool beautiful days to come and memories of Octobers past.

—*John Nichols,* The Last Beautiful Days of Autumn

PROLOGUE

The ball soared high into the cool November night. It rose and rose until it escaped the dim lights of Memorial Stadium. The ball briefly disappeared as it flew above the lights, and then suddenly it was descending, rapidly, but not to me. Dwain would field this kickoff. Dwain caught the ball sure-handedly, and his muscular legs began to churn straight ahead.

I once tried to stop these same churning legs when I was a fifth grader playing for McKinley and Dwain was a sixth grader at Lincoln. We played that game on a barren, grassless playground, and we played hard. I thought Dwain was the hardest runner I ever tried to tackle. I expected ball carriers to try to dodge me, but Dwain lowered his head and plowed straight ahead. He truly punished our small defensive backs as he bulled out huge chunks of yardage, never breaking a long run, but gaining eight, ten, fifteen yards consistently.

➤

Today these legs were not slashing, darting, and trampling defensive backs. They were stilled. Dwain weighed less than one hundred pounds when the cancer finally made its way from the esophagus to the stomach, liver, lungs, and heart. The cancer had not so much eaten him up as it had starved him to death. As one of the honorary pallbearers, I was seated on the second row with our two former high school coaches: the sixty-year-old, six-foot, six-inch, three-hundred-pound Homer Simmons, our line coach, and Gene Corrotto, now sixty-nine years old, former head coach at Norman High School. Just in front of us sat the six pallbearers who wore white boutonnieres to distinguish them from the honorary pallbearers who wore red boutonnieres.

➤

Dwain ran straight ahead a few yards and then veered to the right to follow his blockers as the play had been designed. As one of the potential return men, I had no specific blocking assignment. If I did not catch the ball myself on these returns, I was to lead the ball carrier and block whomever I could. I was some ten yards ahead of Dwain when he caught the ball. As I turned up field I could see the play developing ahead of us. Corrotto and Simmons designed these kickoff returns with great care; they were thoughtful, meticulous coaches, not the rah! rah! "kick their asses" type. This particular return called for our end and our fullback to double team the first man in from the sideline on the right side of the field.

The Lawton end rushed down the field. As he passed the first wave of blockers unimpeded, he was probably thinking he could make the tackle himself.

Now our return was set up. I can mentally replay this run an infinite number of times. I can stop my mental projector and isolate on any part of this play. I can slow the film down, speed it up, or run it backward. When a seventeen-year-old is pumped up on natural adrenaline and his synapses are firing as they never will again, the effect is to slow down and expand time. Reflexes are so sharp that plays seem to develop in slow motion. Each play seems to last several minutes, and a forty-eight-minute game is an eternity.

Ken Foss and Kerry Lambeth timed the Lawton end's pursuit precisely. Foss and Lambeth were a perfect team on this block. Foss's right shoulder was adjacent to Lambeth's left shoulder as they ran stride for stride and downhill. (Before they tore up the greatest natural grass in the history of football to install Astroturf, Owen Field had a severe slope to allow for drainage. If you were running from the middle of the field to the sideline, you would actually be running downhill.) Foss and Lambeth pinned the Lawton boy between their helmets in perfect synchronization. The very best figure skaters are not better coordinated in their movements than these two young high school athletes, one black, one white, were on this particular play. Foss, the white player, and Lambeth, the black, drove this boy literally off the field. The Lawton end was erased, blown away! The crowd did not so much cheer and applaud, as they seemed to gasp at this incredibly perfect block.

>

Foss and Lambeth were not among those of us who sat staring at the coffin containing Dwain's thirty-seven-year-old body. In fact, there were not many people in the funeral home on this day. Other than the pallbearers in front of me, there were only a few of our classmates, probably fewer than ten. Other than Corrotto and Simmons, the only one of Dwain's teachers to attend was also a football coach, our junior high coach, Dale Ernst. I am sure Corrotto and Simmons had attended more services of this type than all the algebra teachers and English teachers put together. As soon as they heard Dwain had died, they went independently to visit his parents, something I regrettably could not bring myself to do.

I listened, or more precisely did not listen, as the minister chosen for this service spoke words that had no meaning for me: "sound and fury signifying nothing." This minister had never seen Dwain, who had not lived in Norman since he graduated from the University of Oklahoma as a Phi Beta Kappa. Dwain had been a pharmacist for the public health service in Bethesda, Maryland, for the last fifteen years. I had not seen Dwain for about seven years myself, and I had probably seen him a total of three times since he had moved to Maryland. But he had been my best friend. Like Sonny and Duane in *The Last Picture Show,* we made our almost obligatory rite of passage together to "Boys Town" in Nuevo Larado, Mexico, after my high school graduation. We drank beer together and shot snooker together for hours on end at the Campus Sport Shop, which no longer exists. I always assumed Dwain would one day move back to Norman, work in a drugstore, or open his own store, and we would go out and play golf. We could simply resume where we left off as adolescent boys and continue our games.

➤

When I saw the block of Foss and Lambeth, I knew, somehow, this would be no routine play. I geared myself for my role as a blocker and raced up field. Dwain was following close behind. Our blockers had the Lawton team sealed off to the inside. For a moment it looked like clear sailing up the sideline, but suddenly three Lawton boys escaped our blockers and stood directly in our path. These players were to present no problem, however. They were knocked over like so many bowling pins by our three-hundred-pound middle guard Randy King. Randy was incredibly fast for a person of his bulk, and he was going downhill as he propelled his massive body through the air. The Lawton players were helpless. It looked like the stadium had caved in on them. This time the crowd did roar. It was the same primal, bestial roar that emanates from stadia everywhere when a particularly vicious block or tackle has maimed or crippled someone.

➤

Randy was not at Dwain's funeral either. As I looked at the row of pallbearers in front of me, I was sure we had to be thinking the same thoughts. These six men in front of me were all classmates of Dwain's, all graduated one year ahead of me. They were all thirty-seven years old. All but one had been a member of our team that night when Dwain made his return. Now a couple were CPAs, one a mail carrier, one a municipal functionary, one an independent oil speculator, and one already a former head coach at Norman High School. He was the second of my teammates who had failed to succeed Corrotto, which was understandable, even predictable. I am sure we were all thinking, "Why was Dwain in that casket instead of another one of us?" Cancer of the esophagus is supposed to strike old people who drink and smoke to excess. Three months before his death Dwain had been running five miles a day and training for his black belt in karate.

➤

There was now only one man between me and Dwain and the goal line. This was the Lawton safety, a quick, wiry boy and a smart player. I knew he was not going to try to make the play himself. He would try to slow us down and wait for the pursuit to overtake Dwain. I lunged at him, but did not leave my feet. He grabbed my shoulder pads and tried to throw me aside, but I was inspired by the two great blocks I had just seen. I kept my legs churning and kept my balance. I did not knock the man off his feet, but I tied him up long enough for Dwain to cut back and run the remaining forty yards or so and score.

➤

My five former teammates now seated in front of me had been on the field during that run, throwing their blocks for Dwain, walling off the Lawton players. Now we sat silently listening to the hymns, organ music, prayers, and eulogy. I knew about the midlife crisis of the late thirties and early forties, when you usually experience your first emotional awareness of death. An intellectual awareness of death implies that you know other people will die; an emotional awareness of death implies that you know you will die. This emotional awareness of death strikes most people around forty, when a close friend dies, someone their own age. Sometimes during this period of you life you begin to measure time not in terms of how long you have lived but rather in terms of how much time you have left. When I try to explain this concept to my college psychology classes, the eighteen- and nineteen-year-olds chew gum, dip Skoal, and look out the window. The forty-and-over students nod their silent affirmation.

We were trailing Lawton 7–6 before Dwain returned that second-half kickoff ninety-five yards for a touchdown. Dwain scored two more touchdowns that night and Lawton did not score again. Dwain's return and the two magnificent blocks had inspired us to play at a level that we had never before achieved. I often wonder whether any of us ever reached such a level in any endeavor again. We defeated our conference rival that night by a score of thirty-something to seven, and a few weeks later we won the state championship.

>

After the graveside services, I met with three of our former players and our two coaches at a local restaurant for drinks and conversation. Someone recalled that it had been twenty years since we had won our championship. Dwain's death, ironically, brought us together for this reunion. I had not seen some of these men since high school, and I probably would never see some of them again. Our mood was surprisingly not downcast as we engaged in this male-bonding ritual. The conversation turned to the OU–Southern Cal game that was to be played later that autumn day. Corrotto and Simmons had been great players at OU. Gene Corrotto was the captain of the 1938 OU team that was undefeated through the regular season and that allowed its opponents a total of only twelve points (as in two touchdowns) all year before losing to General Robert Neyland's Tennessee Volunteers, in the Orange Bowl. Homer Simmons had starred at OU from 1941 to 1943 and had survived the Marine Corps and the invasion of Saipan to play professionally for the Philadelphia Eagles.

Corrotto thought that the OU secondary seemed to be unsure of what they were supposed to be doing, and Simmons said their linebackers were dropping too deep on pass coverage. These observations proved to be prophetic as the University of Southern California (USC) exploited these very weaknesses, completing passes in front of the OU linebackers, and if the OU defensive backs came up to play the run, the Southern Cal quarterback would lob the ball over their heads for a huge gain. USC won the game on a last-second third-down pass.

On September 26, 1953, Bud Wilkinson's Sooners were beaten

by Notre Dame. I was eight years old. OU did not lose again until November 16, 1957, at which time I was one week away from my thirteenth birthday. These are the years (eight to thirteen) that psychologists call the latency stage of development. It is the time of life when a person selects the role models appropriate to his/her gender. In other words, it is the time of life when our heroes are chosen.

Young boys like Dwain and me naturally would want to identify with strong, masculine young men who are winners, and their coach, Bud Wilkinson, was a classic father figure. "The Great White Father," he was called, because of his prematurely gray hair.

It was not just prepubescent boys who were caught up in the mystical spell of Wilkinson's Sooners. It was also middle-aged men who would faithfully attend all the games; it was the elderly women who never went to the games but would never miss a radio broadcast. On game days in Norman, everything stopped for almost three hours as these autumn rituals were enacted. Bits and pieces of the football broadcasts filtered through the open windows and the doorways of homes and shops along the ghostly streets of Norman on game day.

One season shines above all others in this Arthurian era that was Norman, Oklahoma, in the 1950s. The autumn of 1956 is the best remembered by all Sooner fans who are old enough to recall the exploits of Tubbs, McDonald, Harris, Pricer, Gray, and others. It is the best remembered by the professors at the University of Oklahoma who knew these young men as students and as athletes. It was the season in which the Wilkinson philosophy of football and a tremendous group of athletes combined to produce the most dominant team in the history of college football.

Autumn comes with cool invigorating air bringing football games and the World Series. Of these two sports, it is baseball that is most frequently used as a metaphor in literature. In Mark Harris's tremendous novel, *Bang the Drum Slowly,* the baseball season is a metaphor for the life of Bruce Pearson, a third-string catcher who dies of Hodgkin's disease. The great baseball writer Roger Angel had a short essay on how baseball, alone among American sports, because it has no externally imposed time limit, has the ability to cheat time, to make time stand still. One merely has to keep batting: theoretically a team could bat forever, stopping time. Angel wrote, "Since baseball time is measured in outs, all you have to do is succeed, literally; keep hitting, keep the rally alive, and you have defeated time. You remain young forever." Bernard Malamud in *The Natural* employs the metaphor of a baseball player defeating time brilliantly. But it is precisely for this reason that football may be the truer metaphor for life, albeit less poetic, because we cannot really stop time. Our allotted days fall away just as the minutes and seconds disappear from the football clock. Football is perhaps truer to life in another sense, because in baseball the winner is always decided. In (NFL) football this is not true. A game may end in a tie. Then what is to be concluded? Dwain's score card read: thirty-seven years, a high IQ, one wife, two children, and not very much money.

In autumn, students alive with youthful energy and expectations for their futures return to college campuses. Campuses are beautiful in autumn with their ochre shades of red, brown, and orange— sensual, exciting earth tones. If, as T. S. Elliot said, "April is the cruelest month," then surely October is the most beautiful. In the autumn of 1956 a unique group of men returned to the campus of the University of Oklahoma. These men were born in the 1930s, in the heart of the Great Depression. As young boys, they perhaps saw their fathers or older brothers leave home to fight in World War II. These men lived their childhood in days of sacrifice. The goals and values of the class of '57 were molded during a time vastly different from the present television and high-technology era. Nineteen fifty-six, however, was a time of relative calm. The junior senator from Wisconsin, Joe McCarthy, had been formally censured two years previously. World War II and Korea were over. America was nearly ten years away from Vietnam and about five years away from the major civil rights demonstrations that disturbed our social consciousness and shook our values during the turbulent sixties. Ike was in the White House—or on the golf course.

These men, particularly these seniors, who returned to the University of Oklahoma in 1956, played the game of college football better than it has ever been played before or since. This senior class was all victorious during their years of college eligibility. They played thirty-one games, winning all thirty-one. The seasons of '54–'56 formed the heart and soul of OU's forty-seven-game consecutive winning streak.

The '56 Sooners are to college football what the '27 Yankees are to baseball. The Sooners fashioned their own version of "Murderer's Row" with victories of 45–0 over Texas, 40–0 over Notre Dame, 67–14 over Missouri, 54–6 over Nebraska, and 53–0 over (then) Oklahoma A&M.

In '56 the Sooners also established a new collegiate record of 391 rushing yards per game. They set the record for the most first downs (222) in a single season. This team also led the nation in scoring with 466 points. The Sooners scored fifty-one touchdowns by rushing. In only one game did they fail to score more than four touchdowns. They led the nation in total offense that year, and they established two school records that stood until OU began playing eleven-, twelve-, thirteen-, and even fourteen-game seasons: most yards gained by returning intercepted passes (423), and most touchdowns (70). Their record of 46.6 points per game is still the best in Sooner history.

The '56 Sooners had not only a great offense, but they were second nationally in total defense also, allowing their opponents only 193.8 yards per game. They recorded six shutouts and allowed only fifty-one points to be scored against them all year, the second-lowest point total allowed by a team that year.

The combination of the best offense and second best defense in the nation, along with their third consecutive undefeated season, made the Sooners the overwhelming choice as national champions in 1956 for the second straight year.

In terms of individual honors, the Sooners could boast of

center Jerry Tubbs, who won the Walter Camp Memorial Trophy given by *Collier's* magazine to the outstanding player in the nation. Halfback Tommy McDonald won the Robert W. Maxwell Trophy given to the outstanding player in the nation. Halfbacks Clendon Thomas and McDonald finished first and fourth, respectively, in individual scoring. Eleven members of this team went on to play a total of fifty-nine years in the NFL, and six of these made All-Pro teams. Five members of this team became consensus All-Americans: Tubbs and McDonald in '56, Thomas and guard Bill Krisher in '57, and Bob Harrison (in '56 the alternate-team center) in '58. Wilkinson, Tubbs, and McDonald are members of the College Football Hall of Fame, and McDonald is enshrined in the National Football League Hall of Fame.

➤

In the years that have passed since Dwain's death, I have tried to understand why his kickoff return is so vivid to me and why my memories of him are so ineluctably tied to football imagery. I wondered why football had become such a pervasive force in my life and in the lives of my old teammates who served as Dwain's pallbearers.

The answers to these questions are, I believe, to be found in autumns long past, in the days when Dwain and I were ten, eleven, and twelve years old, pulling our football pads over skinned knees with sore and swollen hands. If you grew up in the shadow of Memorial Stadium in the fifties when Bud Wilkinson was winning every week, football can capture your boyhood dreams. What you do not realize as a young boy is that this captor may never release you. When you are a young boy watching your heroes, you still have your dreams. For a twelve-year-old, anything is possible. You can be a Sooner and play for Wilkinson. You can catch the pass that wins the game. This is, of course, the difference between the boy and the man. As a man you have outgrown your dreams and you are left with memories.

➤

Our little reunion of Dwain's pallbearers broke up in time for us to return to our respective homes and watch the OU–Southern Cal game on TV. We were all compelled to watch.

Driving home, I thought about how today's game between USC and OU would be so vastly different from the games Dwain and I had known as kids. He and I watched Bud Wilkinson win national championships with one-hundred-and-ninety-pound guards. Today's players are bigger, faster, and stronger. The pre-eminence of the black athlete has altered the game dramatically.

As I settled down to watch the game, I thought of the old homily that coaches across the Southwest had used for years to inspire their players. This is the story about the third stringer who begs the coach to let him play in the "big game." The coach is, of course, reluctant, but finally relents and puts the kid in the game. The boy makes every tackle, intercepts passes, scores touchdowns, and single-handedly wins the game for his team. After the game the coach asks the boy how he was able to play so well when he had never shown such ability before. The boy replies, "Coach, my father died yesterday. He was blind all his life and this was his first chance to see me play."

Dwain and I watched with great enthusiasm as our heroes crushed their opponents in the autumn of 1956. I wondered if Dwain could see the OU–USC game today, as we watched the Sooners so many, many years ago.

The autumn of '56 was a season in the sun for these great athletes. This is the way they remembered it.

An Autumn Remembered

He was God.

—*David Baker, Sooner halfback/quarterback '56–'58*

Bud Wilkinson

St. Louis, Missouri, Wednesday, March 26, 1986

Bud Wilkinson had presence—a commanding physical presence that put others in awe of him. This was true when he was coaching at Oklahoma in the fifties, and it was still true thirty years later when he was in his early seventies.

Wilkinson's coaching career was behind him: he would never again lead a team into competition. No longer would young men be guided and molded by the Wilkinson philosophy. His hair was whiter and thinner than it was in 1956 when *Sports Illustrated* said he displayed the "handsomest profile in football" and *Look* called him the "Golden Man of the Gridiron." William Furlong in the *New York Times* magazine referred to Wilkinson as "a fleshy apotheosis, a tall, dimpled, somewhat cerebral individual of forty-two with outrageously good looks and an almost maddeningly flawless personality." In 1986, Wilkinson, still a handsome man, had retained the stature, the vital health, and the unmistakable physique of an athlete. He was still as impeccably dressed as a *Gentlemen's Quarterly* model, and his light-blue eyes seemed every bit as bright and alert as they did in 1956.

Outside his twelfth-floor office, which afforded a view of the Mississippi River and the majestic St. Louis Arch, a cold early spring rain beat down. Wilkinson removed his London Fog overcoat. Underneath the overcoat he was wearing a hound's-tooth jacket, gray slacks, and a blue-and-maroon-striped tie.

His office, like the man himself, was neat, organized . . . "maddeningly flawless." Displayed around his office were pictures of Wilkinson with John F. Kennedy, Dwight Eisenhower, Henry Kissinger, and Bob Hope. Behind his desk hung a plaque commemorative of the Amos Alonzo Stagg Award, which was presented to him in 1984 by the American Football Coaches Association (AFCA). The Stagg Award is given "in recognition of outstanding service in the advancement of the best interest of football."

The AFCA president Dave Maurer said, "My problem is limiting reasons why we present our most prestigious award to Bud Wilkinson. There simply is not enough time to cite all this man's contributions to football and to America." He was right. Charles Burnham ("Bud") Wilkinson has won virtually every honor and award there is to win in football. As an All-American at the University of Minnesota, he played on two national championship teams, '34 and '36. At the University of Oklahoma, he coached three teams that won national titles in '50, '55, and '56. He is a member of the College Football Hall of Fame. In 1949, he was named "Coach of the Year" by the American Football Coaches Association.

In his acceptance speech for the Stagg Award, Wilkinson said, "I would like to share one thought with you that has increased in meaning for me over the years. When I was an athlete and a coach, we talked a great deal about the 'will to win.' It's obviously a very basic thing.

"But as time has passed, I have had recognition of a much more basic quality that's called the 'will to prepare.'

"It's not too hard to get the best effort when people are in the stands. The bands are playing, and the cheers are there. But at 6:30 in the morning on the fifth day of double practices you now test the individual and his desire to excel and become as capable as he can be in his sport. The same thing is true in business and it's true in college.

"If you have the will to prepare, things will usually work out quite well and the will to win will take care of itself."

Several of Bud's former players hailed these remarks as the quintessential Wilkinson. Two years after winning this prestigious award and thirty years after coaching the Sooners to back-to-back national championships, Bud Wilkinson, sitting behind his huge mahogany desk, elaborated on this theme of the "will to prepare."

"People in any athletic endeavor talk about the will to win and that's supposed to be a very key factor, but the will to prepare is much more important than the will to win. When the game is on, whether it be a golf match, a football game, the NCAA basketball tournament or whatever, the athlete is in a highly charged emotional environment. The stands are full. The TV cameras may be there. The cheerleaders are there. The athlete's parents are there. The will to win a contest is not that dramatic, but you have no chance to win unless you have had the will to prepare. The will to prepare means you give your best effort in practices every time you practice. The example that I used was the two-a-day practices. On the eighth morning at 6:30 A.M., everyone is stiff and tired and nobody really wants to be there. Football is not a fun game in practice, but if the athletes have the will to go out and try to improve as much as they can at that moment then they have the will to prepare. The will to prepare immediately translates into the ability to win and is a forerunner to it.

"The misunderstood thing about football is that the only people who really enjoy practice are the people who throw, catch, or kick the ball. The other players practice because it is required, which is why football is such a wonderful game, because it requires so much dedication on the part of people who don't get their share of the credit.

"Team dissention about who is getting the most publicity is something I never worried about. You talk to your team about this in spring practice or early in the fall practices. It's a foregone conclusion that the people who are going to get the lion's share of the publicity are the people who are going to be running with, catching, and throwing the ball. Defensively, the linebackers and defensive halfback are going to get most of the credit. The people that are involved physically in every play, the linemen, rarely get the recognition they deserve. That's just a fact of life and the people who are playing must understand this."

John Updike, in 1961, wrote, "Ted Williams is the classic player on a hot August weekday when the only thing at stake is the tissue-thin difference between a thing done well and a thing done ill, because he was one of those who cared about themselves and about their art." Updike could have been describing Wilkinson.

Wilkinson was one who cared on a hot August day, and it can be very hot in August in Oklahoma. On the eighth day of two-a-day practices, he cared about a block thrown well or a play run ill. It was Wilkinson's unremitting attention to detail and to excellence that comprised his will to prepare, which resulted in OU victories.

When Wilkinson spoke of the '56 Sooners, he consistently emphasized the word *team*. "The '56 team had great athletic talent," Bud said. "But they also had the desire to become a team in the very best sense of the word. I don't believe that they had any awareness of the records they were establishing at that time. I don't believe you think about records and winning streaks while you are playing/coaching: at least I didn't. I know this almost sounds like a dreadful old cliché, but the only game that is important is the next game you're going to play. Winning streaks are not by design, they just occur. What you are attempting to do is to have your team play as well as it can play every time they play. Of course, one must take into account the skills of the players, injuries, and all of those things."

To Cliché or not to Cliché

To call a statement made by Bud Wilkinson about football, particularly a statement he made in 1956, a cliché would be a little like the sophomore who came away from a performance of *Hamlet* and pronounced it

---

to be "nothing more than a bunch of clichés." If a particular football expression has become a cliché, it is very possible that Bud Wilkinson said it first.

Wilkinson was always more concerned with the effort his players were putting forth at any given time than with the score of the game. This was true whether his teams were behind, which they seldom were, or ahead by thirty points, which they often were.

"The fundamental idea," Wilkinson said, "is that when we play we must realize we are playing ourselves. This is the first thing you say to a team. You must discipline yourself well enough to get the best out of yourself all the time. Now, transferring this idea into a game situation to explain it a little better . . . you may be in this particular contest against a guy who is physically much better than you are. He is going to defeat you most of the time, but the important thing is, did you try as hard as you could try on every play? It's not your opponent you're trying to beat, it's yourself. In other games you may oppose someone who can't play very well at all. You're so much better physically than your opponent that it's no problem to defeat him; but again the real issue is, did you make the best effort you could make on every single play? If your players understand this philosophy, then they really don't know what the score is. They're trying to run every play as well as they can on both offense and defense." This probably explains why Wilkinson's teams were very seldom upset. Winning streaks of thirty-one and forty-seven games testify to that fact. Wilkinson was able to imbue his players with the belief that they were really playing against themselves, so they played as hard against Kansas State or Iowa State as they did against Texas.

Wilkinson's influence on the state of Oklahoma extended far beyond the gridiron. When he came to the University of Oklahoma in 1946, all was not well in the Sooner State. The 1930s were Dust Bowl and Great Depression days in Oklahoma. There had been a tremendous out-migration from the state because farmers could not make a living. John Steinbeck had written of this exodus in *The Grapes of Wrath*. In 1946, Oklahoma was still struggling to shake off this "Grapes of Wrath," "Okie" image. Steinbeck had few fans in Oklahoma. The OU library did not obtain a copy of *The Grapes of Wrath* until the late fifties.

Wilkinson's winning football teams gave the state something positive with which to identify. Gradually this "Grapes of Wrath" image began to dissipate and blow away just as the actual dark clouds of dust had finally blown away ten years earlier. Great football began to replace the "Okie" image of Oklahoma in the national consciousness.

Happy By-product

One happy by-product of football fever in Oklahoma is that it has finally cured the state of a swollen inferiority complex stemming from the Depression days of the Dust Bowl when so many Oklahomans were forced off their farms and had to move west to California and subsist as migratory farm laborers. The "Okie" label of those days—immortalized for all to see in John Steinbeck's *The Grapes of Wrath*—was a long time dying.

Tex Maule
Sports Illustrated, November 18, 1957

It was not by accident that the University of Oklahoma became a national power in football. Fielding a great football team at OU was a prime objective of the university's board of regents.

The issue came up at a regents meeting in 1945. One regent remarked that because of the negative publicity over *The Grapes of Wrath*, both the book and the movie, many Oklahomans actually felt a little apologetic about living in the state. What, he asked, could the university do to dispel this image and instill pride in the state?

Regent Lloyd Noble, a millionaire "wildcatter" from Ardmore, provided the answer. Why not hire a new coach (Dewey "Snorter" Luster's contract had just expired) and field a great football team?

After all, the war had just ended, and there were four years' worth of high school seniors returning from the service. The university could recruit the best athletes from this abundant supply (there were no scholarship limitations in those days) and field a great football team immediately.

However, Wilkinson was not the coach selected to lead the Sooners out of the Great Depression era. The regents chose, instead, the better-known "Sunny Jim" Tatum, who brought Wilkinson as his assistant. But Tatum stayed only one year before moving on to Maryland. In 1947, Wilkinson was elevated to the head coaching job, and Gomer Jones became his line coach.

Before he came with Tatum, Wilkinson had served a year at his alma mater, the University of Minnesota. Before that, he had been an assistant coach at the University of Syracuse (where he completed his master's degree in English) for seven years. When World War II came, he attended the Iowa Pre-Flight School, where he met Missouri coach Don Faurot and discussed with him the merits of the T-formation.

One would assume a university would aspire to a more intellectual goal than the fielding of a great football team, but the University of Oklahoma opted for athletic prowess over academic excellence. In the fifties, President George Cross often remarked, "We are trying to build a university the football team can be proud of." Dr. Cross, of course, intended this statement to be taken facetiously, but the underpaid OU faculty recognized the embarrassing truth of this remark. However ignoble their purpose, the OU regents could not have chosen a better coach to dispel this negative image of the state than Bud Wilkinson. The tall, articulate man from Minnesota was the antithesis of the "Okie" image. Wilkinson was the perfect role model for his players' and the state's psyche. He was a fine athlete, an All-American. He was a fine student, having won the Big Ten's medal for athletic and scholastic proficiency, and he was a winner. He took OU from the Dust Bowl to the Orange Bowl.

Wilkinson won his first national championship in 1950, his

fourth season after becoming head coach. But ironically, his '49 team was actually better.

"We had another team during this era that was way above average," Bud said, in his characteristically modest way.

The '49 team was a totally different team personnel-wise. Although they came from the same basic area, they were older. Most of them had been in the service and some of them had been in combat. They were more mature than the average high school seniors. The '55 and '56 teams and all the teams after '49 were made up of legitimate high school seniors. But in '49 OU had Darrell Royal, who had played two years on a very fine army team, and Dee Andros, a former marine who was in the second wave at Iwo Jima.

49'er Stats

How good was the 1949 team? The 1949 Oklahoma team was undefeated and ranked second in the nation. Statistically, they were first in rushing defense, second in rushing offense, third in total offense, and sixth in total defense.

Both the 1949 and 1956 Sooner editions had halfbacks named Thomas who led the nation in scoring. In 1956 Clendon Thomas scored 108 points on eighteen TDs to lead the nation, and in 1949 George "Junior" Thomas was first in scoring with 117 points on nineteen touchdowns and three extra points. However, one of Junior Thomas's touchdowns in 1949 against Oklahoma A&M became infamous among certain Aggie fans who happened to be seated in the south end-zone bleachers of Memorial Stadium. Tom McMichael and John Pratt were sitting with several other A&M fans as they watched the play develop. It appeared that Thomas had made a good gain but had been pushed out of bounds. Pratt turned to McMichael and said, "Well, they finally got him out."

McMichael said, "Yes, but the son-of-a-bitch is still running."

Pratt looked back and saw that McMichael was right. He watched incredulously as Thomas continued to run outside the boundary for about twenty yards before stepping back inside in time to cross the goal line. No whistle had blown and the touchdown stood.

"That's why these guys are so hard to beat," McMichael said.

Red-Sweatered Blockers Thick around Him

The "official" OU account of Thomas's run was given in Bud's weekly newsletter following the game. The somewhat flowery prose undoubtedly belongs to Harold Keith, who did an outstanding job as OU's sports information director for over forty years.

"[Darrell] Royal faked a handoff to [Lindell] Pearson and swung around the Aggie right end. The Aggie end crashed, whereupon Royal lateraled to George Thomas who circled the end and headed for the open spaces with our red-sweatered blockers thick around him.

"Down the west sideline they flew with our crowd of fifty thousand roaring. Then our busy downfield blockers began to do their savage duty. Jim Owens bumped the linebacker. Leon "Mule Train" Heath knocked down the defensive half to open the gate wide.

"Running with beautifully controlled speed, Thomas weaved through the havoc wrought by our forwards sprinting downfield ahead of him. Wade Walker screened off a man. [Charley] Dowell took out the safety. Thomas faked outside, then swerved to the middle and jogged across the goal line after a ninety yard touchdown run that I am told is the longest an OU back has ever made in modern times. It was a thrilling sight."

Port Robertson, along with his other responsibilities as academic counselor and wrestling coach, was also the freshman football coach at OU. He said of Wilkinson, "Bud is what athletics is all about really. He was the most self-disciplined individual I've ever been around. That was his key platform with athletes. He wanted them to develop self-discipline. Bud exemplified that to a degree that few people ever achieve. He had a total concern for the kids. Obviously, he had to have on the football field, but quite frankly he was very interested in the graduation rate and he was interested in the boys becoming good citizens. He was concerned with the total well-being of the youngsters to a degree that few people are. A lot of people recognize that kids ought to go to school and that they ought to get degrees, but what you really need are people willing to work at it every day, not just during football season. I think, knowing Bud and Gomer, and granted I am prejudiced, but I was there eighteen years with them both and then another five or six years with Gomer. I think they had about as much of a total concern for the youngsters as it is possible to have."

Wilkinson was very proud of the fact that a high percentage of his players received their degrees. The 1956 *Sooner Press Guide* reported that 88.3 percent of Sooner football lettermen were receiving their degrees. This is no longer true at OU or any other major football power. "We have gone from the era of the student-athlete to an era of the athlete adjusting to what he has to do academically to stay eligible," Bud said. "It's a different world."

Bud made these comments in 1986. According to statistics compiled by the National Collegiate Athletic Association (NCAA), OU's graduation rates for football players in the years 2000, 2001, and 2002 were 17 percent, 47 percent, and 6 percent, respectively. One wonders what he would have thought about these figures.

Bud believed the major factor in bringing about this different perspective on the athletic/academic issue was the change from one-platoon to two-platoon football. In the one-platoon system of the fifties, players had to learn many skills. This is not necessary today. Bud said, "In two-platoon football you recruit a guy with one particular skill. He doesn't have to be an all-round player. All you've got to do is keep him eligible. If you go back to the 'good ol' days'

[Bud smiled at his own words here] or whatever you want to call them, the player had to learn to do a lot of things and it's a natural carry-over that he is a college student and that he will get a degree.

"People are always critical of football, but recruiting in football even today is maybe 20 percent of what it is in basketball. You only have eighty or so schools that really try to compete in major college football and that even includes the Kansas States that can't win. [Obviously this was said before the Bill Snyder era.] In basketball you don't have very many seven footers out there and there are over two hundred schools competing for them. Basketball is 80 percent more intense than football recruiting."

Wilkinson discussed at length the changes in recruiting that have occurred since the 1950s. "One of the things that has changed recruiting so dramatically is the speed of transportation. Everyone tends to overlook this, but the jet airplane has made everyone's campus four hours from wherever the boy is. Lew Alcindor would never have gotten to UCLA if it were not for jet airplanes. At that point in time we were the closest major university to the Texas panhandle and really to New Mexico, too. Texas Tech was not in the Southwest Conference then, so you had totally different circumstances."

John Wooden, Alcindor's coach at UCLA, was one of the first to realize the importance of the jet airplane. He often said that one of the most important factors in having a successful program is being near an airport. Wilkinson said, "This was not true when I came to OU, but by the time I left [1963], it was, and really I didn't adjust to that as well as I might have. I've thought a lot about it and really I didn't realize that we had enough of a reputation to attract players from other states because we never tried to. I went to the University of Minnesota. I grew up in Minneapolis and I had always been ingrained with the idea that you go to college to become an educated person, if possible, and the school that you attend is the school where you want to be educated—and football is an extracurricular activity. Obviously that's not true today, but it was basically true during the time I was at Oklahoma."

In the late fifties and early sixties, Bud saw that recruiting was becoming a much more critical part of college football, and he did not care for many of the changes in recruiting practices. During one of his last seasons at OU, Bud said, "I can understand why a boy from New York would want to come to Oklahoma to study engineering, but I cannot understand why anyone would come here just for football."

Being realistic about it, Bud said, "We probably could have attracted some people from out-of-state, but we weren't set up emotionally, financially, or in any other way to handle it." Standing in sharp contrast to this philosophy is the 2005 recruiting class of Bob Stoops that included players from thirteen different states.

"But again with respect to recruiting, I cannot overemphasize the difference between one-platoon and two-platoon football, and I'm in favor of one-platoon football. The reason I favor one-platoon football is that the factors that are coachable, that is, learning to do things you naturally don't do well, these skills can be coached in one-platoon football. In two-platoon football you recruit these skills. In two-platoon football a player needs only one skill, and the best example I can think of is the wide receiver who can run a 4.4 or 4.5 forty. I don't mind him catching that pass for a touchdown if he has to line up and play defense on the next series. Two-platoon football is a totally different game.

"If you don't have the talent today there is no way you can coach well enough to overcome the lack of talent. When we had one-platoon football, coaching was 50 percent more important than it is today. The factors of attitude, team spirit, conditioning are more important in one-platoon football than in two-platoon football."

A Game of the Heart

It's absolutely true we have to have athletic ability. You can't deny that or belittle it, but I am totally of the opinion that because football is a morale game, because it is primarily a game of the heart, and I don't mean to sound sentimental, I believe you must first find a boy of character, a boy who must first be a good enough student to do college work without undue difficulty, and to be able to graduate from college. If he doesn't have that much academic ability, he doesn't belong in college, that's all there is to it.

Bud Wilkinson
From an interview published in *Sports Illustrated*, September 12, 1955

"Coaching in the fifties was much more intimate," he said. "I think intimate is the proper word here. Then you didn't have the size coaching staffs you do today. The head coach of any school today primarily is responsible for recruiting and for the design of the basic offense and defense, but at that point he passes the control to his offensive coordinator, defensive coordinator, and whoever is responsible for the special teams. In the days of one-platoon football, the head coach had to coach. Today it's all recruiting and I don't mean that negatively at all."

Bud proceeded to describe his recruiting policies in the fifties: "We had a hypothetical line. (There were some exceptions to this, of course.) But basically, if you draw a line from Dallas to Midland, Texas, we would have a chance at anyone who lived north of that line. If we tried to recruit anybody who lived south of that line, we were going to get beat by Texas or Baylor or somebody. We had a few players from Dallas, but we had an awful lot of them from west Texas, Jerry Tubbs, Bob Harrison, and Ed Gray. [Gray, in '56, was the Sooners' right tackle and co-captain. He died in an automobile accident in April 1977.]"

Bud believed that limiting recruiting to one geographical area had its advantages in terms of team unity. He explained, "These men had grown up reading about the Sooners and wanting to be a part of this tradition, and when they became a part of it, making the team, without overstating, was like the fulfillment of a dream. The fact that we played well meant that by the time a kid got to Oklahoma he was already 'psyched up' so to speak.

"If you look at the rosters of college kids today, the majority of the players are from the school's geographical area, for the most part. Texas will have more kids from Texas; Pittsburgh will have mostly Pennsylvania kids, with a few from West Virginia, and so forth, but the player who has the rare skill may come from anywhere, and he's the guy who will play a major role in whether you win or lose. Marcus Dupree is a good example.

"I think the lifestyle in Oklahoma and Texas in this era reflected the moral, religious, work ethic belief that existed then," Bud said.

Lean and Hard

The players are cast in the leathery, stringy, tough mold of the longhorn cattle, which lived on cactus and a spoonful of water during the early days of Texas and Oklahoma. They look lean and hard and the soft sound of their speech comes as a surprise. They have the spare toughness of a mesquite tree and the endurance of a coyote, and they have a deep affection for their windswept, rugged homeland. They come from ranches and small farms and from backbreaking work on oil rigs and from a country where courage is an expected and usual quality.

Tex Maule
Sports Illustrated, November 18, 1957

Although Bud's teams established many offensive records, he based his coaching philosophy on defense. He explained, "The worst thing that can happen to you as a coach is for your best athletes to be on the bench with you and not in the game. It takes more skill to play defense than it does to play offense, but all the publicity flows to the offense. A number of coaches are really not strong enough to have their best athletes playing defense, which they should. If the other team doesn't score, you don't lose and if you don't lose you're undefeated and no coaches get fired if they are undefeated. In football you get the ball two ways, by stopping your opponent and forcing them to kick or you let your opponent score and they kick off to you. You don't win games receiving kickoffs.

"The first time you tell a player something, they don't hear you. The second or third time they may understand, but by the fifth or sixth time they understand and believe, hopefully, which is the important factor.

"In talking to our team, in spring practices and early season practices, we would tell them the most consistent statistic is that you get the ball with a first-and-ten thirteen times a game. Today, because of different rules about stopping the clock to move the chains it may be more like fourteen or fifteen. So, I would try to convince our team that we've got thirteen chances to score. If we get three fifteen-yard penalties, we've got ten chances. Let's say one guy blows his assignment four times. We've got six chances. What this means fundamentally is that we cannot afford to make any errors at any time because you have to give the defense credit for being able to stop you sometime.

"We were playing Texas one year. This was one of the years we were not supposed to beat them. We had talked to our players a lot about the first-and-tens statistic. Our defensive team began to keep track of this. When they stopped Texas the first time, they said, 'Twelve more times,' then 'eleven more, ten more,' as in a crew race. We knew we only had so many strokes to go."

Bud's analogy of the crew race illustrates that he may have been in Oklahoma but he was not of Oklahoma. There are more people on a crew racing team than there are people in Oklahoma who have ever seen a crew race. Oklahomans can relate to bird dogs, shotguns, pickup trucks, and chicken fried steaks but not crew racing.

"When I talk about conviction and belief," Bud continued, "the word *religion* is too strong a term, I guess, but the player must have conviction. The easy way out is for the player to say, 'We're

playing the wrong offense or the wrong defense' or 'I'm playing a position that does not properly utilize my talents and
my mother knows this is true.'

"As a coaching staff you've got to be strong enough to have
the players say, when they are unable to get the job done, 'I'm
just not good enough and by God, I'm going to get better.' If
you can establish this kind of belief in your players early on,
then once they believe it, the incoming freshmen and sophomores join the group and you have momentum going."
Certainly any coach would appreciate the profundity of that
statement.

In explaining Bud's phenomenal success, his former players stressed three factors: his organizational skills, his ability
to handle both players and assistant coaches, and his ability
to motivate players.

Billy Pricer, OU's fullback in 1956, said, "Bud was really a
psychologist. I've said it many times. You could feel like quit-
tin' football and droppin' out of school and after talkin' to Bud
for about fifteen minutes you'd come out of his office over
there in the old field house singin' 'Boomer Sooner' and feelin'
like you owned the University."

Clendon Thomas, an All-American halfback at OU, said,
"Bud was an exceptional man. I've never seen anyone handle
his coaches and his players like he did, certainly not in pro ball,
and I played for Sid Gilman and Buddy Parker. Wilkinson surrounded himself with good coaches. He surrounded himself
with quality people, which tells you a lot about the man psy-
chologically. This tells you he was very secure. The insecure
coaches I played for in pro ball surrounded themselves with
coaches they could belittle."

Wilkinson never belittled anyone. It was one of his very
exceptional traits as a coach that he would never criticize his
players. Bud explained this principle, "I have always operated
on the assumption that everyone is doing his best. Errors are
bound to occur. You wouldn't need to practice if there were no

errors, but you are not downgrading anyone because they make a mistake. You assume a boy is trying his hardest so you help him get better."

Wilkinson pushed himself harder than he pushed any of his players. While at OU he would arise between 4:00 and 5:00 A.M. to begin his workday at 6:00. A typical day for Bud during the season would be seventeen hours. He would often not get home until 10:00 or 11:00 P.M. Even then he would find it difficult to sleep, although he would try to relax by reading or playing his electric chord organ. Then he might return to the training room late at night, where he would often find his trusted line coach and fellow insomniac Gomer Jones waiting for him, sit in the steam room and finally fall asleep on the automatic massage table.

We Don't Really Set Out to Build Character

Colleges don't exist to field football teams. There is no great intellectual gain in football. The aim of football is—or should be—the aim of the university: to develop talent to the highest degree. All the philosophical expressions attributed to football are by-products of the game; oh, they're real—they exist—but we really don't set out to build character. That's a by-product of what we do.

The boy who stays up until two o'clock in the morning three weeks before the game probably has not hurt his physical condition at all, but he's put a dent in his mental armor. If a player hasn't conditioned himself previously, he'll probably not have the fortitude or the courage—football won't mean enough to him—to recover a punt when he's tired and it's ninety-eight degrees on the field.

Bud Wilkinson
From an interview with the *New York Times Magazine,* November 9, 1958

Wilkinson's coach at Minnesota was the highly successful Bernie Bierman. Wilkinson did not believe he made a conscious effort to emulate Bierman, but the coach certainly had a great influence on Bud. Wilkinson said, "I think everyone has to be himself, but you gradually assimilate experiences you have in coaching as an assistant or a head coach, learning all the time. Certainly some of the things I learned from Bierman became part of my coaching convictions.

"One of the things I learned from Bierman was to try to have my players rested and free of bumps and bruises for games. At OU our tough practices were our preseason practices. When we got within a week of our first game, our endeavor was to be as rested as we could possibly be and still be prepared to play. I picked this up from Bierman. At Minnesota we had excellent teams [winning national championships in '34 and '36] and we 'looked' fast, but Bernie had the theory, and he was the only coach at the time that was having no contact within a week of the first game. We had the heavy blocking dummies at Minnesota just like we did at Oklahoma, so we could hit things full speed, but we were not getting any bruises and bumps. The common practice in Bierman's day would be to have a light workout on Monday, scrimmage on Tuesday, Wednesday, and Thursday and have a light workout on Friday, but Bierman changed this. At Minnesota we were not any faster than the people we were playing; we were not any quicker, but we were so much fresher that we looked that way, which is why we won, and having experienced that I always tried to follow the same theory."

Wilkinson was an innovator who was not content to borrow and copy from others. He took the basic concept of the T-formation, a quick attack before the defense could adjust as they do against the single-wing, which requires a deep center snap. Wilkinson added the small twist of spacing his linemen farther apart to create the "split-T." The splits between the linemen were taken to spread the defense and to make them cover more area rather than to create blocking angles. Of course, if the defense does not split or widen out with the offense, blocking angles are created. Splitting the linemen created a premium on speed and quickness rather than size and strength as in the old single-wing, which featured power plays with a lot of double-team blocking. Bud recruited and trained linemen in the 190–210-pound range who were quick off-the-mark and beat their opponents to the attack.

Wilkinson was the first to use the "alternate" team concept, which allowed him to replace a tired team with eleven fresh men. Many talented players are required in such a system and he often had the luxury of two teams of almost equal ability. He also pioneered the Oklahoma "fast-break" or "quick-huddle" offense. The OU fast-break was the ultimate weapon for Wilkinson. On a hot Oklahoma autumn afternoon, alternating two talented and well-conditioned teams that sprinted back to the huddle to run plays as quickly as possible or perhaps ran plays without a huddle, Wilkinson's Sooners simply wore down their opponents. The heavier, slower teams could not keep up with the Sooner fast-break.

Wilkinson explained the philosophy behind the alternate-team system and the fast-break offense. "One of the worst situations possible for a team is to have players know they are not going to play," Wilkinson said. "If a player knows he's not going to play, he won't practice as effectively as he will if he knows he's going to get into the game. This is something Bear Bryant did that people overlooked. Alabama would play eighty people. If eighty people were dressed, eighty people would play. Many of these would play only on kickoff coverage or on the kick receiving team or the punting team, but they would practice hard. They were trying all the time and that's how you get better.

"The analogy of pro basketball is probably the best example here. Let's say Clendon Thomas is your best right halfback. There's a point where Clendon's fatigue becomes a reality. At that point a fresh man may be better than Clendon for four or five plays until Clendon gets it back again. The pro basketball coaches I've talked to say the whole secret of coaching pro basketball, because all the guys are super, super, athletes, is to analyze how long each guy can go before he needs a blow, that's the whole thing.

"Even though a player wants to make his best effort every play, it's almost a subconscious reaction that, if he knows he's going to play sixty minutes, he's going to pace himself. Someone who's going to run a mile doesn't run it with a series of sprints. He's got to pace himself. Our players knew they were going to have physical relief within a short period of time, so they could go all out. They didn't have to pace themselves because they knew they didn't have to play sixty minutes. Knowing they would be relieved was the important fact for our players. All the factors of momentum, speed, quickness and all those things were a result of this conviction that the players had to have. You've got to be realistic about it; if our guys felt that they were never going to be substituted for, they couldn't make their best effort on every play."

The fast-break offense didn't just happen. It was a part of Wilkinson's overall scheme. "We didn't do anything by accident. This goes back to the things you've got to have your people believe. Sometime early in spring practice or early in fall practice, we would tell our players 'We're not any better physically than the people we're going to play.' [It would seem a modern-day coach might have a difficult time selling this point to his team, or at least to any blue-chip recruit who is told what a special player he is and how much a team needs him. How would a coach convince this player that he's not physically better than his opponents?] We would repeat this message over and over. Let's not be ridiculous enough to suppose we have superior offensive talent.

"It follows from this that, hopefully we are as good.

"It follows from that, that each team will have the ball thirty minutes.

"It follows from this, that in our thirty minutes, if we can put the ball in play, twelve, thirteen, or fourteen more times than our opponents, then the yardage we gain on these plays will enable us to win the game.

"The key to running plays quickly is getting back to the huddle. Most people, when the whistle blows, leisurely adjust their pads, and amble back to the huddle. Our guys were taught to spring back to the huddle and they would do this even though it's physically tough because they believe in what I stated: this is how we will win!

"Somewhere along the line somebody is going to run the two-minute offense throughout the game. Everybody does it in the final minutes of the game, and they move the ball super. The offense has the advantage of knowing when the ball will be snapped and what the play is. The offense sets the tempo and to me it's not very sensible on the part of the offense to let the defensive coaches see what the down and distance is and substitute players in anticipation of the play they think is likely to be called. If the offense keeps things moving, the defense doesn't have a chance to substitute. They can't. They must keep the same people in the game; they've got a static defense."

Wilkinson was known as a great motivator, a master of the Knute Rockne half-time speech, but in '56 he needed only one such speech. His '56 Sooners were so dominant that they trailed an opponent at half time in only one game, the Colorado game at Boulder, which they eventually won 29–17 after trailing 19–6 at the half.

Oklahoma fans wanted to know what Bud said to motivate his players at half time and inspire them to dominate Colorado in the second half after such a lethargic first half. Bud, thirty years after this memorable game, went into considerable detail with his explanation.

"I've never felt that what anybody says at half time is all that important unless you've already preconditioned everyone. Colorado had a great team. Several of their players went on to play professional football. We had beaten Notre Dame the week before, but we were ready to play, but we had a kick blocked [which Colorado returned for a TD] and Tommy McDonald returned a punt for a touchdown, which was called back.

"I remember distinctly, at half time, we went through the

normal offensive and defensive changes and, in summary, I said, 'Fifty-thousand people out there think that you guys are beat and maybe you think so, but there is one guy here who has total confidence that you can win, and that's me!'

"The game came down to one play. We took the second half kickoff at our twenty and we came up with a fourth and two, and we went for it. I said, 'We're not going to kick!' At 19–6 we took the gamble that we could make the first down, but if we didn't make it they would have the ball on our twenty-eight yard line leading 19–6." The Sooners made the first down, although the strategy today would probably be to kick.

"Our quarterback always called the plays. [Today, of course, the quarterback never calls the plays. They are signaled in by coaches who are relaying them from coaches in the press box.] We didn't call that much from the bench. On rare occasions we would call a play, but whether we were going to kick or not, that's something where the quarterback would look to me and I would signal whether to kick or go for it. The players wanted to go for it too. We were a good defensive football team, but when you're that far behind a good team, possession of the ball is a vital thing, and it worked out, we got control of the game.

"Making that first down gave us a big surge of confidence and we scored on the drive to make the score 19–13." However, the Sooners also needed a clutch fourth-down pass from McDonald to Thomas to record the TD. Facing a fourth and one from the Colorado six, Jimmy Harris called the successful pass-run option.

"In 1956 we were a better football team than our opponents," Bud said. "But we won a lot of games in '57 when we could have gotten beat, and the same is true of the other winning streak we had in '49, '50, and '51. We were not as good as some of the teams we played, but our players thought if we just hung on tough enough something would happen, and the important thing is that our opponents felt the same way. The longer we could stay close to our opponent, the more their confidence began to ebb and ours improved, so we beat some teams we shouldn't have beaten."

For many fans, one of the most memorable facets of Wilkinson's coaching career at OU was his weekly television program. Unfortunately, there are no tapes of these shows. Viewers did not watch these shows in living color on oversized, plasma-screened Sonys and Mitsubishis. They watched the black-and-white picture on their Zeniths and RCAs, and they watched them only once. They did not record them on DVDs. The fifties was a low-tech time.

Wilkinson was the first coach to have a television show, preceding Woody Hays by one year. In 1954, a year in which Bud's TV show was nationally syndicated, one rumor (which Bud denied) placed his income from all sources at over $100,000. Wilkinson's shows were much different from the standard format of today's coaches' shows. Bud's shows had a didactic quality. In his professional manner, Bud patiently explained many of the basic fundamentals of the Split-T as well as many techniques of blocking, tackling, passing, kicking, and so on. Howard Newman, the show's host, would pose a question to Wilkinson, who would typically say, "Perhaps I can explain this a little better with the 'little men.'"

Wilkinson's "little men" were small wooden figures, about the size of chess pieces, shaped to resemble football players in their pads and helmets. With these little men, Bud would show his audience the defense they could expect to see Kansas using next Saturday, or perhaps he would explain how the blocking had developed to free Tommy McDonald for a long punt return. After these shows young boys would rush out to practice the skills Bud had demonstrated. They would kick and punt and pass and dream—dream that they would one day play for Wilkinson.

Wilkinson's shows were as popular with female viewers as they were with men. Although many women might not be particularly interested in the intricacies of the Split-T, they would tune in to gaze on the well-favored features of Wilkinson.

Bud said he did not necessarily plan a didactic approach for his shows. "I don't think I ever looked at it as educational from the standpoint of teaching or anything like that, because television programming has to be entertaining or people won't watch it.

Most people have an interest in football because of the press coverage it receives, and of course in Oklahoma it's a major activity. So, explaining 'why' was always a big factor in everything I did. Getting back to coaching, you don't tell a player to do something this way. You begin by telling him why he must do this. If he understands why, then he will follow through and learn. It will become important to him. If you approach coaching from the standpoint of 'OK, this is what you do, you block this guy,' the player doesn't know why you're doing this and he can't put the same degree of emphasis on it he otherwise would."

Wilkinson would typically close out his show with a homily, which, through an allusion to sport, would illustrate some moral principle. Newman might ask, "Bud, when the team is in the huddle, do any of the other players try to tell the quarterback what signals to call?"

Wilkinson would respond, "No, Howard, the players must know that in order to be a successful team, you can only have one person, the quarterback, calling the plays. It is the job of the other players to obey the commands of the quarterback. So, you young boys and girls remember; it is your job to obey your parents. They are the quarterbacks of your team. If you obey your parents and do as they bid, you will undoubtedly be much more successful and happier in your lives, just as the team who listens to the quarterback will be more successful." Such was the repartee young viewers of the *Bud Wilkinson Show* would hear.

Perhaps the single most remarkable episode of all Bud's TV shows occurred midway through the 1961 season. The Sooners had just lost 14–22 to Colorado. Their record was now 0–5, and they appeared to be headed for their worst season ever. Worse, even, than the 3–6–1 mark they had posted the previous year.

Bud shocked his Sunday viewers following the previous day's loss at Colorado when he said, "The University of Oklahoma will not lose another game this season." This was an unbelievable statement coming from Wilkinson, who, even when he had great teams, would make statements such as, "We will have to be most fortunate if we are to defeat Kansas State next Saturday." The Sooners did not have a great team in 1961. They had already been shut out 0–10 by Kansas and had not scored more than two touchdowns in any game. So, their chances of making good on Bud's boast seemed poor, especially since they still had to play road games with Missouri, Army, and Nebraska.

However, after a 17–6 victory over the moribund K-State Wildcats, OU defeated Missouri 7–0, journeyed to New York to beat Army 14–8 in the last college game ever played in Yankee Stadium, and beat Nebraska 21–14 in Lincoln before returning to Norman to defeat Oklahoma State 21–13. Bud's prophecy was fulfilled.

There was one Sooner fan who was not surprised by Bud's prediction. It was a twelve-year-old girl by the name of Jill Kendall. Jill, whose father, Dr. Jack Kendall, was an English professor at OU, lived a few doors down the street from the Wilkinsons. Jill saw that Bud always walked home from the stadium after games. He liked to wait until all the reporters and photographers left the locker room and then take a leisurely walk home to erase the tension of the game.

After she had learned Bud's routine, Jill would "just happen" to meet him by the lockers and walk home with him. The tall, handsome coach in his fedora and the pigtailed girl in her pleated skirt and bobby sox would walk home together in the lingering twilight of these Indian summer days. The seemingly formal and reserved Wilkinson, whose mere presence rendered two-hundred-pound tackles tongue-tied, would politely answer any questions the young girl asked.

On their walk home after the Colorado game, Wilkinson told Jill that he was sure OU would win the rest of their games. Jill was surprised then, but she was not surprised when Bud said the same thing the next day on his television show.

When Bud said OU would not lose again the rest of the season, local gamblers did not take this lightly. They, too, believed.

After hearing Wilkinson's bold prediction "Friendly" Frank

Logan, an inveterate snooker and parlay card player, rushed downtown to the H & H Pool Hall to find Hookie the Bookie. Hookie was playing moon with a couple of chumps and seining out the doubles, which he had marked. "What's the line on OU?" Friendly Frank asked.

"Plus six," Hookie replied.

"I'll take a hundred on OU," Logan said, waving the cigar smoke away from his face.

Hookie took out his little note pad and wrote down Logan's bet. "Boy, you're really plunging, ain't you! You want any other action?"

"No."

"What, no four and five teamers?" Hookie asked.

"No, just OU."

"Well, maybe you're finally wise'n up, Logan," Hookie said. "You know what the big boy in Fort Worth used to tell me. He used to say, 'If you want to play a single game or a two teamer, don't call me after ten. But if you want to play a three teamer or more, call me anytime!'"

On game day Logan went down to the Town Tavern to watch the OU–Army game on their big twenty-four-inch TV. He ordered a T-bone steak and a schooner of beer. The waitress brought his check for the T-bone (two dollars and twenty-five cents), but she made Logan fork over the two bits for the beer up front.

Logan was about to ask the waitress where she had gotten the colorful new tattoo of a butterfly on her forearm, which he had just noticed, but before he could get the words out, Sooner halfback "Iron Mike" McClelland broke away for a seventy-five-yard touchdown run. The Town Tavern erupted in cheers and Logan got so excited he picked up his steak and threw it across the room. Logan's steak knocked over the gravy bowl of Blind Martin, who did not give a damn about football and was only trying to eat his lunch in peace.

A Norman Landmark

The Town Tavern was a Norman landmark. It stood on the corner of Asp and Boyd Streets about three football fields north of Memorial Stadium. It was a reference point and meeting place for football fans. Its specialties were that southwestern staple, the chicken-fried steak, onion burgers, and pan-fried steaks, along with frosty schooners of beer. Before the games, ticket scalpers congregated without its portals to prey upon the less sanguinary fans. Inside, printed in bold lettering and clearly visible from any table, were the scores of each football game the Sooners had played since 1947 (the year Wilkinson took over). These schedules were, in a sense, a type of calendar, the Oklahoma version of the Gregorian calendar, which marked time in two epochs: Before Wilkinson and After Wilkinson.

What had Bud seen in the five losses to make him so confident OU could win their last five games? "I wasn't that overwhelmingly confident," Bud admitted twenty-five years later. "You've got to believe you're going to win, and we needed to do something dramatic to have our players believe we were going to win.

"I don't mean to be critical of anybody who ever played for me, but we did not have the same degree of talent in 1961 as we had earlier. This was my fault and my staff's fault in that we didn't do as effective a job of recruiting then. But this delves into our approaches to recruiting. The Oklahoma/Texas area has a high degree of athletic ability per one thousand population. The fact that there are so many people from this area that are on big league baseball rosters supports this statement. But, in that area for about three years, we just didn't have that many good athletes. It was just a drought. I think we would not have been able to win those games [in 1961] if we had not had a tradition of winning. I think our players believed the things that I had been talking about, and even though we had been beaten five times, they were still play-ing against themselves; they were not playing their opponents."

This turnaround in 1961 and Bud's prediction, or challenge, as it were, that he would not lose again provides insight into the man, the human. Despite the claims of William Furlong and David Baker, Wilkinson was not really a deity. Like lots of other men he enjoyed a drink now and then, smoked cigars, got a divorce, and then remarried. But Wilkinson was so poised, so smooth, that one may not really understand that behind this gra-cious public persona, Bud was a proud, intense competitor who hated to lose at anything. He was embarrassed about the 1960 season and the first part of the 1961 season, and he said, "This is enough, by God. We just won't lose any more."

Wilkinson recovered from his '60 and '61 disappointments to have two fine seasons in '62 and '63, winning sixteen and losing five. Then after seventeen seasons and a record of 145–29–4, Wilkinson left OU.

He entered politics as many had long thought he would. In 1964 he ran for the U.S. Senate as a Republican on the ticket headed by Barry Goldwater. Although he was obviously a popu-lar figure in Oklahoma, this was one contest he did not win. Lyndon Johnson's Democrats crushed the Republicans nation-wide that year, but Bud narrowly lost to the liberal Fred Harris.

After his ill-fated venture into politics, Wilkinson worked as a color commentator for college football telecasts. Although one critic described his delivery as "unctuous," he had a long career with ABC and ESPN.

Following a fifteen-year hiatus, Bud made a return to coach-ing when he became the head coach of the St. Louis Cardinals of the NFL. When Wilkinson, then sixty-two years old, was hired, one cynical scribe wrote, "The Cardinals wanted to find a living legend to coach their team and they did—barely."

Wilkinson proved he could still coach by winning six of his last eight games in 1978. The next year Bud was fired by Cardinal owner Bill Bidwell over a disagreement about who should be quarterbacking the team. Bidwell wanted to see second-year man Steve Pisarkiewicz calling the signals, but Wilkinson preferred to stay with the veteran Jim Hart. Wilkinson refused to capitulate, and Bidwell fired him. Bud was not particularly surprised at being summarily dismissed by Bidwell. His father, Charles Patten Wilkinson, had warned him long ago, "No matter how able or successful he may be, every coach everywhere eventually reaches a point where a lot of people want someone else."

At the time of this interview, Wilkinson held an executive position with the Public Employee's Benefit Services Corporation (PEBSCO), which designs and administers deferred compensation programs (essentially IRA and annuity-type benefits). Bud's youngest son Jay, an All-American at Duke University in the early sixties, was then the president of PEBSCO, and his other son, Dr. Pat Wilkinson, was an eminent eye surgeon with the Dean McGee Eye Institute in Oklahoma City.

As has always been his policy, Bud would not compare his '56 team to any of his other Sooner teams, and he wasn't too interested in speculating about which team may have been the "Greatest of All Time." He said simply, "The athletes get better all the time. Another way of looking at this issue is, was Bobby Jones better than Ben Hogan or Jack Nicklaus or whomever you want to name? The only satisfactory response is that if you were the best at the time you played you can forget the other arguments.

"The people who played at the University of Minnesota at the time I played have been very successful in their lives. They haven't gone out and conquered the world but they are well above the fiftieth percentile, and I'm sure this is true of the '56 OU team. I don't think you'll find a loser on the whole team."

Norman, Oklahoma, January 2005

Charles Burnham Wilkinson died of congestive heart failure February 9, 1994, in St. Louis, Missouri, at the age of seventy-seven. He had suffered a series of strokes, which had left him blind and virtually paralyzed at the time of his death.

He was already in declining health on September 13, 1991, when his friends and former players hosted "A Tribute to Bud Wilkinson" in Oklahoma City. Chris Schenkel, his longtime broadcasting partner at ABC, was the featured speaker, and Kurt Gowdy was the emcee. Thirty-two of Bud's former All-Americans were on hand for the black-tie affair.

One of these All-Americans was chosen two and a half years later to deliver a eulogy for Wilkinson at his funeral in St. Louis. Darrell Royal, who quarterbacked the Sooners from 1947 to 1949 and later went on to become a coaching legend himself at the University of Texas, said of Bud: "Never at any time did Coach Wilkinson raise his voice at a player, other than in encouragement. Never did I see Coach Wilkinson berate or criticize a player.

"Coach Wilkinson taught me that the greatest asset a player has is his pride. Playing under Coach Wilkinson, you were always able to maintain your pride.

"Never did I hear Coach Wilkinson make an alibi when we lost. Coach Wilkinson taught me that you don't need to explain victory, and to the press, you cannot explain defeat.

"Time changes everything except what we choose to recall. I'm going to remember the good times . . . many, many wonderful memories. They will be easy to recall."

Coach Bud Wilkinson, center Jerry Tubbs, and quarterback Jimmy Harris

OU head football coach Bud Wilkinson is carried off the field after his 1956 Sooners defeated Notre Dame 40-0 in South Bend, Indiana.

Norman, Oklahoma, Friday, August 31, 1956

Crew-cut and tanned from their summer work on farms, ranches, and oil rigs, the '56 Sooners turned out for picture day. The Sooners had won thirty consecutive games and were hoping to repeat as national champions.

About fifteen hundred miles away another young man from Oklahoma was finishing up a brilliant season. In Washington, D.C., with President Dwight Eisenhower looking on, Mickey Mantle of Commerce, Oklahoma, blasted his forty-seventh home run of the season. This homer put Mantle four games ahead of Babe Ruth's record pace of sixty homers in 1927. Mantle's homer came in an afternoon game, for in those days baseball was still essentially a daytime game the way God and Mr. Wrigley intended. No one had even thought of playing a World Series game at night. The Fall Classic was still considered important enough to be played before dark.

New York City, New York, Sunday, September 9, 1956

Elvis Presley made his first appearance on the *Ed Sullivan Show*, singing "Love Me Tender," "Hound Dog," and "Love Me," and the music industry has never been the same. According to *Billboard* magazine, Presley had the most records (seventeen) on the charts in 1956. Pat Boone was second with five charting records, followed by Fats Domino, Little Richard, and the Platters with three each.

Norman, Oklahoma, Sunday, September 16, 1956

The AP preseason football poll was released today. The Sooners were number one with 111 first-place votes. Michigan State was second with twenty first-place votes.

The Sooners did receive some bad news, however, as All-American and Heisman Trophy candidate Tommy McDonald suffered a hyperextended knee injury in practice. Ken Rawlinson,

OU trainer, said McDonald could miss the Sooners' opening game on September 29 against North Carolina.

In baseball, the Brooklyn Dodgers gained the lead in the National League pennant race as Don Newcombe shut out the Chicago Cubs 3–0 on only three hits.

No spring nor summer has such grace as I have seen in one autumnal face.

—John Donne

Norman, Oklahoma, Saturday, September 22, 1956

On this, the first day of autumn, the Sooners conducted a lengthy scrimmage in preparation for their opening game, which was just one week away.

Oklahoma City, Oklahoma, Monday, September 24, 1956

Bud Wilkinson, speaking to the Quarterback Club of Oklahoma City, said, "I know football coaches are always saying the margin between winning and losing is very small, but fans fail to realize that the margin is as narrow as it really is."

Commenting on the Sooners' first opponent, North Carolina, which lost its first game to North Carolina State 20–6, Bud said, "I don't think our players will underestimate North Carolina, but I imagine everyone else will. If we win by one point I will be happy. But that first game is the toughest to win and I certainly wish we had it behind us."

Bud made the drive from Norman to Oklahoma City in his new Cadillac, which had been presented to him earlier that year by the Muskogee, Oklahoma, Quarterback Club. The Muskogee club wanted to honor Wilkinson for winning the national championship in '55. The club also wanted to recognize the academic achievements at OU so they made a presentation to President Cross. They gave him a cigarette lighter.

It all began on an autumn afternoon—and who, after all these centuries, can define the fineness of an autumn day?

—John Cheever

We played a typical opening game.

—Bud Wilkinson

Oklahoma 36   North Carolina 0

Norman, Oklahoma, September 29, 1956

This game featured the return of "Sunny Jim" Tatum to the University of Oklahoma campus where he had been head coach in 1946. Tatum and OU president Dr. George Cross had not parted company as the best of friends. Tatum's free spending had the athletic department several thousand dollars in debt. Tatum, in violation of conference rules and against a direct order by Cross, had given each of his players one hundred and twenty dollars in cash after the 34–13 victory over North Carolina State in the 1946 Gator Bowl. Apparently the players could not decide if they wanted new shotguns or golf clubs, so they decided to take the cash.

Persuade Hell!

Tatum left OU in the spring of 1947 to become the head coach at the University of Maryland. After his departure, Cross ordered an audit of the athletic department's financial affairs and found a deficit in excess of $60,000. It appeared that the athletic director Jap Haskell did not know (or perhaps did not want to know) about Tatum's profligate spending. In either case the university's board of regents abruptly relieved Haskell of his duties.

Not long after Tatum had assumed his coaching duties at Maryland, Dr. Cross received a phone call from him. Tatum told him, "The sportswriters here are giving me a little trouble. They're talking about me causing Jap Haskell to lose his job as athletic director."

Cross said, "Well, you were responsible, indirectly at least. Haskell lost his job not just because you overspent the budget but because he didn't know about it."

Tatum then told Cross, "I want you to issue a statement immediately saying that I had nothing whatever to do with Haskell losing his job."

"Jim, I can't do that. It's not true," Cross replied.

"If you don't issue that statement," Tatum said, "I'm going to issue a statement saying that OU paid its team six thousand dollars to play in the Gator Bowl, and there won't be a single one of those boys who made that trip that will ever be eligible to play there again."

Cross realized how potentially damaging such a statement could be, and he quickly called Maryland university president Curly Byrd. (Byrd had been the football coach but was elevated to the presidency when Tatum was hired. Today the Terrapins play their games in Byrd Stadium.) Cross explained the situation to him and said, "I'm not going to issue any such statement. It would cripple OU football for the next five or six years. But, Curly, remember he's your boy now. How is it going to look for you to have as your football coach a guy who

> admits he violated all the rules and paid a team to play
> in the Gator Bowl? If you could persuade . . ."
>   "Persuade hell!" Byrd said. "I'll tell him to keep his
> damn mouth shut!"

Before his death in 1964 at the age of forty-five, Tatum compiled a coaching record of 100–35–7. In 1983 he was posthumously inducted into the National Football Foundation's College Hall of Fame. Buddy Burris, a three-time All-American guard at OU ('46–'48), perhaps got it right when he said, "Tatum was a con man, a dictator, a tyrant, and one hell of a football coach."

Tatum and Wilkinson had matched wits nine months earlier in the Orange Bowl. Tatum was coaching at Maryland then and the Sooners and the Terrapins were undefeated going into this showdown. Wilkinson's Sooners won the game 20–7 to nail down the national championship.

However, Tatum brought a much less talented North Carolina team to Norman with him on this day. North Carolina had suffered through six straight losing seasons.

There were several ironic occurrences during this remarkable season. Only one of the Sooners' four home games was a sellout (this game with North Carolina). The Sooners had only one game televised (Notre Dame), and they did not go to a bowl. They were ineligible to appear in a bowl game under existing Big Seven rules because they had been to the Orange Bowl the year before.

Temperature at kickoff was ninety degrees—Wilkinson weather. The hotter it was, the better Bud liked it. The Sooners, under Wilkinson, were always superbly conditioned. Oklahoma's practice of substituting two complete teams on an almost equal basis simply wore down their opponents, particularly on hot days.

Oklahoma scored three touchdowns in the final 6:30 of the first half to seal the victory. The alternate team drove fifty-two yards for the first touchdown. David Baker began the drive with an eleven-yard gain behind the blocks of Delbert Long, Hugh

Ballard, and Joe Oujesky. Baker also ended the drive by taking a handoff from quarterback Jay O'Neal, running ten yards, and then pitching the ball back to O'Neal, who ran the remaining seven yards for the score.

The second touchdown was set up by Billy Pricer's seventy-eight-yard quick-kick. Wilkinson, a great advocate of field-position football, often used the quick-kick as an offensive weapon. On these quick-kick plays, center Jerry Tubbs would snap the ball through the legs of quarterback Jimmy Harris directly back to fullback Pricer. Pricer would then take a quick "rocker-step" backward and punt the ball. The opposing team, which had not been expecting a kick, could not make a return and would be pinned back in their end of the field.

After Pricer's kick, North Carolina could not advance the ball. McDonald returned their punt eleven yards. Clendon Thomas and Pricer had gains of thirteen and ten, respectively, before Thomas got away for twelve yards and the score, running behind the blocks of Jerry Tubbs, Bill Krisher, Tom Emerson, and John Bell.

North Carolina, now trailing 14–0 with only 3:01 to play in the first half, took to the air. Thomas intercepted and returned the ball ten yards. Then he lateraled to McDonald, who raced for forty more yards before being driven out of bounds on the North Carolina ten.

From there, OU scored on their second play. A pass from Harris to McDonald and an extra point by Pricer made the score 21–0 at the half.

OU failed to score in the third quarter, but in the fourth, the alternate unit began an eighty-two-yard drive, which the starters finished with McDonald getting the score from two yards out.

On their next possession, the Sooner starters drove to the Tarheel thirty-six yard line. At this point, Bud inserted the third team into the game. By this time the visitors were so worn down by the heat and the first two Sooner teams that they quickly yielded a touchdown to quarterback Lonnie Holland. The extra point was no good, but a few plays later Steve Jennings tackled Ron Marquette of North Carolina in the end zone for a safety. This made the final score 36–0.

OU had totally dominated the game, piling up 411 yards to 140 for North Carolina. The Sooners employed twenty different ball carriers (five complete backfields) in this game. However, the news was not entirely good for the Sooners because both the starting left tackle, Wayne Greenlee, and the starting left guard, Ken Northcutt, suffered broken ankles. Neither of these young men would play again in '56. Northcutt returned to play for the Sooners in '57 but Greenlee chose to complete his degree on schedule, rather than accept a medical hardship, and did not return.

After the game, McDonald said of North Carolina, "They seemed like they were sort of out of shape. Every time we turned around, they were calling timeout. They were hurt by the heat. We weren't even tired."

The Sooners had thoroughly impressed Tatum. "They're all they say they are and greater," he said. "I never saw a greater squad. Did you ever see backs run harder and faster? They really hit. At the end of the game I was having trouble getting guys to go in there."

Even though the Sooners equaled their own record of thirty-one straight victories with this win, Bud tempered the victory celebration with a note of caution, "Our future opponents are all working hard and improving each week. Several of them played much better this Saturday than last, a tribute to their enthusiasm for practice. A football squad doesn't stand still. It either improves or becomes poorer by its practice attitude. Every opponent we face will work extra hard and make a tremendous effort to defeat us. If we let them surpass us in practice, they will defeat us in the games."

On this day the leading rusher for the Sooners was not one of the "Touchdown Twins," Thomas or McDonald. OU's leading ground gainer was a sophomore halfback from Bartlesville, Oklahoma, David Baker.

David Baker

Norman, Oklahoma, Thirty Years after the Game

"I was scared to death, literally scared to death." David Baker was seated behind his desk in his State Farm Insurance Agency office in Norman, speaking of his first college game at OU.

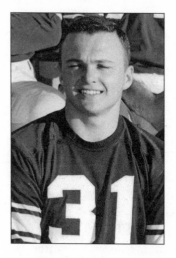

"Because of the image you've got of OU, you're saying 'I can't perform to that level' and you're afraid you can't. I was literally petrified. I almost would have done anything not to have gone out on that field against North Carolina."

Baker, thirty years later, kept trim by jogging. He looked like he was pretty close to his playing weight and appeared to be in excellent physical condition. He was neatly dressed in khaki slacks and a plaid long-sleeved sport shirt, with no tie. His blue-gray eyes flashed intently, and he gestured forcefully as he spoke of his former team.

"I came in my freshman year with four or five other quarterbacks, one or two of which were high school All-Americans. No way could I outperform any of them offensively, but they couldn't play defense. They couldn't tackle their mothers. So, I got to play." Three years in the defensive secondary of the San Francisco Forty-Niners of the NFL attest to David Baker's ability to play defense.

"I couldn't really play offense all that well," Baker said. "I didn't have that kind of speed. But I could contribute because I could play defense. Bud said, 'If they don't score on you, you're not going to get beat.'"

Baker had been a quarterback at Bartlesville High School, so he was surprised to find himself playing halfback in his first varsity game. He would subsequently play quarterback at OU, but in 1956 he was playing left half on the alternate team, backing up All-American and Heisman Trophy candidate Tommy McDonald.

Baker was even more surprised at being the punter for the alternate team. In those days, before unlimited substitution (a player was allowed to come out of the game and reenter once per quarter), teams were not afforded the luxury of kicking specialists. So, if a punt, or any type of place kick, were dictated, it would have to be executed by a player in the game at that time (a player who played a regular offensive position as well as a regular defensive position).

"I had been a high school classmate of Bobby Green at Bartlesville," Baker explained. "Well, I ended up punting and people back home said, 'What are you doing punting?' They knew what a good kicker Green was, and they thought everything OU did was just the most outstanding thing in the world. They knew I couldn't kick anywhere near as good as Green." Bobby Green, who was unsuccessful as a total player at OU, had an outstanding thirteen-year pro career in the NFL punting for Pittsburgh and Chicago.

Baker had a one-word explanation for his decision to come to OU—Wilkinson. Baker, like so many other boys in Oklahoma, grew up amid the compelling mystique of the Wilkinson era. "When I was in the seventh grade, OU was playing in the 1951 Sugar Bowl against Bear Bryant's Kentucky team. I was so nervous that I couldn't even listen to the game. So, I would go outside and shoot baskets hoping that when I came back in they would have won the game. [OU did not win this game. Kentucky snapped their thirty-one-game winning streak 13–7.] The media coverage then was nothing to what it is today, but still that's all you would hear about, OU football."

The shadow of Memorial Stadium was a long one. It reached to villages and hamlets as far away as Bartlesville in the northeast corner of the state. It reached to Lawton, Hobart, and Hollis in the southwest corner of Oklahoma. It engulfed the cities and towns of the Sooner State, places with names such as Anadarko, Apache, Cheyenne, Konowa, Muskogee, Okarche, Okemah, Oologah, Quapaw, Sallisaw, Seminole, Tahlequah, and Wewoka, names that linger as a reminder of the white man's rape of the Indians, the true natives of this territory. This giant shadow crept over Ardmore and Duncan and even across the Red River into the Lone Star State of Texas.

The town of Norman is almost exactly in the center of the state. The surrounding countryside is so flat that in '56, approaching Norman from any direction, the first landmark to catch your eye would be the press box of the football stadium, which was the tallest structure in town. The stadium loomed several feet above the treetops and the campanile of the McFarlin Methodist Church, which was the second tallest building in Norman. In that image lies a great truth about Oklahoma.

Baker seemed to have a very clear memory of this season of long ago. He listed the first twenty-two men by their positions, and he gave his observations, as a young sophomore, of this '56 season, when freshmen were ineligible. "I realized that we were far superior, and this is particularly true of the first eleven players. You actually played with twenty-two people then. The first unit would start and play seven minutes or so, then the alternate team would come in and play the next six or so minutes. The alternates would play the middle part of the second quarter, and usually the first team would finish out the first half. The first team would play about 60 to 65 percent of the game; the second team would play 35 to 40 percent." Obviously, the term alternate was not simply a euphemism.

"We had a lot of good quality on the second team, but we were not near the superior physical ability of the first team. The first team was one of those rare bunches that just had everything fall right. They recruited a bunch of super kids out of Texas. They got the best out of Oklahoma. You had an awful lot of seniors on that team. They all seemed to mature at the same time." Then Baker used a term that has become a cliché today—chemistry.

"You had the right chemistry on that team. But that doesn't mean there were not some personality conflicts. We definitely had some personality conflicts on that team, but they didn't interfere with the team's performance. When the guys got on the field it was a question of who could help us do what we needed to do at that moment. If I didn't like you, I could discuss that with you after the game.

"Another thing that this team had—and I can't say how this contributed to the football success, but I think that it contributed to the atmosphere—was that a lot of players who never got to play in the games stayed around and were good students and practiced every day. Henry Bonney, who became an attorney, and Bill Harris, who also became an attorney, were excellent students. Somehow they were possessed of a quality that says 'there is more to life than football.' Most kids, when they are nineteen or twenty, don't understand this. But we had kids on that team that did understand that. There were so many kids on that team that were good students. Tubbs, [Dr.] Tom Emerson, and Jay O'Neal were excellent students." It is apparent from these remarks that David Baker had thought a great deal about the abilities of this team— abilities and qualities that go beyond blocking and tackling and running. David Baker was possessed of the type of mind that makes these analyses. Indeed, Baker's intelligent and serious demeanor was often broken by a smile or a laugh, but he obviously had an incisive analytical mind.

"Wilkinson told me once, something that Tubbs had told him after the season. Tubbs and some of the other seniors got together and made a pact that they would try to get better every day. I think this goes along with Wilkinson's theory of preparation. When your best players have that kind of goal, then somehow it rubs off on all the others, even though they may not have been told.

"Everything fell into place that year. I think Wilkinson would have to say that. If he were to come back and have that same situation today, some things might not fall into place."

Baker recalled Wilkinson's warning about potential upsets. "Even the weakest opponents would prompt Bud to say such things as, 'We will have to be very fortunate to win.' Or 'We expect a very tough game and we will have to have a superior effort if we expect to win.' I remember being a little confused. All my so-called intelligence told me that what he was saying was a bunch of junk, but at the same time, who was I to question him? Today we question authority more than we used to; our whole society does. Maybe this is good sometimes, but maybe sometimes it's not so good.

"His authority was never challenged. We all revered him so. Not just his coaching, but physically he kept himself in good shape. He dressed neatly. Everything about him was just what you would want to be. You could never do anything with Wilkinson that would be construed as being too familiar. You just couldn't get that way with him. We had a few guys, who, around people they felt comfortable with, would make a joke about Wilkinson. But not too often." Obviously Baker's respect for his former coach had not eroded over the years.

Baker played professional football with the San Francisco Forty-Niners. This was long before their Joe Montana/Super Bowl days. The Forty-Niners were only an average team when Baker was there. He suddenly found himself in a situation where his team was often on the short end of the score, something that he experienced only twice in his three years at OU. This wasn't exactly fun for him but it didn't devastate him, either.

"At San Francisco, we won more than we lost. Not much more, but usually we won a few more games than we lost in my three years there. As an athlete you feel that you could have won some of those you lost, so you don't ever get your hope destroyed. As long as that's true, I don't think that [losing] affects you too much. I don't think it would really affect you unless you were with a terrible team and went 1–15."

Baker then launched into a reminiscence of his rookie year with the Forty-Niners, invoking the names of great players from autumns past. "LA had traded for Ollie Matson. The headlines in the sports pages and in magazines were, 'By Golly LA's Got Ollie.' Well, we played them in an exhibition game my rookie year. This was the first time I'd ever been in the Coliseum. LA came out with those rams horns on their helmets . . . and don't ever let anyone tell you a team's uniform cannot be intimidating," Baker said emphatically, "because it can be, particularly if you've got some insecurities that are just waiting to be developed.

"They had us down 41–7 at the half. We'd run three plays and punt. I felt like I had run down under twenty-three million punts. They beat us 54–14. They took everyone out the second half. Two weeks later we beat them 34–0. See those pictures behind you?" Baker said, gesturing at some pages from *Sports Illustrated* that were framed and hanging on his office wall. "*SI* sent their people out there because they could see LA coming on. LA had Ollie Matson, John 'Jaguar' Arnett [and Clendon Thomas]. They were supposed to kill people. We kicked 'em 34–0. So you realize you've got the tools, it's just a matter of using them. [A couple of tools Frisco had were Hugh McElhaney and Y. A. Tittle.] If you got destroyed to where you feel like you don't have the tools, well, I guess that would be a different story."

Since his playing days Baker had developed a new perspective on physical fitness. He considered himself lucky not to have had any serious injuries. He never had to have surgery. He had no physical problems resulting from any football injuries. But, he commented on how athletic training techniques had improved over the years. "We were not trained to take care of our bodies. We were trained to get ready to play a game. We were never told what our bodies were all about.

"When I first began teaching physical education [at Bethany Nazarene College in Oklahoma City], I realized I did not know what was going on physiologically in the human body. I had not been trained that way. You ran sprints or laps, not because it would be good for you in thirty or forty years, but because you were told to. We were not trained then, that to be physically fit would help you function better later in life."

Baker particularly took issue with the old practice of feeding steak to players on the night before a game or for breakfast on the morning of the game. "High protein fiber is one thing that builds up lactic acid, which is the thing that irritates your nerve endings. Probably marathon running has done the most to inform people of proper nutrition. If you had told a guy he's going to eat spaghetti and pancakes and stuff like that—they'd think you were crazy.

"At OU, our trainer, Ken Rawlinson, used to give us Cokes at half time. That was almost unheard of then. It was almost like a sin to give an athlete a Coke. We didn't get water like they do today—we didn't get it like we should have. There was not the sophistication in training techniques that there is today."

Coaches used to consider it a sign of toughness to practice two or three hours without water. Many coaches used to believe athletes would surely founder if given water during practice or games. Because of this benighted macho mentality, many athletes were running the risk of severe cramps, potassium loss, and heat stroke. Today virtually all teams provide water and/or saline solution for their players. Some teams even administer these saline solutions intravenously. It would surely come as quite a shock to the old-timers to enter a locker room at half time and see the players lying supine on training tables with IV needles sticking in their arms. If this trend continues, will emergency-room-type medical practices replace the motivational half-time speech? Will modern-day coaches tell their players to "lie down and shoot up for the Gipper?"

Although training techniques were not as sophisticated in the 1950s as they are in the 2000s, Wilkinson was certainly aware of the athletes' need for water. He explained, "When I was playing and during the early part of my coaching career, it was a part of the conditioning discipline that you did not drink water during practice. This was supposed to make you tough. Then in the early fifties, the Marine Corps did a study, which proved that the body needed a certain amount of fluid. They had a scale of temperatures and humidities related to the amount of water a person would lose if he were engaged in rigorous activity. From that time on, we began to take water breaks during practice on hot, humid days and we would try to get the players to take salt tablets."

Baker's experience in teaching physical education for ten years made him reevaluate what he believed athletics to be all about or what it should be all about. He described himself as a football fan "in a different kind of way."

"I enjoy going to games like other people, but I go for different reasons . . . I don't go as a fan to hoop and holler. My wife, who has no athletic background, just loves it. She yells and hollers. She says, 'I can't understand it. You don't say a word.' She thinks I'm not enjoying it. No, I'm enjoying a lot of other things about it. I might be watching some kid who got hurt and realizes his career may be over. I watch his reaction.

"I leave in the middle of the second quarter if the game is out of hand. In fact, we got down on the campus corner on game day about seven o'clock in the morning. By game time, if I had to go home, the things I truly enjoy have already been accomplished.

"I'm talking about the sociology of sport, the way sports affects people, the little old ladies who wear their red-and-white uniforms. What makes these people do this kind of thing? I have never seen a former athlete come to an OU game wearing a red outfit. It's just something you don't do. I don't put the people down who do it. I know they enjoy it. The guy who is cutting hair down in Durant, Oklahoma, feels better when OU wins because they're his team." The psychological term for this phenomenon Baker was speaking of is identification; that is, identifying with persons or institutions of illustrious standing, which is to say Lloyd Noble and the regents were right.

Each autumn, Normanites watch in fascination as the throngs of Sooner supporters invade the city in their game-day regalia. By assuming a position in front of the student union, it is possible to observe many outlandish expressions of sartorial fanaticism. There are husband-and-wife teams in matching red-and-white bib overalls. There are women who long ago passed the hash mark or middle age dressed in OU cheerleader outfits. One can only speculate as to whether or not these people behave more rationally in other moments.

Another phenomenon that puzzled Baker was the sudden increase in attendance at OU football games, which began around 1969. "Up until that time you could still buy season tickets to OU games. Today [1986] you can't," Baker observed. "Something happened in the late sixties and I really don't understand it," Baker said. "Suddenly the thing to do was to be at an OU football game." OU went through some lean years in terms of wins and attendance in the 1990s, but now with Bob Stoops at the helm, season tickets are again a rare commodity, even with the expanded seating capacity.

In the opinion of Port Robertson, this increase in attendance was not necessarily a positive factor. He said, "I don't think the fact that we didn't have sellouts then and we do now is a great tribute to our program. We are the greatest nation of spectators on the face of the earth. The interest in football is greater now. You've got more publicity and more coverage on TV today. I don't think it is a real strong, healthy thing to have a nation of spectators rather than participants." Recent findings on the epidemic of obesity among Americans (especially among children) would seem to prove Port's point.

Baker was very forthright in assessing the changes in football since the fifties. "The biggest change is one thing—the black athlete—period." Baker recalled the first time he ever saw Prentice Gautt, OU's first black football player. "Gautt came in the dorm and he was built like no human being I'd ever seen in my life. I came from Bartlesville where the kids were not integrated. I'd never been around black athletes. This kid came in in just a T-shirt and khaki pants. My god, I'd never seen a kid built like that in my life. If you've ever seen the classic black athlete, there are no white athletes built like that. None. There is a difference. Their muscles just rippled and they haven't done any weight training. They are just built that way."

Baker mentioned another black Sooner halfback from a later era who awed him physically. "When I saw Marcus Dupree, there was no way anyone could have convinced me this guy was a running back if I had not recognized him." Marcus Dupree, at 230–240 pounds, was OU's fastest player in 1982. Bill Krisher, a 215-pound tackle, was OU's biggest man and certainly not the fastest in '56.

"You must never get so full of nostalgia that you let yourself become an All-American when you weren't even All-Conference," Baker said. "You must keep things in perspective.

"Jimmy Harris could play today. McDonald could play today. None of us could make it as running backs except McDonald. Clendon Thomas would really have to hump it with what they are trying to do today." White guys don't run with the ball at OU (or anywhere else) anymore. White boys might throw a football, but they don't run with it. OU has not started a white running back since the early seventies.

"There is one thing I can't buy about the modern athlete," Baker said. "We weren't any tougher. We weren't created any tougher, but we didn't get hurt as much back then. I don't know if it's because they've got bigger kids today who are faster, so you take a few more licks. We didn't have people miss practice and games. We just didn't do that."

Baker did not believe there would be any more all-victorious classes such as the seniors of the '56 Sooners because of parity brought about by scholarship limitations.

The only consideration, he thought, that could possibly serve to somehow lessen the accomplishments of his '56 Sooners might have been their opponents. "I don't believe the schedule was as tough in '56 as what we would have to play today. The Big Seven was not very strong. Texas was down. But even so—we crushed 'em. We stomped on 'em. There is no way that any team today is as superior to the people they play as OU was in 1956."

Norman, Oklahoma, January 2005

In order to sign Baker to a football scholarship, Bud Wilkinson had to out-recruit Kansas's Phog Allen and Oklahoma A&M's Henry Iba, who wanted to recruit him to their respective schools to play basketball.

Baker still holds the OU bowl record and the Orange Bowl record for the longest interception return for a touchdown—ninety-four yards. He was named All-Pro all three years he played with the San Francisco Forty-Niners, '60–'62, and led the club in interceptions each year. He held the Forty-Niner record for the most interceptions (ten) in a season until Ronnie Lott tied it in 1986.

After serving two years in the army he returned to Bethany, Oklahoma, where he was the head basketball coach for five years and served another five years as director of athletics at Bethany Nazarene College. He then spent twenty-seven years with the State Farm Insurance Company in Norman. He was also a recipient of the Timothy Award, one of the Nazarene Church's highest honors.

David Baker died on September 4, 2002, at the age of sixty-five, after a long struggle against emphysema.

Brooklyn, New York, Sunday, September 30, 1956

The Brooklyn Dodgers clinched the National League pennant today. Duke Snyder and Sandy Amarose each hit two home runs and Jackie Robinson hit one homer as the Dodgers beat Pittsburgh 8–6. Don Newcombe (27–7) secured the win for the Dodgers.

In the American League, Mickey Mantle was wrapping up his Triple Crown season. Mantle finished with 52 homers, 130 RBI, and a .353 batting average. Casey Stengel's Yanks had already won the pennant and were set to meet the Dodgers in the series.

Brooklyn, New York, Wednesday, October 3, 1956

Sal "the Barber" Maglie beat the Yankees 6–3, and the Dodgers took a 1–0 lead in the World Series.

Brooklyn, New York, Thursday, October 4, 1956

Today's World Series game was rained out.

Brooklyn, New York, Friday, October 5, 1956

The New York Yankees used seven different pitchers in losing to the Brooklyn Dodgers 13–8. The series now moved to Yankee Stadium with the pinstripers trailing two games to none.

Bronx, New York, Saturday, October 6, 1956

The Yankees rebounded to win today's series game 5–3. Enos "Country" Slaughter was their hero, hitting a three-run homer. The INS wire service called Slaughter "a bald old gentleman who entered baseball shortly after its invention."

The forty-year-old Slaughter had been picked up on waivers from Kansas City on August 25. To make room for Slaughter, the Yankees waived veteran shortstop Phil Rizzutto, and nostalgia broke even.

We were pleased that our players did not take Kansas State lightly.

—*Bud Wilkinson*

Oklahoma 66   Kansas State 0

Norman, Oklahoma, Saturday, October 6, 1956

The empty stadium waits. There are no fans, no players, no bands. The grass is freshly mowed and the chalk-dust yard lines are straight and sharp. It is early in the day. The field is still damp from the morning dew. The grass has lost its summer coat of green and faded to yellow.

Soon strong legs will tear up great chunks of turf. Players will leave stains of blood and perspiration on the field, and their uniforms will be covered with grass stains, chalk dust, blood, and sweat. One team will win; one will lose. Nothing of great significance will happen. These are not nations at war. These are college boys playing a game.

After the game the groundskeepers will repair the damage done to the field. Janitors will sweep up popcorn boxes, hot dog wrappers, and whiskey bottles from the stadium. A week later the field and the stadium will look just the same as they do now. Nothing will have changed.

Yet, in a way, a lot will have changed. The game becomes a part of the players. Once played, the game can never be unplayed. It will be headline news tomorrow, then second page, and finally a footnote, but it will always be part of a great body of folklore, statistics, and history that will exist even after the players grow old and die. The game, in a sense, will always be.

Surely no series in the history of football has been as one-sided as OU vs. K-State. Kansas State beat Oklahoma in 1969 and 1970. Before that you had to go all the way back to 1934 to find another Wildcat victory. K-State never defeated a Wilkinson-coached team.

Wilkinson Vs. Wildcats		
Year	OU	KS
'47	27	13
'48	42	0
'49	39	0
'50	58	0
'51	33	0
'52	49	6
'53	34	0
'54	21	0
'55	40	7
'56	66	0
'57	13	0
'58	40	6
'59	36	0
'60	49	7
'61	17	6
'62	47	0
'63	34	9
Totals	645	54
Average	37.9	3.2

The easy victory allowed the Sooners to eclipse their own record of thirty-one straight wins. In his weekly newsletter, Wilkinson apologized for the lopsided victory. "Scores such as we had in this game are unfortunate. We simply had too much manpower for Kansas State, and the extremely warm weather [88 degrees] tired the Wildcats more than usual. We were sorry our margin of points was so large, but the circumstances were such that it couldn't be prevented."

Clendon Thomas ensured the Sooners of their homecoming victory by scoring the first three TDs of the game on short runs. Eight different backs scored for OU and fifty-five players got into the contest. OU totaled 479 rushing yards to K-State's 172, and the Sooners had seventeen first downs to the Cats' four. Thomas finished with 82 yards on eight carries, and Tommy McDonald, who ironically did not score in the rout, had 79 yards on six carries. OU's first unit had the ball on offense only four times and scored each time.

The Sooners ran a few plays from their Swinging Gate formation. "It was just an old Francis Schmidt [Ohio State] play," Bud told reporters. Wilkinson and his assistants liked to put in one or two such "trick" or "gimmick" plays each week. The players liked to run the new formations because they helped to break up the monotony of practice and they usually worked successfully in the games.

Oklahoma's Swinging Gate

E C   G G T T E

LH   FB   RH

QB

After Thomas's three tallies David Baker continued the Sooner scoring, returning a punt fifty-seven yards for a touchdown. The fifth OU touchdown was set up by Steve Jennings's block of a K-State punt. The fourth team finished out the first half for the Sooners.

The alternate team started the second half for OU, but the starters came back into the game midway through the third quarter and Jimmy Harris moved them forty-three yards on six plays with Billy Pricer getting the TD from two yards out. After this score the first team retired for the afternoon.

The alternates scored again, when Baker, after taking a hand-off from Jay O'Neal, lateraled to Carl Dodd, who raced thirty-three yards for the Sooners' seventh touchdown.

The third team recorded the next TD when halfback Johnny Pellow ran the ball in from the six. Bud inserted the fourth team again, and Jakie Sandefer soon scored from the five.

The tenth and last Sooner touchdown was made by Ernie Day, who was listed on the depth chart as the sixth-team left halfback. Day scored from three yards out after Sandefer had broken away for a fifty-four-yard gain.

After the game, the Kansas State coach, Bus Mertes, who had started five-foot, four-inch Jerry Hayes at halfback, put things in perspective. "The scoreboard tells the story. There is not much I can add to that 66–0 score."

I loved to hit people.

—*Bill Krisher*

Bill Krisher

Edom, Texas, Thirty Years after the Game

Driving east from Denton to Greenville on Highway 380 one crosses the fertile dark soil of north Texas. This is a land of pickup

trucks and tractor caps. These tractor caps—or baseball caps, if you prefer—are either genetic mutations or else they have been surgically attached. If you see a man in this area wearing a tractor cap, you never see him not wearing one.

There was once a sign on the outskirts of some small hamlet along 380 (it might have been Princeton, Farmersville, Floyd, or maybe Campbell) that proudly boasted, "The blackest soil and the whitest people in the world."

Continuing south and east from Greenville along Highway 69 a subtle change in the landscape emerges. The trees begin to obscure more and more of the rich soil. Somewhere around Emory one enters the piney woods of east Texas.

Bill Krisher, the starting right guard for the '56 Sooners, lived among these beautiful tall pines. On this day Krisher and some of his friends and associates were having lunch at the Woodshead Restaurant in Edom, Texas, which is not far from Ben Wheeler, Texas. The Mercedes and Cadillacs in the Woodshead's lot were a stark contrast to the pickup trucks parked at Bea's Diner in Emory a few miles down the road.

Later that day, seated in a large antique chair inside his custom-built log home, Krisher recalled, "Yes, it was hard to get psyched up to play teams like Kansas State. But one of our strengths at OU was that we had five teams and the AOs [All Others]. We had a lot of folks, and you're looking at people pushing you all the time. So the motivation wasn't necessarily coaching. It was somebody trying to take your job, trying to beat you out. I think we had a situation, if I'm not mistaken, where a guy could challenge you for your position and we'd have a one-on-one and see who could beat who.

"That was the one thing that made us so tough in '55," Krisher continued, "with that fast-break team, when we did such a good job in the Orange Bowl against Maryland. A great deal of that was generated in practice because the team would be breaking the huddle real quick and getting up to the line. Bud saw us doing that and we started the fast-break stuff.

"There were some games, like Kansas State, where we played only half a game. We were trying to get the other guys into the game. We respected them for all the time they spent in practice running the plays against us, and we liked to see the third and fourth team get in and play."

Krisher said he began to realize this was no ordinary team when Coach Wilkinson brought his camera out to take pictures of the players. "Bud could draw a play up on the board, and we could go out and run that play to perfection in two or three plays," Krisher said.

"I feel like we had a camaraderie and a discipline that was really great, and I credit a lot of it to the Christian influence on our team. They were a solid group of guys who believed in training and taking care of themselves and paying the price. You were more afraid of your teammates catching you [breaking training] than of the coaches catching you."

In 1956, Krisher, whose nickname was "Man Mountain," was

the biggest man on the team at 215 pounds, about average for a Bob Stoops running back. Even in '56 Krisher played against men who outweighed him by twenty or thirty pounds. "When I went into pro ball I weighed about 220, I had to run with the backs since I was just too fast to run with the linemen." Krisher's college roommate, Benton Ladd, recalled that he was indeed, very fast. "Bill Krisher could run," Ladd said. "His legs were huge and you wouldn't think that he had speed but he did. He could keep up with most of the backs for forty yards."

However, Krisher eventually had to sacrifice some of his speed for bulk in the pros. "I got beat to death," he said. "I had to go up to about 245 to survive in the pros [as an offensive guard]. That's about where I am today." In the twenty-first century there are many offensive linemen who are a hundred pounds heavier than this in both the pros and college.

After leaving OU, Krisher played with the Pittsburgh Steelers in '58 and '59. In 1960 he joined the Dallas Texans, which later became the Kansas City Chiefs. Krisher spent two years with the Texans, where he was named to the American Football League All-Pro team. He retired from pro ball after the 1961 season to work full time with the Fellowship of Christian Athletes (FCA) in their national office in Kansas City. "I enjoyed playing very much," Krisher explained. "I just felt the Lord calling me into full-time Christian work. That's why I retired from pro ball. I physically could have played a number of more years."

In 1965 Krisher resigned from the FCA to manage a Morgan horse farm in Vermont. In 1968 he returned to the FCA to become director of the southwest region. Krisher remained with the FCA until 1979 when he again resigned, this time to become the executive director of Meaningful Life, the position he held at the time of this interview.

"Meaningful Life is a Christian organization," Krisher explained. "We run a Christian retreat center here. My responsibility is having weekend retreats and having a ministry to single parents and kids who have some problems. We also have weekend retreats for couples, and we have some churches who use the facilities on weekends."

Meaningful Life was headquartered on 420 acres of beautiful east Texas timberland called Wendy's Meadow Ranch. Purchased by Dallas builders Bob and Andy Hickman, the ranch was named in honor of Bob's son, Wendy Dean Hickman, who died of a heart attack at the age of seventeen. At the organization's inception, Krisher was hired by Bob Hickman to be the executive director of Meaningful Life.

"We started with nothing," Krisher said. "We dug a lake. We built four cabins, named Matthew, Mark, Luke, and John, and a six-thousand-square-foot barn with a racquetball court, ping-pong, bumper pool, meeting room, weight room, and a tack room. We bring people out of the busy city life to relax. They can walk, ride horses, fish, and swim. We are trying to reach out to people that maybe the church or other organizations are not reaching. We're hoping we can win them for the Lord so they can go back to their churches and be stronger witnesses for Christ. We do the ministry to them and sometimes we bring in speakers."

The board of directors of Meaningful Life read like a Who's Who of Texas football: Roger Staubach, Bob Breunig, and Grant Teaff were part of this panel, along with Kyle Rote Jr. In addition to his role with Meaningful Life, Krisher also served on the board of trustees of the Paul Anderson Youth Home along with Kyle Rote Jr., Roger Staubach, and Tom Landry.

Bill and Lana Krisher and their two sons, Chad, eighteen, and Eric, twenty, lived in a custom-built log home on twelve acres near Wendy's Meadow Ranch. Several large oak rocking chairs sat serenely on Krisher's large front porch. To enter the Krishers' house was to step back in time a hundred years. Their home looked like it should have been featured in *Country Living* or some other decorator magazine. Every article in their home was an antique, every chair, every bed, every table. Indeed the antique industry seemed to be the major form of commerce in this area of Texas. There were several antique stores at both Edom and Ben Wheeler. In fact, that is about all there was in these two towns. Canton, Texas, twenty miles to the west, hosted a huge flea market and antique bazaar one weekend each month.

The old-timers say Canton was once the site of public hangings. People who came to see the hangings began trading animals (horses, cows, mules, and so on) at first, and later started to trade other articles. This trading evolved into the present-day antiques selling and trading, according to the folklore.

Krisher was wearing blue jeans, a flannel shirt with a hunting vest, and Adidas running shoes. The '56 crew cut had grown long enough to just cover the tops of his ears. Krisher, a consensus All-American for the Sooners in 1957, thought his blocked extra point against Colorado in that year was perhaps the most memorable personal achievement in his career at OU. He shoved a Colorado blocker into the kicker, blocking the kick and allowing OU to escape with a 14–13 victory to keep their winning streak alive at forty-five games.

Dissenting from many of his former teammates, Krisher believed the '57 team was probably as strong as the '56 unit. "We had as much in '57. I think the great desire of coaches around the country to beat the champs finally caught up with us. I think there were a lot of film exchanges and some people figured out some of our plays. If we had had a few more minutes we would have won that game [Notre Dame '57] or at least tied it." This was the only blemish on the record of Krisher's class of '58. Their three-year record at OU was 31–1–0. The '56 seniors compiled a record of 31–0–0. And the '56 sophomores were 30–2–0.

"Carl Dodd was an excellent quarterback. Jimmy Harris might have been a little better. Harris was probably a little faster than Dodd but Dodd did a good job in '57. He played excellent ball. The thing that encouraged me was that after we lost that game, we didn't lose any more and that takes some character to do that. I think our '57 team was as good as our '56 team but the circumstances were different, the building of pressure, winning forty-seven games in a row, and building to a crescendo of a game like Notre Dame. I don't think anybody played below their ability. I just think Notre Dame got up for it. Terry Brennan wanted to keep his job." Brennan had tried to recruit Krisher to play for Notre Dame.

Krisher, as did almost all of his teammates, recalled the bone-jarring tackle that Jerry Tubbs made on Paul Hornung in the '56 Notre Dame game. "I think that's the hardest hit I've ever seen in my life, when Tubbs hit Hornung on the second play of the game. I was right next to him at the time." Krisher played middle guard on defense, lining up directly in front of the center, with Tubbs and Billy Pricer right behind him as linebackers.

Krisher and Tubbs often had to match up against each other in practice. Krisher said they had to work out a kind of a buddy system for their own survival. "Tubby and I would agree on certain things so we wouldn't kill each other. I'd tell him I wouldn't ring his helmet if he wouldn't cut block me at the knees. He didn't like to have his helmet rung and I didn't like to be cut [Krisher had suffered a knee injury in his freshman year], so we had an agreement when we scrimmaged against each other. We used to laugh about it because we could have really hurt each other if we had really gotten after it."

Krisher enjoyed playing both offense and defense in college. He said he really had no preference. "I liked both offense and defense. I just enjoyed hitting people. It was a unique era in that you played both ways. It takes some ability to play both ways to where you're changing your mind to go from tackling to blocking to running to defending. The type of mental adjustment that a player had to make at that time, and this is where I think some of the great coaching was done, having things so well organized with all the different defenses you had to run with the slants and stunts and everything, and then to be able to perform at that level going both ways. I'm glad I played in that era. I never played on Astroturf. I played on grass and I enjoyed it immensely. I know they've got better equipment and better training now and as far as pro ball is concerned you make a lot more money now than you did then by a long shot. But I wouldn't take for the years I played. Basically you look at our society today, and everybody is wanting to copy the fifties in cars, music, and everything; it's all a fad, the fifties fad. It was a fascinating time." Rock music critic Marcus Greil believed that for many, many people 1956 represented the ultimate in style. A lot of fifties fans think things have never been better. The music hasn't gotten any better; the clothing styles haven't improved; and there has never been a better haircut than the ducktail. Certainly this was the "Golden Era" of OU football. Sooner fans have never felt more pride in their players and coaches than they did in 1956.

Krisher spoke about his coterie of friends at OU; however, he gave the impression of being much more locked into the present than did many of his teammates. It was not that he was unwilling to talk about the past, and it was not that his teammates were still living in the past. However, Krisher seemed more removed from this era than some of the others. He seemed to be more immersed in his present life of ministry. He often seemed to recite his experiences from rote memory as one tells an old familiar story. Other former players gave the impression, as they talked, that they were reliving these experiences. Krisher's present seemed to be more important, more real than his past. "There was a group of us that bummed around together," he said, "because of similar lifestyle and Christian commitment. That was one of our real strong suits. We traveled all over the state showing films and witnessing and sharing our faith. Clendon Thomas, Chuck Bowman, Don Nelson, Billy Pricer, and Tom Emerson were basically the group of us that got together so much. You have cliques on teams, and these guys had some mutual interests."

Krisher said he often sees many of his former teammates. "I see Tubbs quite a bit because I'm up at the Cowboy office a lot." (At the time of this interview Tubbs was a linebacker coach for the Dallas Cowboys.) Through the FCA, Krisher helped start a Bible study group for Dallas Cowboy football players.

"Clendon Thomas and I stay in close touch. Chuck Bowman and I stay in close touch. He's now taken over the region of the FCA I had. I see Carl Dodd once in a while. There is an awful lot of camaraderie among OU players, not just from the mid-fifties, but there is an unusual camaraderie and closeness of OU players all over the country. I'm talking about guys who played in the late forties. It was an unusual group in the forties, fifties, and sixties, but it seems like the seventies and eighties was a whole new breed of folks.

"I'll tell you what amazes me even today, is the number of people that remember me because I played at OU. More so than because of anything I did in pro ball or in the FCA or anything. Evidently we were a remembered team. I have never thought I was a great athlete at all. I just played because I enjoyed playing and whatever accolades I got I have to give the credit to the Lord because I didn't deserve anything I got. I wasn't a fan. I didn't go grab a paper to see if my name was in it. I guess I was getting some publicity because, even today, I am amazed at the number of people who mention that team.

"I guess I never read the sports page because of my high school coach at Midwest City, Oklahoma, Jake Spann. He told us to never read the sports pages. He hated sportswriters. I understand he used to have fistfights with them. They hated his guts. He said don't read the sports page because you can only believe half of what you read. [Pete Gent, in *North Dallas Forty*, stated this theme more laconically when he wrote, "Sportswriters don't know shit."] So I never read the sports page. To this day Mom has scrapbooks of me and articles that I've never read.

"Kids today have greater nutrition, and of course today they have the weight training programs, which we didn't have," Krisher said. Many people probably thought Krisher lifted weights because he had the thick neck and large upper body of a weight lifter, but this was not the case. He said, "They wouldn't allow us to lift weights, because a couple of guys hurt their backs lifting weights. There was no weight work at all. The guy who started it all was Alvin Roy at

LSU with Johnny Robinson and Jerry Stovall. They were the ones who really got the weight lifting started, and it caught on."

Krisher, however, is not envious of today's athletes. "I wouldn't change anything. If I went back to do the whole thing over again, I'd do everything just like I've done. We even won our alumni games. You talk about learning football! That was where I learned it fast. I had to play against Jim Weatherall, who was an All-Pro. I was a college kid out there trying to play against those big suckers. That taught me a lot real quick. I enjoyed coming back to play in those games immensely. I thought it was a great thing."

The OU varsity-alumni game was discontinued in 1981, primarily for financial reasons. Another factor that led to the alumni game's demise is that the pro teams would no longer allow their players to risk injuries playing in the game, so it had become more and more difficult for the alumni to field a team.

However, in the fifties, many professional players did return to play in these games. Men such as "Indian" Jack Jacobs, a great passer and punter in Canadian football, "Cactus Face" Duggan, Weatherall, Homer Simmons, Leon "Mule Train" Heath, who still holds the Sooner record for the longest run from scrimmage (ninety-six yards), and Dee and Plato Andros returned several times to play in alumni games. Jacobs and Duggan, who both played until they were nearly forty years old, would remove their helmets to smoke cigarettes on the sidelines.

Although a very high percentage of players in Krisher's era earned their degrees, he was somewhat irresolute on the issue of requiring tougher academic standards for athletes. "[NCAA regulations] ought to be in line with what the average student can do. I don't think athletes should have unjust demands put on them, because if I tried to figure out the number of hours I put in per week on football and still tried to keep up with academics, while fraternity kids were running around doing their thing . . . I was working hard. I put in forty-eight to fifty hours a week on football and still had to make my grade point. I had to miss classes because of travel, and I had to come back and make up all those labs.

"We had a lot of freshmen who couldn't cut it academically. They would party and goof off and eventually end up at another school. Some of them were better athletes than what we had left, but the ones who made it were the ones who had made their grades, who would toe the line and follow discipline."

Whether it is more difficult for an athlete than a nonathlete to make his grades is a debatable subject. The major factor working against the athlete is time. It may be that a player will not have any time to study until 9:30 in the evening, when he may be so tired from classes, practice, and meetings that he won't be able to accomplish much, even if he has the best intentions. Weekends are almost totally lost for football players with regard to academics, especially if they play a road game. When the team goes on the road, Friday classes have to be missed. Then on Saturday, after the game, the team will not get back to campus until very late at night. On Sunday morning they will have to report to the training room to have injuries treated and perhaps run through a light workout. They may have Sunday afternoon off between lunch and the evening meal, but after Sunday's dinner, there are team meetings to go over the scouting report of next week's opponent. On Monday the weekday schedule begins all over again.

A Day in the Life of a Student-Athlete

A football player who is serious about earning his degree might have a schedule much like this one during the season. If the athlete is trying to earn only enough grade points to stay eligible, he can have almost any class schedule he wants.

7:00 A.M.	Breakfast—training table—attendance required
8:00 A.M	Class
9:00 A.M.	Class
10:00 A.M.	Lab

11:00 A.M.	Class
12:00 P.M.	Lunch–training table—attendance required
1:30 P.M.	Report to training room to get treatment for injuries and have ankles taped
2:30–4:30 P.M.	Football practice
4:30–6:00 P.M.	Get treatment in training room for injuries
6:00 P.M.	Dinner–training table—attendance required
7:00–9:00 P.M.	Team meetings—watch films, go over scouting report for Saturday's game
9:30 P.M.	Back in room to study

The time that an athlete's sport detracts from his studies is definitely a disadvantage. However, athletes have at least two advantages the nonathletes don't have. First, the athletes have the advantage of counselors (coaches and/or graduate assistants) to help them plan their class schedules. These counselors are able to tell the athletes which professors to avoid and to recommend certain professors who are amenable to working with athletes.

Some professors are more understanding than others about classes that must be missed because of road games and assignments that may have to be turned in late. At every university there are some professors who are known "jock lovers" and will give athletes every break, and there are other professors who will go out of their way to make it tougher on the players. Secondly, the athletes have the benefit of tutors paid for by the athletic department. For the nonathlete such tutors either may not be available at all, or if they are available, the cost may be prohibitive.

So who has the best chance of academic success, the athlete or the nonathlete? If one compares the percentage of athletes who graduate with the percentage of nonathletes who graduate it appears the advantage is to the athletes. Port Robertson, who for

Bill Krisher

thirty-seven years monitored the academic progress of athletes at OU, said, "Our graduation record for athletes has always been far in excess of the graduation rate for the general student body." This is true even though the percentage of athletes who graduate today (1986) is much lower than it used to be. Robertson said, "We used to graduate 85–90 percent of our kids. Now we don't graduate 40 percent. It's a sad, sad thing."

Krisher said he seldom returns to Norman to see games now. "I've got tickets on the fifty yard line and I never use them. I give them to friends. My weekends are taken up with my ministry and what I'm doing now. My son, Eric, is very interested in OU so I took him to the Nebraska game last year, and I did the chapel service for the Nebraska team because Tom Osborne is a good friend.

"I've gone to the Texas game one time in the last twenty years. You can see so much better on TV. If you want to watch football, that's the place to watch it. I loved to play. I loved to hit people. I enjoyed playing but I'm not what you would call a dyed-in-the-wool football fan. I'd rather be at home with my family here in the afternoon than take all the time to go to a college or pro game." This is not too difficult to understand; east Texas is a beautiful place to be in the autumn.

A good season for staying is Autumn; there is work
there for everyone before the very short days . . .

—From an anonymous eleventh-century Irish ballad

Dallas, Texas, January 2005

"It really doesn't seem like it has been almost fifty years since I played at OU. I would say more like twenty-five. Time goes by so quickly that, as you look back on it, you don't realize how much change has taken place in fifty years.

"I'm in good health. I have a little back problem, but most people my age [seventy] do. I had a hip replacement a few years back, but I have no problems now at all. It just went fine." Indeed, Krisher did appear to be in excellent health. He looked much the same as he had twenty years earlier, with just a few more gray hairs perhaps.

Bill Krisher recently celebrated another fiftieth anniversary: one that is at least as important to him as the anniversary of his championship season. In 2004 he marked fifty years of membership in the Fellowship of Christian Athletes.

The FCA was incorporated in 1954 when Branch Rickey and some other Pittsburgh businessmen underwrote its first year's budget. Bill Krisher was a charter member. In fact, the original site of the FCA's national headquarters was established on the second floor of the City National Bank building in Norman, Oklahoma. Two years later these offices were moved to their present site of Kansas City, Missouri.

When the Fellowship of Christian Athletes held its first national conference in Estes Park, Colorado, in 1956, Bill Krisher, along with some of his OU teammates, Carl Dodd, Ross Coyle, Bill Brown, Clendon Thomas, Chuck Bowman, and Bob Harrison, was in attendance. "Port Robertson was really the main thrust behind putting this group together," Krisher said. "Port was really one of the 'Founding Fathers' of the FCA."

In 1993 Bill Krisher resigned as the director of Wendy's Meadow Ranch and left the bucolic serenity of the east Texas piney woods to return to Dallas. "The fellow who owned the property was getting into gambling, so I had to get out of that," he explained. For a couple of years after this Krisher worked as the director of the Paul Anderson Youth Home before rejoining the FCA to serve in his present capacity as senior director of development for the Dallas area.

"I still get requests, about twice a month or so, from fans who want autographs. They will send a picture or something to be signed and returned. Some of it is from pro ball, but most of it is from OU. So obviously the interest in this era is still out there.

"The only regret I have about the '56 team is that we could not play in the Orange Bowl, because the rules, then, didn't allow us to go two years in a row. So, there we were, the national champs sitting at home watching everybody else play."

Bill Krisher, in 2005, was certainly not just an "Old School" cynic living in the past and disparaging modern players and coaches. He spoke highly of the Sooners' current gridiron combatants. "I just can't say enough about what Bob Stoops and Joe Castiglione have done at OU," he proclaimed. "They have done wonderful jobs. They brought back the winning tradition and they have done it with class and dignity, and they always welcome us old-timers back." Not all of Krisher's old teammates shared his opinion of Mr. Castiglione. In fact, one of them said, "He's done a lot of good things and raised a lot of money for the athletic department, but I wouldn't want to buy a used car from him."

"It's funny when you go back for reunions," Krisher said. "When you look at the guys who played in the forties and fifties, their noses are smashed in and their faces are all scarred up. But if you look at the guys who played in the sixties and later, they look fine. You can tell when they started to play with face masks.

"But . . . the thing that is great about Oklahoma," Krisher continued, "is that no matter when you played you're accepted. There are no distinctions or exceptions for anybody. If you're from OU and you're a ballplayer, you're accepted. No questions."

Bronx, New York, Sunday, October 7, 1956

The Yankees evened the series at two games each by beating the Dodgers 6–2. Mickey Mantle hit a tremendous home run that cleared the center field wall 464 feet from home plate. Knuckleballer Tom Sturdivant of Oklahoma City was the winning pitcher.

Bronx, New York, Monday, October 8, 1956

In what remains as one of the great enigmas of sports, Don Larsen pitched the one and only perfect game in World Series history as the Yanks beat the Dodgers 2–0.

Of all the great pitchers who have been in the World Series it is incredible that Don Larsen, a man with a lifetime record of eighty-one wins and ninety-one losses, would be the man to pitch a perfect game. Brandon Boyd and Fred C. Harris, writing of this phenomenon years later in their tremendously witty *The Baseball Card Flippin', Tradin', and Bubblegum Book,* said, "In the seventy-five or so years that the World Series has been played there have been perhaps 1,200 pitchers who have pitched in it. Of these, Don Larsen is the only one to have pitched a perfect game. Like Sophia Loren's marriage to Carlo Ponti, the continuing popularity of Danny Thomas and the political career of Spiro Agnew, there is no rational explanation for this. It just is."

The last man retired by Larsen was Dale Mitchell, who was no doubt the greatest baseball player ever to play at the University of Oklahoma. While at OU, Mitchell recorded a batting average of over .500 for one season. The '56 season was Mitchell's last in the majors. Mitchell, a lifetime .300 hitter, seemed surprised that a pitcher of Larsen's meager talents could strike him out under any circumstances.

One of those who did not watch on TV as Larsen pitched his perfect game was Bud Wilkinson, who was speaking at the Oklahoma City Quarterback Club about the Sooners' next opponent, the University of Texas Longhorns. Bud said, "Texas quarterback Johnny Clements, on record, is the best passer in college football today and," Bud continued, apparently forgetting that Jimmy Brown was still playing for the University of Syracuse, "Walt Foundren is probably the best runner. This game means a lot to Texas. I hope we can play as well as we can and I hope that if we do that, it will be good enough to win. I don't know if that will be good enough, but I hope so."

Brooklyn, New York, Tuesday, October 9, 1956

With two outs in the bottom of the tenth inning, Jackie Robinson drove in Junior Gilliam to beat Bob Turley and the Yankees 1–0 to even the World Series at three games each.

Brooklyn, New York, Wednesday, October 10, 1956

Yogi Berra smashed two home runs off Don Newcombe to lead the Yankees to a 9–0 victory over the Dodgers and to the World Series championship. Twenty-three-year-old Johnny Kucks pitched the shutout for the Yanks.

Bob Consodine wrote, "This will be a series to be rolled off the tongue of fandom like fine brandy for generations to come." Indeed, it has been.

Dallas, Texas, Thursday, October 11, 1956

Two days before the Sooners and Longhorns were to meet, 26,500 screaming fans gathered in the Cotton Bowl to see Elvis Presley in concert.

The next day the *Dallas Morning News* wrote: "Presley started off with 'Heartbreak Hotel,' doing a staggering, shuffle-footed dance with the microphone. Sometimes he went into a really classical Indian war dance. Other times it was sheer voodoo acrobatics as he threw his famous pelvis from the 50 yard line to the 35."

*Our starting team fumbled four times. In a close game,
which we will have every week from now on, poor
mechanical play will be the margin by which we will
be defeated. I certainly hope we can overcome our
errors through diligent practice in the days ahead.*

—Bud Wilkinson

Oklahoma 45   Texas 0

Dallas, Texas, Saturday, October 13, 1956

In 1956, when there were no interstate highways, the journey
from Norman to Dallas was long and arduous. It might take
almost twenty hours to drive to Dallas, watch the game, and drive
back to Norman or Oklahoma City. Highway 77 meandered
through Purcell, Wayne, Wynnewood, Davis, then over the steep
grades and tricky curves of the Arbuckle Mountains to Ardmore
and finally across the Red River into Texas. Each of these small
towns had its red sandstone monument to the WPA, either an
American Legion Hall, an armory, or perhaps an amphitheater.
These reminders of the depression are plentiful in Oklahoma.
Some have been torn down so that Pizza Huts, McDonalds, and
Wal-Marts could be built, but many have survived. The sidewalks
on the University of Oklahoma campus are stamped with mes-
sages that read WPA 1937.

Each year thousands of Oklahomans made this long pilgrim-
age to the Cotton Bowl. Several opted for the more leisurely train
ride and took Santa Fe's Super Chief, which was still possible, for
in 1956 passenger trains had not yet been assigned to the endan-
gered species list.

Abe Lemons, the longtime Oklahoma City University basketball coach and humorist in the tradition of Will Rogers, told a rather poignant vignette apropos of the disappearance of the passenger train. Abe said when he was a boy living in Walters, a small town in southwestern Oklahoma, his father came to him one day and said, "Come on, Abe, we're gonna take the train over to the game preserve at Lawton [a distance of about forty miles]. We'll go see the buffalo over there. There'll come a time when there won't be no more buffalo to see."

Abe said of his trip, "So we rode the train over there, saw the buffalo, and took the train back to Walters. I was really glad I took that little trip with Dad because now we have way more buffalo than we need but there aren't any more trains."

The easy victory over the Texans made the journey home seem less tiresome for Sooner fans. As the early fifties models of Fords, Chevys, Pontiacs, Studebakers, Ramblers, Buicks, and Cadillacs climbed the Arbuckles, heading north, the occupants of these vehicles were still marveling at the ease with which Thomas and McDonald had run through the Texas defenders for 263 yards and six touchdowns on twenty-nine carries.

McDonald returned the opening kickoff fifty-four yards, and the Sooners scored in seven plays. Clendon Thomas recorded the first TD from two yards out.

It seemed that Texas had not given up yet as they threw Jimmy Harris for a twenty-nine-yard loss on a broken pass play in the second quarter. On the next play Tubbs snapped the ball through Harris's legs directly to Pricer, who prepared to quick-kick. However, instead of kicking, Pricer handed the ball to Thomas, who ran forty-four yards to the Texas twenty. McDonald scored a few plays later.

Later in the second period, Pricer did quick-kick, a sixty-two-yard beauty, and after the subsequent Texas punt, OU had the ball on the Longhorns' forty-seven yard line. Harris spiraled a perfect pass, which McDonald snagged on his fingertips and carried in for the score just twenty-seven seconds before time expired in the first half with OU leading 19–0. McDonald described his catch after the game: "You know we missed that pass in practice all week long. That was the best pass Jimmy and I have ever completed. I'll tell you one thing. I strained every gut in my body catching it. I got it with the last joint of my fingers."

After intermission the starting eleven took the kickoff and marched eighty yards for another touchdown. Again, McDonald sparked the drive by running for twenty-one yards and making another spectacular pass reception. On fourth down McDonald hauled in the pass at the Texas eight yard line with a diving catch. Clendon Thomas ran the ball in from there.

Although the alternate unit failed to score against Texas, they played well on defense. After the alternates forced a Texas punt, the starters came back into the game and scored in two plays. McDonald ran forty-four yards for the TD this time.

In the fourth quarter, Bill Krisher knocked the ball away from Walt Foundren, who could manage only twenty-six yards on eight carries for the day. Thomas got an easy touchdown after McDonald had completed a twenty-seven-yard pass to John Bell, who took it down to the one yard line.

As he had done the previous week, Ernie Day from Muskogee recorded the Sooners' final touchdown. Day intercepted a pass, the fifth interception of the game for the alert Sooner secondary, and ran twenty-five yards for the TD in the last minute of play.

Because of the limited substitution rule in 1956, OU was forced to play the last three plays of the game with only ten men on the field. Dale "Cowboy" Sherrod had been ejected for fighting, and Wilkinson did not have any other players eligible to reenter the game. "That's what's wrong with the rule in a nutshell," Wilkinson said.

A Wave Breaking Evenly along a Beach

Coach Bud Wilkinson's proud, skillful veterans have never lost a game in their entire college careers. Last

> Saturday playing against what was in the beginning an adequate, reasonably capable University of Texas football team, they showed why as they won 45–0. They showed it in the sudden, lifting charge of a line, which moved all of a piece, like a wave breaking evenly along a beach. They showed it in the meticulous, precise play patterns they braced against the faded green background of the Cotton Bowl turf.
>
> Tex Maule
> *Sports Illustrated,* October 22, 1956

This was undoubtedly Tommy McDonald's most productive game of his great Sooner career. He personally accounted for 282 yards of offense by rushing sixteen times for 140 yards, completing one pass for 27 yards, catching two passes for a total of 61 yards, and returning a kickoff 54 yards.

*There's nothing like it when you get that ball on a punt
and know that you've got a wonderful bunch of fellows
ready to step in and cut down tacklers as they come up.*

—*Tommy McDonald, 1956*

*It's not what you accomplish in life that's important; it's
what you stand for.*

—*Tommy McDonald, 1986*

Tommy McDonald

King of Prussia, Pennsylvania, Thirty Years after the Game

"Absolutely! Yes, I remember that Texas game," Tommy
McDonald said. "In the first two games that year, an opposing

player was hitting me whether I
had the ball or not, but in that
game my linemen opened up
some great holes.

"In '55 the AP picked me on
their All-American team; that was
the only organization that picked
me as an All-American. This was
a big surprise to me to find out I
had been picked to the AP All-
American team as a junior. I
wanted to have a good senior year
and maybe make some other All-
American teams, but the first two
games of my senior year were ter-
rible, absolutely horrendous. [Most backs probably would not

consider ninety-eight yards and two touchdowns on fifteen carries horrendous.]

"It was just fate. For some reason everything will go just right on some days. I mean just extra, extra right. Then there will be some days when things will go just sort of right and then there are days when it just seems like the bottom of the world falls out; you drop balls, you fumble. Now I've never had one of those days, but I know guys that have had them. I do remember that Texas game, yes, I do. I remember I returned a kickoff for forty some yards, the opening kickoff, I believe. I should have broken that damn thing for a touchdown. I really should have. I've seen the films.

"I remember in the Texas game right before the half I caught a ball, and I'll never know how I caught the thing because I caught just the last half of it. Jimmy Harris threw it really well, and I just put up my arms because I thought he had overthrown me. I don't know how I did it, but I'll be damned if I didn't catch the last half of the ball."

Tommy McDonald, the quickest and swiftest of the '56 Sooners, was Oklahoma's breakaway runner with the same potential for the long, game-winning run that Greg Pruitt, Joe Washington, and Barry Sanders gave their respective teams. When OU fans recalled and mentally replayed a game, McDonald's runs, catches, and touchdowns were most prominently remembered. A back with such noticeable talent draws a lot of attention from defenses, so other facets of the offense begin to open up. Often the difference between a great team and one that is merely good is a back with McDonald's game-breaking ability.

Because of his exploits at OU and his twelve-year professional career at the glamour position of wide receiver, McDonald's name is the best remembered of the '56 Sooners. As an All-American in college and later an All-Pro, Tommy McDonald was a prominent player to American football fans for many years. His picture appeared on the cover of *Sports Illustrated* three times. John Underwood of *SI* (October 8, 1962) called him "the pro's best pass catcher."

This same *SI* article stated that McDonald looked a lot like Kirk Douglas. Thirty years later, he looked a lot like he did in the late fifties and early sixties, a slightly older version of Kirk Douglas perhaps. His body was still lithe and youthful. It was only in his face, especially around his eyes, which he covered with wire-rimmed glasses, that McDonald showed some of the strain of having been tackled by people such as Dick "Night Train" Lane, Erich Barnes, Johnny Sample, Jerry Stovall, and Larry Wilson.

If other suburban Philadelphia residents should encounter Tommy McDonald in the supermarket or at a restaurant, unless they knew him, they would not guess him to be a twelve-year veteran of professional football. At five feet, nine inches, 175 pounds, he simply does not look big enough to have bumped heads with the monsters of the Midway and Doomsday defenses of the NFL. Ironically, it may have been McDonald's lack of size that brought him to OU in the first place.

"When I graduated from high school my mother tried to get Notre Dame to give me a scholarship, but they wrote back and told her I would get more playing time at a smaller school. They told her that if I came to Norte Dame I would probably be on the bench. I remembered that when we played Notre Dame.

"When I left Albuquerque to go to OU, the local papers were mad at me because I didn't go to the University of New Mexico. They even had me investigated because they tried to say Oklahoma gave me a car.

"The University of New Mexico, at that time, was de-emphasizing football. They were thinking about dropping it, but the papers really blasted me for leaving Albuquerque, saying I could have been a big duck in a little pond, but now I was going to be a little duck in a big pond. It really upset me! I thought, 'How can you people do this to me?' Instead of hoping I do well, they say something like that." The emotion registered in McDonald's voice and his gestures revealed that this incident had indeed upset him greatly.

"I really didn't have that many scholarships offered to me. I'm not the biggest guy in the world, so there were not a lot of people fighting over me because of my size, but fortunately the number-one guy upstairs blessed me with speed. I won the 100, the 220, and the 180-yard low hurdles in high school, and Bud was fascinated with speed. I didn't have tremendous speed. I mean Billy Sims would throw grass in my face. I was about a ten flat 100 guy. I was the fastest guy on the Oklahoma team in uniform, but Robert Derrick [a third-team halfback in '56] could beat me if we ran in shorts and T-shirts. If we put a uniform on, I could outrun him.

"The University of New Mexico, SMU, and Oklahoma offered me scholarships; now is there a big choice?

"I didn't want to go to SMU because while I was sitting outside the coach's office, he was in there chewing out one of the players. He was just screaming at him. He lost me right there.

"When I look back on that now, I realize that I was in such an immature stage of my life at that time. I don't know what sold me on Oklahoma. I knew it was a big school and we would be playing Notre Dame. When I met Bud I saw what he was, and to me people mean a lot more than other things."

Tommy McDonald was always a little different from his teammates. He was the only member of this team who did not come from either Oklahoma or Texas. Young men who grew up in Oklahoma and Texas in the forties wore a thick coat of humility, spoke with a soft southwestern drawl, and would look down at the ground if someone paid them a compliment. Tommy McDonald could never be described as humble. He was not bashful about receiving a compliment. He ran fast and he talked fast. He had a high-speed turbo-charged personality more characteristic of . . . well, a Yankee. Jerry Tubbs, by comparison, seemed to be going through life on cruise control.

Wilkinson heard about McDonald from his friend Dud DeGroat, the coach at the University of New Mexico. DeGroat and Wilkinson were asked to travel to Europe by the United States Department of Defense to conduct coaching clinics in the summer of 1953, and this is when Bud learned of McDonald.

Wilkinson had been trying to recruit another boy from Albuquerque, a linebacker named Teddy Jack Rhodes. Wilkinson thought he had a chance to get Rhodes because he knew he was not interested in going to the University of New Mexico. DeGroat knew Wilkinson wanted Rhodes and he told him, "There's another kid out there that everybody says is too small, but if Rhodes is coming to Oklahoma you should try to get McDonald to join him."

Bud took his advice and brought both young men to OU. Rhodes, the player Wilkinson was most interested in, at least initially, was injured in his freshman year and never played at OU. McDonald became an All-American. "McDonald was a high school star," Wilkinson said. "He had the aggressiveness and the quickness, but he was not going to go to New Mexico and Dud knew that, so he helped us behind the scenes." It is hard to imagine one major college coach helping another "behind the scenes" given the kind of bloody recruiting wars waged over high school seniors in today's game.

Obviously, McDonald never regretted his decision to come to Oklahoma. "Everything was so special about being there at OU then. I mean Port Robertson was such a great guy. We had a great trainer in Ken Rawlinson. I almost never got hurt, but two weeks before we were to play our first game in '56, I had a hyperextension of my knee. Ken Rawlinson was such a super guy he took me to see a specialist who was in town that day for a coaching clinic. This specialist said, 'You're finished, you're not going to be able to play the rest of the year!' You talk about crying! I let it out! He said, 'We're going to have to put this in a cast!' That's why I think the mind has a lot to do with injuries." Another player, lacking McDonald's drive and determination, would have had the perfect excuse to sit out the grueling practices. He could have claimed his "cast of courage" and no one would have blamed him, but McDonald's competitive spirit would not allow him to take this option, which never occurred to him.

"Wilkinson was ahead of his time," McDonald said. "He was

so creative. His imagination was so great. It's a shame Bud went to the St. Louis Cardinals, because as far as I'm concerned, he probably picked one of the worst owners in the National Football League in Bidwell. He's a kook. I saw Bud at a coaching clinic, and I said, 'I'm glad you got into professional ball, but you probably picked one of the worst owners to go with. I doubt if you'll be there two years.'

"I think the personalities added to that team. I don't think it was just all talent. I think personalities add to the charisma and the magic that a team has, and I think that's exactly what we had at the University of Oklahoma. I just happened to be one of the guys who went there when we had a hell of a class. We went through three years of varsity football and never lost a game. I'm very proud of that record.

"I had a lot of friends at Oklahoma. Byron Searcy and I were great friends. Ed Gray and I would cut up together all the time. Jerry Tubbs, Bo Bollinger, Kurt Burris, and Bob Burris were great friends of mine. Jimmy Harris could almost be like a brother to me.

"I think a quarterback can make or break you because if he doesn't throw you the ball, you may as well stick your finger in your ear and go off and pout in a corner. Nobody can do anything without that little piece of leather. Jimmy was an excellent play caller. Jimmy Harris probably had more to do with us winning that senior year than anybody because of his play calling. There was nobody who could run the option better. He knew when to keep the ball, and he could pitch it off at the last minute. I think Jimmy Harris was the man we could least afford to lose on that team."

Great hands, speed, and quickness were the talents that McDonald possessed, but fans and players were impressed with McDonald's enthusiasm for football. No player ran back to the huddle faster than McDonald. If football ever had a "Charlie Hustle" his name was Tommy McDonald.

A Funny Kid

McDonald is a funny kid in that he figures any play that doesn't go for a touchdown is a failure. When he carries the ball and doesn't score, he's mad and wants to hurry up and get another crack at it. Most players who carry for 25 yards or so on a play, lie on the ground, get up slowly, and turn their backs to both sides of the field to make sure everyone sees their number—not McDonald. He jumps up and runs back to the huddle, running almost twice as fast as if he had the ball. It's nothing we taught him. It's something that God gave him, or his parents or something. We didn't do it.

Bud Wilkinson
Daily Oklahoman, 1956

McDonald could not really explain how this practice began or where he picked it up. "That was just born in me. I didn't develop it. I don't know where it came from. I did that all through high school. As soon as I'd get tackled, I'd jump up and run back to the huddle."

With seventeen touchdowns in 1956, McDonald was fourth on the list for national scoring honors. Sooner right halfback Clendon Thomas scored eighteen touchdowns and won the national scoring title. McDonald acknowledged that he and Thomas were certainly rivals for the scoring title. "Any time you've got two good players like that on a team, you can't help but have rivalry. If you don't think there is going to be rivalry, you're living in a fantasyland. Thomas and I were never really buddy-buddy, but I don't think you have to be buddy-buddy with everyone on the team. That is not what a team is really all about.

"I know at least three of Thomas's eighteen touchdowns were scored on passes from me. [This is true. McDonald threw Thomas touchdown passes against Colorado, Missouri, and Oklahoma

A&M.] So if I had wanted to be totally selfish and win the scoring title myself, all I had to do was not throw him the ball. I think against Colorado it was a fourth-down play, we were on their five yard line or something like that, and the defensive halfback came up on me and Clendon was wide open. I very easily could have overthrown him, but I am not that kind of a guy." The play McDonald recalled was OU's second touchdown against Colorado. It came on a fourth and goal from the six. If McDonald had been the kind of guy to overthrow Thomas, the Sooners, who were trailing 19–6 at the time, would almost certainly have lost the game.

In contrast to some of his teammates, McDonald said he was very much aware of his statistics. "I don't care who the individual is. Everybody is concerned about his stats. They may say they don't care about their statistics, and an individual may say that he's a team player and he's not concerned about his stats, but I'll tell you he's a bold-faced liar!" McDonald said, most emphatically. "Anybody who tells me he's not concerned with his stats speaks with forked tongue."

Mac Stats		
1955		
Category	Yards/Points	Nat'l Ranking
Scoring	96 pts.	3rd
Total offense	967 yds.	14th
Rushing	707 yds.	
Punt returns	207 yds.	9th
1956		
Category	Yards/Points	Nat'l Ranking
Scoring	102 pts.	4th
Total offense	1,036 yds.	11th
Rushing	817 yds.	8th
Punt returns	150 yds.	15th

Although McDonald would later gain fame as a pro receiver, he set a couple of Oklahoma passing records: the highest pass completion percentage for one season by a halfback, 70.8 on seventeen of twenty-four passes with no interceptions, and the most consecutive pass completions, eleven. "I'm not too proud of 'em," McDonald said. "They were just little flips. Anybody could do it."

McDonald, who won the Maxwell Memorial Award honoring college football's player of the year in 1956, also finished third in the voting for the Heisman Trophy. "Hell no, I never thought I'd win the Heisman," McDonald said. "No way. Actually I'm glad I didn't win the Heisman, because most guys that won the Heisman did not do well in professional football." Indeed, no Heisman Trophy winner had ever been voted into pro football's Hall of Fame until O. J. Simpson and Roger Staubach were inducted in 1984.

McDonald, who became a member of college football's Hall of Fame in 1985, was obviously not pleased about his exclusion from the pro Hall of Fame. "The people who are voting [for the Hall of Fame inductees] need to see a psychiatrist. There are a lot of guys that are not in there like Fran Tarkington [who was voted in later that year]. Sonny Jurgenson didn't go in the first year he was eligible."

McDonald's case for induction was a very strong one and he would eventually get his wish, but he would have to wait another twelve years. In his twelve NFL seasons, McDonald caught 495 passes for 8,410 yards (an average of 17 yards per reception) and scored eighty-four touchdowns.

When McDonald played in the NFL, teams played twelve- and fourteen-game schedules. Now teams play a sixteen-game season, so modern players have more games per year and more chances to surpass McDonald's totals. However, at the time McDonald retired from pro football (1968), only two men, Jimmy Brown (106) and Don Hutson (99), had scored more touchdowns than McDonald. O. J. Simpson (61), Larry Csonka (64), Raymond

Berry (68), and Gayle Sayers (35), who are all members of the pro Hall of Fame, did not score as many TDs as McDonald.

McDonald was understandably very proud of his touchdowns. "To me, the most important accomplishment is not how many balls the guy catches, it's what he does after he catches the ball, and that's what I'm really proud of. Drew Pearson caught 489 balls to my 495. He scored forty-eight TDs. I caught six more passes and scored eighty-four TDs." Or, to further emphasize this point, Charlie Taylor had 649 receptions, 154 more than McDonald, and scored seventy-nine touchdowns, five less than McDonald. McDonald averaged a touchdown every 5.9 receptions.

McDonald's professional career began in 1957 with the Philadelphia Eagles, who won only four games and lost eight that year. The next year was even worse as they sank to a 2–9–1 record, but in 1959 they improved their record to 7–5. In 1960 the Eagles were 10–2 and defeated the Green Bay Packers to win the NFL championship with McDonald catching a thirty-five-yard touchdown pass from Norm Van Brocklin, who McDonald said was the man who taught him how to run his pass routes.

McDonald could not say whether his two national collegiate titles at OU or the NFL championship with the Eagles gave him the most satisfaction. "Both were great," he said. "We had a fantastic team at Oklahoma, and nobody will ever touch that record of forty-seven consecutive victories. I can't say one means more to me than the other. They are both extra, extra special. We had great teams, great individuals, and great coaches. Wilkinson obviously was a great coach, and Buck Shaw, my coach with the Eagles, was great, too."

McDonald also could not (or would not) choose between his two quarterbacks at Philadelphia, Van Brocklin and Jurgenson. "You have to put them in different categories. They were two different types of throwers. They were both great players. I would be perfectly happy to play for either one of them." Both apparently liked to throw to McDonald.

In 1964 McDonald was traded to the Dallas Cowboys, a move that did not turn out well for McDonald, and he stayed with Dallas only that one year. "Tom Landry was one of the greatest coaches around, but the situation just wasn't right for me. I refused to go back to the Cowboys because I knew playing there just wasn't going to work out. I had a little personality clash with one of the quarterbacks. [He would not say which one.] When the quarterback won't throw you the ball, it's like trying to change a tire without a tire tool."

From the Cowboys, McDonald went to the Rams, where he had a very good year in '65, catching sixty-seven passes for 1,036 yards and nine TDs and making the Pro Bowl. "I had a disastrous year with the Cowboys. Then I went to the Rams and made the Pro Bowl, so that shows you how important it is for the quarterback to like you," McDonald said. After two seasons with the Rams, George Allen traded McDonald to the Atlanta Falcons, where he led the team in receptions with thirty-three. "I knew it was hopeless down there," McDonald said. (The Falcons were 1–12–1 in '67.) "I asked to be traded." He was traded to Cleveland, where he finished his career in 1968.

After his retirement from pro football, McDonald formed his own corporation, which is involved in the painting and selling of color portraits. He explained how he got started in this business. "This artist did a painting of me from a photograph. I couldn't get over how he could do that from a photo. [McDonald, who had received numerous rings, watches, and other awards throughout his career, began to see some possibilities for these portraits.] So, I formed a corporation in 1967 and got this guy to paint for me. Pretty soon the painting got to be too much work for one man, so I hired another artist to work with him. Soon the work got to be too much for the two of them and they had to get other artists. When I started, I never realized how many organizations other than touchdown clubs and quarterback clubs want portraits like this. Banks and insurance companies have ordered many,

many of these to present to someone who is retiring or to give a 'Distinguished Service Award' to someone.

"I don't do any of the painting, but my name goes at the bottom of the pictures because I'm hoping that if somebody likes it they'll come to me for another picture. We have about six artists now. We were up to eleven, but within the last few years I've sort of retired. I don't really work at it that much any more. I answer the phone. If somebody wants a painting, we'll do it.

"I'm not what you'd call a money-hungry individual. I don't care about making a lot of money. I'm perfectly happy as long as I can live my life with God, which is my goal in life."

McDonald and his wife, Patty, raised their four children, Sherry, Christopher, Tom, and Tish, in a large, well-appointed suburban home with a swimming pool. If they wished, they could escape to their other home on the New Jersey shore.

Christopher played college football at the University of Delaware, and Tom played football in high school but not college. "I talked him out of playing," McDonald said. "Because, unless you're really droolin' at the mouth and really have to play, like me, it isn't worth it. Tom more or less played to make me happy. I don't need that. I told him, 'Don't make me happy. Make yourself happy.' I'm not one of those fathers who thinks my son has got to play, that it will teach him to compete and get along in life. Bullshit. It doesn't work that way. Football does not teach you how to compete in life and how to get along with other people. That is the farthest thing from what football teaches. It kills me when I hear fathers say things like, 'Football will teach my son how to get along with other guys,' or 'It will teach him how to win and how to lose.'"

Many of McDonald's former teammates remarked that Tommy had not returned to OU for any of the alumni games. He did not come back for the twenty-fifth reunion of his 1956 championship team. "I was running my own business and business comes first, pleasure second," he said.

"I run my business the same way I played football. I'm dedicated to it. I run my company myself. I'm the salesman, the bookkeeper; I have to do everything. I just could not take three or four days off and go back to alumni games.

"I didn't come back to the twenty-fifth reunion, but what people don't understand is that I made a commitment to *Sports Illustrated* to do an appearance for them. I had a chance to pick up three or four day's work for *SI*, and I'm not the kind of guy to cancel out when I've given my word.

"I almost did go back for Port's testimonial dinner in '84 because I have such great respect for Port Robertson. I contributed some money for the truck they bought him. I'm probably more sentimental than anyone who was on that team. The one thing that I have a real problem with is that I let my emotions run away with me. My wife gets so upset with me because I'll get up to talk at banquets and I'll get tears in my eyes. I've found out it's not what you accomplish in life; it's what you stand for. That's the important value. I think most people have a misconception of life. They think you must keep up with the Joneses or get ahead of the Joneses. To me there is more to life than that. It's the kind of person you are.

"I've gotten mad at myself because I haven't gone back, because, as I say I'm probably more of an emotional person than the people going back there. When I see Billy Pricer, I'm not going to shake his hand. I'm going to hug him. If there is ever another reunion of our 1956 team, I know I'll be there."

Norman, Oklahoma, January 2005

Tommy McDonald is alive and well and still living in Philadelphia. He had to wait thirty years, but on August 2, 1998, he was finally inducted into the Professional Football Hall of Fame in Canton, Ohio.

He was introduced by former Philadelphia sportswriter Ray Didinger, who said, "Inside that jack-rabbit body beats the heart of a lion." Didinger remembered that McDonald was the last man in the NFL to play without a face mask. He told the story of how he once suffered a broken jaw but played the next week and scored four touchdowns.

Didinger concluded his remarks by saying, "If I had one wish for today's NFL, it would be that more players played the game the way Tommy McDonald did. We'd all have a lot more fun. He played it the way we did as kids at recess, afraid the bell would ring any time."

Then it was the sixty-four-year-old McDonald's turn, and he had fun. Perhaps sensing that this might be his last time in the spotlight, he put on a show for the national television audience. He turned on his boom box and did an impromptu disco dance to the "melodic" strains of "Stayin' Alive." He then proceeded to the podium and exchanged high fives and chest bumps with his fellow inductees, Anthony Munoz, Mike Singletary, Paul Krause, and Dwight Stevenson.

When NFL commissioner Paul Tagliabue handed him his twenty-five-pound bronze bust, he threw it into the air and snagged it cleanly. He always did have good hands.

"God Almighty, I feel good," McDonald yelled. "God Almighty, can I hear an amen back here? Move over Ronald McDonald, there's another McDonald in Canton and he's selling hamburgers. You sell Big Macs, and I'll sell Little Macs."

Then there was this joke, "The reason I take my wife with me everywhere is because she's too ugly to kiss goodbye."

But McDonald did have a couple of serious moments. He thanked his eighty-eight-year-old mother, who was watching from her home in Albuquerque, New Mexico, and his father, who died in 1994. He recalled his days at Oklahoma. He spoke reverently about being part of a class that never lost a college game. Surely there will be a fiftieth anniversary reunion for this great team, and hopefully McDonald will make good on his pledge to be there.

New York City, New York, Monday, October 15, 1956

Democratic presidential nominee Adlai Stevenson said that Eisenhower's position on H-bomb testing posed a grave danger to the world. Stevenson said he would make it his first priority, if elected, to get together with the Russians and hammer out an agreement on banning future nuclear "super weapons."

Oklahoma City, Oklahoma, Monday, October 15, 1956

Bud Wilkinson told the Oklahoma City Quarterback Club, "There will be a natural tendency to overlook Kansas [with Notre Dame coming up]. Most people forget that college teams are pretty much the same, being composed of eighteen- to twenty-one-year-old students. On any given Saturday when teams of approximately the same weight and speed are playing, any team that decides to play very well against one not ready to play can win the game."

I think Kansas exploded the myth that we have two or three teams of equal strength. They pushed our third unit around a lot in the second half.

—Bud Wilkinson

Oklahoma 34   Kansas 12

Lawrence, Kansas, Saturday, October 20, 1956

Going into this game with Kansas, the score stood at Oklahoma 147–Opponents 0 after three games. Thus, a Sooner letdown (if letdown is the right word for a 34–12 win) was understandable in this game, coming as it did after Texas and just before Notre Dame.

Kansas, the last Big Seven team to defeat OU, beat the Big Red 16–13 in 1946 during Jim Tatum's only year as the OU coach. Wilkinson had yet to lose a conference game even though he was in his tenth autumn as the Sooners' mentor. It was not until 1959 when Nebraska beat the Sooners 21–25 that Bud lost his first conference game to end a string of seventy-three straight league games without a defeat.

Although OU had no trouble winning the game, they were disappointed, especially the seniors, because Kansas had scored. Billy Pricer said, "We really thought no one was going to score on us all year." This was not exactly out of the question because in thirty regular season games, Pricer's class of '57 shut out their opponents fifteen times.

The last team to go through a season without being scored on was Tennessee in 1939. OU's 1938 team, captained by Gene Corrotto, allowed its opponents only twelve points during the regular season. This is the lowest point total allowed by any Sooner team that played a ten-game schedule.

In his alumni newsletter following the game, Wilkinson remarked, "When a team is fortunate to win several games consecutively, some of its followers lose their sense of perspective and are not satisfied unless every opponent on the schedule is defeated by a truly large score. Such an attitude is bad for the game. The purpose of competition is to test yourself not to embarrass your opponent."

OU had scoring drives of fifty, forty-five, sixty-one, thirty-five, and fifty-four yards. They scored twenty points in only eight minutes during the second quarter to lead 27–6 at the half.

Clendon Thomas, who gained seventy-one yards on twelve carries, returned the opening kickoff forty yards to mid-field. Despite a very sore instep, Billy Pricer had a thirteen-yard run on this opening drive, and of course he blocked well for Thomas and McDonald as always. Thomas got the first TD from one yard out on fourth down. Harris, because of Pricer's injury, kicked the extra point and OU led 7–0.

The Sooners held Kansas on their first possession, but when OU regained the ball Jimmy Harris was trapped for a six-yard loss on fourth down and Kansas had the ball on Oklahoma's forty-five yard line.

Bud sent in the alternate team, but KU covered the forty-five yards in only five plays, with quarterback Bob Morris getting the touchdown. OU's Dennit Morris, Pricer's backup at fullback, blocked the extra point try. In comparing teams of the fifties to modern teams, one of the most noticeable differences is in extra-point and field-goal kicking. In the fifties an extra point was a very chancy event. Now extra points are automatic. There are many reasons for this, of course. With unlimited substitution, teams can have kicking specialists; in the fifties you could not. Also the soccer style kickers and smooth artificial surfaces have improved kicking accuracy.

When the starters reentered the game in the second quarter,

they quickly stopped KU and then scored when McDonald, who had ninety-one yards on sixteen carries, ran the ball over from twelve yards out on an end sweep.

The third OU touchdown was scored on a David Baker to Bob Timberlake pass. Then the starters returned just before the first half ended, and McDonald capped a thirty-five-yard drive with an eight-yard run, which was aided by what Bud called a "savage" block by Pricer.

The alternates scored the only OU touchdown in the second half. Morris had runs of thirteen and ten yards in this drive. Baker took a pitch from Jay O'Neal and ran seventeen yards for the TD.

Kansas scored once more in the fourth quarter, against the alternates, on a seventy-yard drive. However, on this possession the referees lost count of the downs on one series and Kansas had the benefit of a fifth down, which enabled them to sustain their drive. With the ball on OU's twenty-seven yard line, KU gained three yards on a run and two yards on a run, then had an incomplete pass leaving them with a fourth and five. They threw another incomplete pass, but instead of giving OU the ball, the refs allowed Kansas an extra play. Kansas picked up the first down and went on to score making the final OU 34–KU 12.

Kansas coach Chuck Mather commented after the game, "This team is far superior to the '54 and '55 Sooner teams. Their speed is so great! They didn't knock us down. We simply couldn't catch up to them!"

Benton Ladd

Oklahoma City, Oklahoma, Thirty Years after the Game

Benton Ladd, alternate-team right tackle in '56, was now a sales representative for a pharmaceutical company. On this day he was

pausing for lunch between his appointments with doctors. He displayed all the skills of a surgeon himself as he adroitly carved his chicken fried steak sandwich. As the smooth swing of a scratch golfer or the deft stroke of a pool hustler would reveal their talents, Benton Ladd's skill with the culinary instruments revealed him to be a man who was no stranger to a chicken fried steak, either on a bun or served with mashed potatoes and gravy.

Ladd was a very sincere, friendly, likable person. His blond avuncular Scot/Irish features smiled easily and genuinely. Although he was a salesman, he nevertheless seemed to be easygoing, rather than tense and hard driving.

"The thing I remember about the Kansas game," he said, "was that nothing seemed to work right. On the plane, on the way back, it was almost like we had lost. Everyone was just completely down. We had been playing some high-scoring games, and we just didn't play well that day. During the flight Bud said, 'We won! You guys are acting like we lost.' The team let down after the Texas game. Playing anyone after Texas is difficult. Texas was our biggest rival, no question."

Ladd did not specifically remember the Kansas game, but he did vividly recall an incident on the following day. Notre Dame was to be the Sooners' next opponent, so OU assistant coach Sam Lyle had watched the Irish play Michigan State the day before and was going over the scouting report with the team on Sunday afternoon.

"Sam was a great big guy and a good recruiter," Ladd recalled. "He was from the south. He spoke well and was a real gentleman. But Sam was also a kind of an off-the-wall type guy. In his scouting report he was talking about Bronco Nagurski Jr., who was a tackle for Notre Dame then. He said, 'This Nagurski guy is a stud.' Then he looked up and saw there was no response.

"'No, I mean it,' he said. 'I saw him in the shower!' Of course he was talking about his muscles, but there was a slight pause and then pretty soon even Bud had tears running down his face from the laughter."

Ladd did not think the Sooners failed to take Kansas seriously. "Football is not just a game," he said. "It's you playing against some other guy. In that sense you may not take somebody too seriously as a team, but when you get down nose to nose with your opponent you're going to take that guy seriously. So, from a lineman's viewpoint particularly, you realize that there is going to be another big guy right across from you. I don't care how good the team is; you've got a fight on your hands and you know it."

Ladd had broken his leg in the Oil Bowl game, an annual game matching the high school All-Star teams from Texas and Oklahoma, just before he entered OU. Since he could not practice with the other footballers, he was given a job working in the coaches' office cutting out newspaper articles pertaining to OU football. Later, while working on his master's degree, he helped coach the OU freshman team. These experiences enabled Ladd to get to know the OU coaches pretty well and observe them closely. "Bud was not hard to see or talk to. Gomer did handle most of the personal problems, but if you wanted to talk to Bud you could go into his office—and a lot of guys did."

As a lineman, Ladd had more direct contact with Gomer Jones. "Gomer had tremendous rapport with people," he recalled. "You wanted to play for Gomer. He was the kind of guy who could climb all over you and smile the next minute. Even if he got after you in earnest, you never got mad.

"Bud didn't criticize players; in fact, none of the coaches really did. Gomer might jump on you to get you to do something, but he wouldn't compare you to other players. It was a darn good coaching staff. Everyone got along.

"Bud really did coach. When we would have a half-line scrimmage, Bud was in charge of that. You didn't have an offensive coordinator then; Bud did all that. Even though [assistant coach] Eddie Crowder worked with the quarterbacks, when it came time for the quarterbacks to go into the scrimmage, Bud was in charge of that.

"One of the things that I think made Bud and Gomer such a good team and made us such a good team was their complete mastery of the Split-T. They knew what they wanted to do and what kind of players they had to have to do it. They had meshed everything together. Bud got along well with people. He demanded a lot but we were willing to give him a lot. He made a science of it. He knew what kind of drills to practice in order to perfect the Split-T. A coach must know what he wants to do and what skills the players have to have. That's where Bud excelled. He knew what he wanted, and he knew he would be successful if he could get the right kind of people and that's what he did."

It Takes Lots of Hard Physical Work

It takes four hours of preparation by the coaches for one hour of practice. We ask boys to give a lot, but we never ask them to make any more sacrifice than the coaches. We divide preparation into two phases. First establish the foundation of football you're going to play—fundamentals, offense and defense and setting players in their position. While we're establishing this fundamental soundness, we come up with the 22 best football players on the squad, regardless of position, and

---

> we fit them into the positions we figure they can play
> best. We find that good football players are good at any
> position. This phase is extremely difficult for both play-
> ers and coaches, and it takes lots of hard physical work.
> Then you get into the season when most of the work is
> mental and that's hard, too, in a different way.
> Bud Wilkinson
> *Sports Illustrated,* November 18, 1957

"Bud and Gomer tried to pick their team during two-a-days when they can really judge the character of the players. They ran a good tough practice. They kept things moving. However, the reason we had such a good team was not that coaches were so tough. It was the competition. We would get our scouting report on Sunday night, and Bud would say, 'We're going to put in these new plays or this formation.' Well, when you went out to the practice field Monday afternoon you might not be able to do everything perfectly but you had certainly better know what to do. If you messed up, Bud didn't jump all over you, he just moved you down a couple of teams. He didn't have to say anything. He had a lot of talent on that team. Part of the mak-ing of that team was that you had to know what to do. Bud was willing to give you some time to learn to do it well, but he expected you to know what to do when you walked out on to the practice field so that he didn't have to spend a lot of time going over and over things. That was part of the discipline. You knew that if you messed up there was someone there who would love to have your spot.

"Our practices were never very long, two hours was probably the maximum, but you were doing something all the time. They would blow the whistle, and you would go from one drill to another. Bud was a real believer in wind sprints and getting you into top shape. They would get you out there after practice, even during the season, and we would run what they called 'perfect plays.' [A perfect play was a play executed flawlessly by every player.] Thirty of those would turn out to be a whole lot more than thirty. We thought they were going to run us to death. Then after practice, they would check your ankle wraps. That was Port's baby. If you were caught without your ankle wraps you would have to run the stadium steps."

Benton Ladd got to know Port Robertson "too well," he said. It was also Port's job in those days to see that the athletes attended classes. "Port really ran the show as far as academics and discipline and things like that [are concerned]," Ladd said. "He would check your class attendance and for every missed class you had, it was twenty trips to the top of the stadium [sixty-three rows] and back. He would let class cuts accumulate. He wouldn't check them every week. He'd get you up before breakfast and toot that whistle and you'd feel like throwing up, but before breakfast you didn't have anything to throw up, so you'd get the 'dry heaves.' He'd toot that whistle and say, 'You won't throw up on my time.'"

Athletes at OU no longer have to "run the steps" as a punishment for class cuts. This is a practice that has gone the way of the Split-T formation. "If a kid isn't any more than an athlete it's a sad thing," Port Robertson said. "I intended for them to go to class. I had some reasoning sessions [a euphemism if there ever was one] with them. If I couldn't get their attention, we would get up at five o'clock in the morning and hit the steps. But I was not naïve enough to think that there were not a lot more classes cut than I was ever aware of." It has probably never been possible to know just how many classes are missed whether one is talking about 1956 or 2005, but one can easily discover how many athletes graduate. Undoubtedly, many more athletes were receiving their degrees fifty years ago than now.

A back injury during his senior year ended any thoughts Ladd may have had about a career in pro football, although at 210 pounds he was undersized for a pro lineman, even then. So, he pursued a coaching career. "I thought I was going to be another Wilkinson, then I found out there is only one," he said.

After graduating from OU, Ladd coached high school football at Hobbs, New Mexico. From there he moved to Tishomingo, Oklahoma, where he served as head coach of Murray State Junior College in '61 and '62. While at Murray State, Ladd recruited many black athletes to play for him. Most of Murray's opponents were Texas schools, which were not integrated then. He recalled that his team and particularly his black players were not welcome in Texas. "It was terrible down there," he said. "They didn't want to serve our black players in the restaurants. We'd tell them that they had to serve us as a team or not at all. It was a real issue. When I was at Murray the Texas teams had played other teams that had black players, but I brought the first black players to their playing fields. We were down in Texarkana one night and a bunch of rednecks came up to the dressing room, maybe a hundred or so, and stood around hollerin' at us."

In 1957 Benton Ladd was a member of the team that included Prentice Gautt, then a sophomore, who was OU's first black player. Even though few, if any, of the '57 Sooners had ever played with blacks before, Ladd said Gautt was well accepted. "If anyone resented Gautt, I never heard anyone say so. I can't remember anyone saying anything derogatory about Prentice."

After the '62 season, Benton Ladd left the coaching profession and he and his wife, Jurhee, moved back to Norman. The Ladds had enjoyed their time in Norman as OU students, so they decided to make their home there. After moving to Norman, Ladd worked one year for an insurance company before getting into pharmaceutical sales. "It has worked out real well," Benton said. "But I liked Norman better the way it was in 1956. Now I live in the south end of the Sherwood Forrest area. I can remember quail hunting in that field when I was in school. In those days Berry was just a dirt road." In 1956, along Lindsey Street, which is now an ugly gauntlet of fast food and filling stations, there was only Doc Berry's inscrutable Hereford bull, watching the throng of football fans motor their way to Owen Field, which is only one mile east of the corner of Berry and Lindsey. The people who miss the old Norman are not the ones who moved away but the ones who stayed, like Benton Ladd.

Moving back to Norman, as the Ladds have done, is a common practice for OU alums. This phenomenon of OU grads returning to Norman is a bit paradoxical. Norman is not a particularly pretty place. It is flat and windy. Its weather is not good. It is too hot and humid in the summer and sometimes very cold in the winter. It may, in no small part, be the charisma and the success of the Sooner football teams that pull so many former students back to their old campus town. There is really nothing else to recommend Norman as a place to live if one has the wherewithal to live anywhere else.

In the years that have passed since Benton Ladd graduated from OU, the demographics of Norman have changed drastically. In the fifties, Norman was a quiet, unhurried little college town of about 28,000. Fifty years later Norman has become a crowded, ill-planned, ill-maintained, and polluted city of 100,000 with sprawling suburbs and tacky strip malls. Norman has totally lost its "college town" ambience and has become a bedroom community for Oklahoma City. There is consensus among longtime Norman residents that it was a much better place in which to live in the 1950s.

In 1956 Jerry Pence ran a Texaco station at the corner of Boyd and Porter. This street corner is located about a half-mile northeast of the football stadium and about eight blocks due east of where the Town Tavern used to be. At Pence's station when a car pulled in to fill up, Jerry or one of his men would come out to check your oil and check the air in your tires. If you wanted your car washed you could leave it at the station and pick it up later or have it delivered to you. At Pence's station you got personal service. There was a mechanic on duty to check your engine. If something was wrong with your car it could be fixed at Pence's station.

Pence's station was torn down many years ago. In its place is a Kwik Shop. At the Kwik Shop you can buy food, beer, and cigarettes at greatly inflated prices. You can play video games. You can buy gasoline and oil, but you pump the gas and add the oil yourself. You give your money to the clerk who is wearing a starched red jacket and has clean, pink, little hands, not the oil-stained callused hands of a mechanic. The difference between the Kwik Shop and Pence's station is a metaphor for the difference between the fifties and the present. What is new is simply new. It is not necessarily better than the old, and it does not really replace the old. Places like the old Texaco make a place a town, a community. They encourage people to linger, to talk to one another. They promote camaraderie. Kwik Shops encourage people to come and go in a hurry, as the name implies—shop quick, hurry up. Kwik Shops don't bring people together. They alienate people.

When Ladd returned to Norman he gave up coaching. This was not an easy decision for a man who had been involved in football each autumn for the last eight or ten years of his life. "The lifestyle of coaching is so good," Ladd said. "It's filled with excitement. You're preparing for games each week and you're playing the games. It's a very exciting lifestyle, particularly during the season. It's something you have to think about a long time before you give it up. But I was in a small school with just room-and-board scholarships and we were competing against the Texas schools, so we were not very successful. Part of the reason I got out of coaching was that I just didn't feel that I was making any progress on the low pay. When I left OU I could have gone to Tulsa Central to coach. They were going to pay me fifty-two hundred dollars. Instead I went to Hobbs, New Mexico, for six thousand. It was a living but that was about all. Although, it does seem like you did more with less then."

Benton Ladd, who had added a mustache and about thirty pounds since his playing days, is still very much a football fan. He attends all of OU's home games and some of the away games. He has been to almost all the Texas games since his graduation. Attending as many games as he does, Ladd sees many of his former teammates. "I see Bill Krisher two or three times a year, and

I see Clendon Thomas and Billy Pricer some. Pricer was one of the guys who really made that offense go. He was probably the best blocking fullback I've ever seen. I see David Baker frequently. He's my insurance man."

Thirty years after he last wore the crimson and cream of Oklahoma, Ladd found that people still remembered his football exploits. "It surprises me all the time, how many people recognize my name from football. When I took over the western Oklahoma territory [for his pharmaceutical sales], I wouldn't have thought very many people out there would remember me, but gosh, almost all of them recognized me. Just recently, I was talking to Dr. Lynn Harrison at the OU Medical School. He's a thoracic surgeon, almost inaccessible now. He said, 'I remember when you played football at OU. I was a young boy then.' I run into this all the time.

"About eight or nine years ago, I was talking to a Dr. Kline, who remembered that I used to play football. He had been a big OU fan all those years, so when I went to see him we would talk about football instead of drugs. He said, 'I'm playing golf this afternoon with Bud.' Well, he gave Bud my card and about three days later I got a note from Bud saying, 'It's good to hear from you, etc.' It takes a special kind of person to do a thing like that. I had not seen Bud in almost ten years.

"People like to associate with that team. A lot of people growing up when OU was really on top, and when they find out I was on that team, they want to know if I've seen Bud lately, or if I've seen so-and-so lately. When I meet people or if they want to come to the house to see the trophies and such, it's a topic of conversation. I'm really proud to have played on that team. I think it has really benefited me socially and professionally." Meeting Benton Ladd, one is easily charmed by his ingenuous personality. He gives no hint of pretentiousness or boastfulness. He is not an ex-athlete living on the glory of youthful autumns. He is a mature man justly proud of his accomplishments.

Although the Sooners were rated as the number-one college

football team in the nation virtually throughout Ladd's entire career, he did not recall that the players attached any particular significance to this. "It doesn't seem to me that we thought about it very much. It was not a real topic of conversation. I know that Bud pointed out that even playing a weak Kansas State team meant playing for number one. If you didn't play well, you wouldn't be rated high. It was something that after the season you really enjoyed, but I don't recall a lot of talk about being number one during the season." Watching football on TV today, one gets the impression that players are only capable of speaking two sentences: "We're number one," and "Hi, Mom."

Ladd and the other linemen, of course, did not receive the publicity that their teammates in the backfield did, but this was never an issue. He said, "You never really thought about it because you know you're a lineman with a unique job to do. You don't really worry about the publicity too much. The only time it might become a factor is if you've got some guy whose personality would be a problem. But I never remember the Bill Krishers or the Tubbses or the Bob Harrisons ever resenting the publicity the backs got."

Ladd, like the other Sooners on that now-infamous day (November 7, 1957) in OU football history, remembers the loss to Notre Dame that broke the winning streak. "It was a tough game. Notre Dame was playing well. We were moving the ball but not scoring. The stadium was just dead quiet after the game. It was hard to believe. Everyone was just depressed after the game. [Sooner tackle Doyle Jennings said, "It's just like death."] But Bud and Gomer and each of the coaches came around and visited with all the players. They stopped at each locker and talked to each player. I think their talking to us helped a lot. That loss was quite a letdown and yet we bounced back pretty well."

Bud may have consoled the players, but the loss was painful for him, also. When asked if there was any relief in seeing the winning streak come to an end, he said, "No! That's one question I can answer unequivocally."

This one loss has in no way detracted from Ladd's love for his alma mater. He said, "OU was a good thing then and it's a good thing now. I have only good memories of it."

Norman, Oklahoma, January 2005

Benton Ladd enjoys retirement, although he moves around a little more gingerly than he once did. "I've had both knees replaced and I had neck surgery," he said. "I'm not sure any of this can be traced back to football because I have arthritis.

"The knee surgery went well. I certainly don't have any pain in my knees now, which is good. My balance is a little bit off, but I think that has more to do with the neck surgery. But, my health is generally good. I go down to the donut shop every morning to have coffee with the old-timers and I can still go fishing, so I'm getting along fine, but these 'Golden Years' are not what you may have been led to believe.

"I'm still very respectful of the people I played with and the coaches I played for," Ladd said. "But really, about the only time I think about my college days is when I run into some of my old teammates, and then I'm always surprised at how old they look, because it just doesn't seem like it's been that long since we were playing."

Whether he thinks about the old days much or not, Ladd seems to enjoy relating stories about his former teammates. "About 95 percent of our guys came from small towns," he said. "We had everything in common. Everybody had basically the same experiences growing up so the camaraderie was really good. There were no steroids or drugs in those days. We had never even heard of marijuana."

In 2005 Ladd remains a great fan of OU football. He still attends all the home games and the Texas game every year, and, like all his former teammates, he is very complimentary of Bob Stoops. "Stoops restored the football program and he did it in a hurry," Ladd said. "Basically he just took the guys that were already there and turned them into pretty good football players.

Benton Ladd

"Stoops really wants to relate the history of OU football to the present-day players because that is where a lot of the pride is coming from. And he has welcomed Barry Switzer back. He never knocks him. He's always positive with him. I think it is just wonderful that he and Barry get along so well."

Ladd came to OU from a strong high school football program headed by Coach C. B. Speegle at Capitol Hill High School in Oklahoma City. "When I was a freshman in 1950," he said, "we played out at Clinton and beat them pretty handily. After the game they took us out to this nice restaurant, and they had this big fried chicken dinner for us . . . all the chicken we could eat with all the trimmings. Well, a week or two later we went over and played Muskogee and lost. After that game we got a half pint of milk, a cheese sandwich, and an apple. That was when I first became aware of the rewards of winning." Ladd and his teammates could certainly be excused for losing the Muskogee game. Muskogee's coach, the venerable Paul Young, fielded many great teams during this era and this was perhaps his best. It included three linemen who later became All-Americans at the University of Oklahoma: end, Max Boydston; guard, Bo Bollinger; and center, Kurt Burris. The 1950 Muskogee Roughers were undefeated state champs and certainly one of the greatest teams in the history of Oklahoma high school football.

Ladd's OU teams reaped the "rewards of winning" in every game—except one. "I remember when we lost to Notre Dame in '57," he said. "Bud had this hat [a gray fedora] that he had worn for the forty-seven straight games we had won. But after we lost he was going to throw it away. Well, Doyle Jennings went by to see him and Bud said, 'I'll get rid of this hat, because we'll start a new winning streak.' So, Doyle asked him for the hat and Bud gave it to him. Then, after Bud died, Doyle gave it back to his son, Jay Wilkinson. I thought that was a nice gesture on Doyle's part." One has to wonder today, how much that hat might fetch on e-Bay.

Oklahoma City, Oklahoma, Monday, October 22, 1956

Bud was asked if he had any thoughts of trying to beat the Irish worse than Michigan State had (47–14). His reply to the Quarterback Club crowd, which was assembled for a luncheon in the Huckins Hotel, was, "I don't have much of an idea that we can beat them at all, but we will try, of course."

New York City, New York, Tuesday, October 23, 1956

OU dropped to second in the week's Associated Press rankings despite thirty-four straight wins. Michigan State was first on the strength of their drubbing of Notre Dame. At this date the Sooners were leading the nation in scoring, rushing, and total offense.

New York City, New York, Thursday, October 25, 1956

Saturday, October 27, 1956, the day of the OU–Notre Dame game, had been declared Knute Rockne Memorial Day at South Bend. Will Grimsley, a fearless football prognosticator, picked Notre Dame (who had already lost three games) to beat the Sooners 20–7. Grimsley wrote, "The Fighting Irish will have the spirit of Knute Rockne riding with them in the over-the-head effort. Paul Hornung, one of the nation's best backs, will have his day of glory."

Withering speed in the backfield and shattering speed in the line made it easy for Oklahoma to trample Terry Brennan's forces in the most frightful demonstration of man's inhumanity to man that the farm belt has witnessed since the Dearborn Massacre.

—Red Smith

Oklahoma 40   Notre Dame 0

South Bend, Indiana, Saturday, September 27, 1956

A record crowd of 60,128 was packed into the Notre Dame stadium to see this game. Red Grange and Lindsey Nelson were there to broadcast the event to a national television audience. This was the only time the Sooners appeared on television in 1956.

Notre Dame had been the last team to defeat OU when they stopped the Sooners 28–21 in Norman on September 26, 1953. The following week OU was tied by Pittsburg 7–7 and then began their winning streak, which stood at thirty-four going into this game. The Irish fortunes had not been so good. They had already lost to SMU and Purdue, and just the week before had been pounded by Duffy Daughterty's Michigan State Spartans 47–14.

Michigan State had left Notre Dame battered and bruised. Paul Hornung, their All-American quarterback, had a very sore thumb, and there was some speculation that he might line up at halfback because he might be unable to take the snap from center due to his injury. This was not the case, however, as Hornung did play quarterback, and suffered four pass interceptions. Hornung commented after the game, "This is the greatest team I've ever played against. It's the fastest team I've ever seen, and they can really work the option play."

Three of OU's six touchdowns were provided by the defense. McDonald and Thomas each picked off one of Hornung's passes and returned it for a TD, and tackle Steve Jennings blocked an Irish punt to give the Sooners possession on the three yard line.

OU received the opening kickoff and marched sixty-nine yards to establish their dominance at the outset. Jimmy Harris rolled out and connected with his right end John Bell, for a fourteen-yard TD pass. This impressive drive prompted the venerable sportswriter Red Smith to observe, "If there is an abler, wiser, unit anywhere than Wilkinson's first eleven, it must be kept under armed guard. If there has been a college team in recent years with greater overall speed, these eyes did not see it."

On Notre Dame's first play from scrimmage, Hornung took the snap from center and moved laterally down the line where, as the *Daily Oklahoman* put it, Jerry Tubbs "hit him like a freight train." This was, without doubt, the single most memorable play of the season. Tubbs's hit made the national TV audience cringe in sympathy for the helpless Hornung. Years later each of the Sooners interviewed for this book still vividly remembered this one single tackle. David Baker called it "probably the most outstanding tackle I ever saw in college football. Tubbs just literally killed him." Clendon Thomas called it the "keynote tackle" because it set the tone for the entire game. This play was certainly symbolic of OU's superiority over Notre Dame on this day. If one were to select one isolated play to put into a time capsule that would represent the excellence of the '56 Sooners, "Tubbs's Tackle" would surely be the play.

After David Baker boomed a quick-kick sixty yards, and Steve Jennings blocked Notre Dame's punt, Jay O'Neal scored on a quarterback sneak. Carl Dodd kicked the extra point, and the Sooners led 13–0. By now all of the 60,128 watching in person and the entire national television audience knew that only the final margin of OU's victory was in doubt.

When the starting team got their hands on the ball for the second time in the game, they covered the sixty-four yards needed for a score in only eight plays. Clendon Thomas carried through a large hole opened by Bell, Emerson, and Krisher for eleven yards and the TD. In his weekly letter to the Alumni Association, Bud praised the Sooners' strong blocking in this contest. "I thought this game showed the tremendous importance of blocking in football offense. Billy Pricer, our senior fullback from Perry, did a truly outstanding job of blocking, as did all our linemen, Don Stiller, Ed Gray, Joe Oujesky, Jerry Tubbs, Bill Krisher, Tom Emerson, John Bell, Delbert Long, Ross Coyle, Byron Searcy, Steve Jennings, Bob Harrison, Doyle Jennings, Benton Ladd, and Bob Timberlake. The men who carry the ball, throw it, and catch it get their full share of publicity; yet, football games are won by the outstanding play of unheralded linemen."

In 1956 unheralded linemen actually had to "block" their opponents with their shoulder pads. The first move for today's linemen is to reach out and grab their victims with their hands. There is absolutely no need, the way the rules are interpreted today, for the bulky behemoths in the line to wear shoulder pads. They never use them for "blocking."

Just before half time Tommy McDonald ran fifty-five yards with a theft of a Hornung pass to make the score 26–0. Paul Hornung, of course, had an outstanding career in professional football. He was obviously a great player, but for him to have won the Heisman Trophy in '56 while playing on a team that went 2–8, in addition to suffering the indignity of four interceptions on national television, is almost as inexplicable as Don Larsen's perfect game.

Jimmy Harris scored once in the third quarter, and Clendon Thomas scored again in the fourth, when he returned an intercepted pass thirty-six yards to make the final score 40–0. Late in the game, the public address announcer gave this final score: "Illinois 20–Michigan State 13." Hearing this the OU players celebrated jubilantly. Wilkinson may have even allowed himself a small smile, for OU would surely regain the top spot in the AP poll.

After the game Bud was enthusiastic in his praise of Billy Pricer. "On McDonald's pass interception and touchdown run, Pricer rushed the passer and made him throw wildly. Then he got up and threw a terrific block on a player who was going to tackle McDonald. Pricer also did a good job of blocking their ends to make our wide plays work."

Billy Pricer was the best blocker I ever saw in college football.

—*Clendon Thomas*

Billy Pricer

Oklahoma City, Oklahoma, Thirty Years after the Game

"When we got up there they made us mad before the game. It was just ethical that the visiting team comes out first and forms  a circle at one end of the field to do their calisthenics," Pricer explained. "Then the home team comes out last because they will get the biggest cheer, and they take the other end of the field. Well, we went down to the far end and started our calisthenics and Notre Dame came out and lined up on the yard markers. They came down through our team's circle and started their calisthenics. Well, ol' Bud was so mad," Pricer said, smiling at the memory of this long-ago incident, "he called us over to the side and said, 'This is the most unethical thing I've ever seen!' He told us to get into our teams and run a few plays and then go back to the locker room, which we did. Well, the crowd started cheering because they thought Notre Dame had chased us off the field. When we went to the dressing room, Bud said, 'You ought to beat them 35–0.' So we beat them 40–0." This remains the only victory OU has ever achieved over Notre Dame.

Billy Pricer had a penchant for nicknaming his former team-mates. Dale Sherrod was Cowboy; Ed Gray was Beaky; Bill Krisher was Man Mountain; and so on. If one were to give Pricer a nickname, it might be Bulldog or Scrap Iron. His physical stature (at the time of this interview, five feet, ten inches, 230 pounds) suggests the sobriquet of Fireplug. If he had played Major League Baseball (and he was a good semi-pro player), the Gas House Gang would have been his team.

Jimmy Harris said, "Billy Pricer was probably the most under-rated player and got less publicity than anybody, but he did as much or more for that '56 team as anybody."

David Baker remembered Pricer as being "tough, tough, tough, but very friendly and easy-going off the field. The only guy I ever knew who never worked out a day before two-a-days began." Pricer took exception to this statement, however. "I don't know where he got that stuff. I'd always run. I'd come in a little over-weight I guess—if you'd call 196 overweight."

Pricer remembers the dreaded two-a-day practice sessions under the blistering Oklahoma August sun. He and his teammates were usually so tired after the morning practice that they would simply return to the dorm to rest and recuperate before the after-noon practice. But one day Pricer and some of his friends decided to go over to the girls' dorms and check out some of the coeds who had come back for rush week.

"Well," Pricer said, "ol' Dale Sherrod [in '56 a reserve quarter-back] and a whole bunch of guys rode over to the girls' dorms in my car. Sherrod was sittin' out on the front fender. We called him Cowboy because he was always swingin' a rope. We were going to buzz through the dorms and see all the girls who were getting ready to walk over to the sorority houses. Sherrod was tryin' to rope a couple of 'em. So we made a circle through the dorms and pulled back out onto Lindsey Street and of all the people we had to stop for—Bud and Gomer.

"After the afternoon practice, Bud said, 'If you boys aren't tired now, we'll see how tired we can get you.' We had just worked out for about an hour and forty-five minutes. Then we went down and ran wind sprints for about forty-five minutes. We were really draggin'."

Pricer remembered another time he upset Bud . . . literally. "We were practicing handoffs one time." In the Split-T, the handoff was primarily the responsibility of the quarterback. The back receiving the handoff was to keep his head up and his eyes open to watch the blocking develop so he could make the proper cut away from potential tacklers. The quarterback was to place the ball firmly into the ball carrier's hands. Bud had a special drill for teaching this technique. Bud would stand behind a blocking dummy and just as the quarterback and ball carrier were executing the handoff, Bud would quickly jump to one side of the dummy. The ball carrier was supposed to see this and react quickly enough to run to the opposite side of the dummy.

"Well," Pricer said, "I went up there and looked down, and of course he stepped the same way I cut and I ran right over him. I was scared to death. I thought he would kick me off scholarship because I really put him up in the cheap seats.

"You could always tell when Bud was really mad at you. He'd send you down to Gomer and the linemen, and they'd punch the crap out of you." Then he added quickly, "I loved Gomer dearly. He taught me everything I knew about being a linebacker."

Pricer's admiration for Bud was equally strong. "We held ol' Bud up on a pedestal. Matter of fact, I still hold him up on a pedestal.

"When we first came to OU as freshmen in 1953, Bud said we had the potential to be national champions and that's what our goal would be. We came through in '55 and '56. [The Sooners were third nationally in '54, Pricer's sophomore season.] When we had our twenty-five-year reunion in 1981, ol' Bud got up and said our record of three successive all-victorious seasons would never be broken. I got goose bumps. I told him I could go out and play a whole game right then."

Pricer recalled how Wilkinson had done a very unusual "psych job" on the Sooners in 1956. The team had just concluded their Friday practice at the Cotton Bowl in preparation for Saturday's game against Texas. After practice Bud told them, "We're not prepared for this ballgame. You're going to get your tails whipped. All I want you to do when Texas beats you is hold your heads up high. It's not a disgrace to get beat by a good ball club."

This speech had Pricer and the other players so upset they decided to stay at the hotel and study their playbooks rather than attend a movie as they usually would on the night before a game. The next morning Bud gave them basically the same speech.

"When we got out there to the Cotton Bowl on Saturday," Pricer said, "he told us to hold our heads up high and that we couldn't win. Then we went out and beat 'em 45–0. Bud came in and said, 'I knew you could do it. All I had to do was get you to think about it.'"

Billy Pricer obviously enjoyed reminiscing about his former team and teammates. He was a gregarious person, and his memories tended more toward personal antidotes rather than in-depth analyses. He folded his massive forearms across his chest, leaned back in his chair, and said, "I remember when we played up at Iowa State that year. We were ahead of 'em pretty good at the half [32–0]. We were kind of just playin' around, so we went in at the half and ol' Bud, of course he had to have something to talk about, said, 'You're not blocking anybody on punt returns. Let's hit somebody on punt returns.'

"So the first time they punted to us in the second half I peeled back to block . . . and all of a sudden it felt like a big Mack truck had hit me. I mean to tell you, somebody just cut me in two. But . . . I couldn't see anybody except the guy I was supposed to block, and he was a good ten yards away from me. 'Man,' I said, 'I'm gonna get that ol' boy's number, I owe him something.' Then I rolled over and looked up and ol' Beaky [Ed Gray] was the only guy around there. I said, 'My God, Beaky, I'm on you're side.' 'I know it,' he said, 'but Wilkinson said for me to hit someone and you were the only guy around.'"

The only story Pricer failed to chuckle about was the one he related about trying to locate a team picture of the '56 Sooners for a friend. Pricer called the OU sports information director's office and asked for a team picture of the '56 Sooners. A male voice replied, "Let's see, '56, was that a good year?"

The football players were not the only all-victorious athletes in Billy Pricer's senior class at OU. Danny Hodge won all his collegiate wrestling matches at OU. Hodge simply overpowered his opponents with his tremendous strength. Hodge, it was said, could crush an apple with one hand and squeeze a pair of pliers so hard he could bend the handles flat against each other. He was a remarkable athlete who pinned most of his opponents.

Hodge, like Pricer, graduated from Perry High School in Oklahoma. He was two years ahead of Pricer in high school, but after his graduation, Hodge spent two years in the navy, so he and Pricer were both freshmen in 1953.

Pricer recalled a match that he and Hodge wrestled in the gym in 1952. It was just before Christmas vacation, and Hodge had returned from the navy and was practicing with the high school team. Pricer explained, "Coach [John] Devine kept telling me he had a boy who was going to work me out. I knew who he meant, of course. So, at sixth hour, I'd peek into the gym and see if Hodge was there. If I didn't see him, I'd go ahead and wrestle. One day I looked in the gym and he was in there wrestling about six guys. So I told coach I had some work over in the woodshop I needed to finish today. The coach said, 'OK.' The next day Hodge was there again so I told the coach I had to go back to the shop. But he said, 'Not today. I've got somebody for you to wrestle.'"

The word quickly spread through the school that Hodge and Pricer were going to hook up. Neither had lost a match in high school, and Perry, Oklahoma, was to high school wresting what Massilon, Ohio, was to high school football. By the time Pricer could get suited up for the match, the gym was full of students and teachers. Pricer knew he might not beat Hodge but he vowed, "He won't pin me." Hodge won 6–4, and in three years at OU no one even came this close to beating him.

Pricer was prepared to wrestle at OU, but Port Robertson wanted him to pull thirty pounds and wrestle at 167. Wilkinson simply said, "No." "So, Port and I parted friends," Pricer said.

In 1956 Billy Pricer handled the punting and the place-kicking for the starting team in addition to playing fullback and linebacker. His average punt of 46.8 yards was the best in the nation, but the Sooners did not have to punt often enough for Pricer to qualify for the national statistics.

Pricer thought that in 1956 there was not as much emphasis placed on individual statistics as there is today. "I probably didn't carry the ball over fifty times all year [forty-seven to be exact]," Pricer said. "They gave the ball to Steve Owens fifty-five times in one game. That's stupid. Statistics didn't mean that much to us. Statistics were not kept as carefully or as thoroughly as they are today. We had two halfbacks, Thomas and McDonald, and my goodness, we could have broken all the records with them. There were a lot of those ballgames that the first team would start the second half and play five or six minutes and maybe not play anymore. You didn't see guys like Owens carrying the ball fifty-five times." In 1956 sixteen carries were the most any Sooner back had in a single game.

"Bud would get the first-unit guys out of there, so we never did hardly have anybody hurt. We didn't want to beat anybody ninety to nothin'. We beat some teams 53–0, but you can't tell a fourth-unit guy, 'Go in there but don't do anything.' Ol' Bud would never run the score up. But I think in '56 we averaged forty-six points a game and had six shutouts."

After graduating from OU, Pricer played five seasons of professional football with the Baltimore Colts before bad knees requiring seven operations forced him to retire. He played on great Baltimore teams that included Johnny Unitas, Lenny Moore, Raymond Berry, Alan "the Horse" Ameche, "Big Daddy" Lipscomb, and Gino

Marchetti. Pricer played in the game many experts consider to be the greatest football game ever played. On December 28, 1958, Pricer's Baltimore Colts beat the New York Giants, who were led by Frank Gifford, Charlie Connerly, Kyle Rote, Sam Huff, and Pat Summerall, 23–17 in Yankee Stadium to win the NFL title. This was the first "sudden death" game ever played in the NFL.

The Colts beat the Giants the following year to take the title again. These two victories by the Colts gave Pricer four national championships in five years: two national collegiate titles at Oklahoma and two professional titles at Baltimore.

Less than a week into Pricer's rookie season with the Colts, "Big Daddy" Lipscomb (who apparently did not realize what an accomplished wrestler Pricer had been) came up behind him and put him in a bear hug. Pricer threw the three-hundred-pound tackle over his shoulder and pinned him. This earned him instant respect among the Baltimore veterans.

"We won the championship in 1958. We played the championship game at Yankee Stadium. We either wanted to play it in Yankee Stadium or in Cleveland because they were the biggest stadiums. My share was just a little under five thousand dollars, and this was the largest paycheck anyone had ever gotten in a single game until then. And nowadays . . .

"These outrageous salaries have got to end somewhere. Guys can be millionaires by the time they get out of school. I just don't understand that. I thought I was 'King of the Road' when I signed a three-thousand-dollar contract. I think McDonald signed for a three-thousand-dollar bonus with Philadelphia. I know in those days that was fantastic money."

The money is what made the pro game so vastly different from college ball, according to Pricer. "You're playing for the money, which takes a lot out of the game. Either you produce or they kick you out. You still have the love of the game. You still enjoy playing the game, but you better produce or you're not going to be there long. That's when you start to feel the pressure."

Pricer, as a young man, had a rock-hard body that seemed indestructible. But like many other former athletes he continued to consume calories and not burn them off. His weight climbed to nearly three hundred pounds, a hundred pounds over his collegiate weight. All this extra weight was too much for his five-foot, ten-inch frame and for his heart. He suffered a heart attack in 1983 and underwent triple bypass surgery.

Three months after his surgery, Pricer's recovery was so complete that his doctor cleared him to take a Colorado ski trip with his family.

"I called the doctor and said I needed something for the pain. I didn't know I was having a heart attack then," Pricer said. "I didn't even think I had one after they told me about it. I thought I had some kind of indigestion or something. They ran me out to Mercy Hospital and the doctor in charge of the emergency room said I had gastritis. But when the cardiologist came, he said, 'I'm the cardiologist. I'll make my own diagnosis.' So he did an arteriogram. He said, 'Mr. Pricer, you've had a mild heart attack.' I still didn't believe it. He said, 'Yes, one artery is completely shut and one is narrowing.' He also said, 'Mr. Pricer, I'll be honest with you. If that one closes up there will be no more Mr. Pricer.'

"'Well when?' I asked. He said, 'We don't know these things, five hours, five days, five years. We need a triple bypass. But it will be expensive, and it will be a big decision for you.'

"I said, 'I don't think there is any decision whatsoever.' We did the surgery the next morning at 9:30. At 7:30 that night I told them I had to get up and sit on the edge of the bed. I was in intensive care two days. The third day they moved me over to a private room and they let me up to walk down the hall.

"Alan Ameche had a triple bypass four years ago and he called me up and welcomed me to the zipper club," Pricer said. "I've lost sixty-two pounds since the surgery. I'm down to 229 now, dang near down to my playin' weight, before two-a-days. They've got me on twelve hundred calories a day. The weight is comin' off and I feel better. I walk three miles every day in forty-five minutes.

"I was diabetic, too. I hadn't had a checkup in four or five years and that's dumb. I didn't know the symptoms of being a diabetic. You can't pass a water fountain. You drink a lot of fluid and you continue to lose weight. I was working out here in the shop [at NECO Industries, an industrial supply manufacturing company that Pricer and his partner owned and operated] and I thought, I'm getting the old muscles tightened up. I was sweatin' and my pants were fallin' off me, and I'd go home and drink about three gallons of water at night.

"I had been in such good health. I guess this just happened in the last four or five years. When I was at OU I never had any weight problem. In fact, in Baltimore, they tried to put weight on me. I kept my appetite, but I wasn't working out. Just walkin' three miles a day is takin' it off."

Pricer seemed to have his physical problems under control. The results of the most recent stress test were excellent. "The doctor said that if I get my weight down a little more, I might be able to get off the insulin. Then I would just have to take a pill.

"We had a heck of a club in '56," Pricer said, returning to a subject that was very dear to him. "When you've got guys the caliber of ol' Bob Harrison on the second team, you know you've got something. He was all-pro! He was a heck of a player! We had guys on the third unit that possibly could have been playing on the first unit for any other team in the Big Seven. I think we had enough confidence in our offense, the old Split-T, that we could have moved the ball on any pro team. We might not have beat 'em, but I think we would have moved the ball on 'em.

"Players today are getting bigger, stronger, and faster. We prided ourselves in '56 in having a fast team. Tom Emerson [220 pounds] was probably the biggest guy we had. We didn't have anybody that was gigantic. If we ran up against somebody that was 260 or 270, they'd be a big blob and we'd just run around 'em. But when guys like John Dutton came along at six-foot, six, 275, that could chase down the little halfbacks, I said, 'Oh no!' Guys are much bigger today but maybe not as quick as we were. I think we could match the speed of teams today, but we would be a small club.

"Pound for pound, I don't think you could beat the '56 Sooners."

Norman, Oklahoma, January 2005

Billy Pricer was a man who loved life. He loved people and he loved food. As he began to put weight back on, his diabetes and, consequently, his other health problems became much worse.

A stroke in 1996 left him paralyzed for a while, but he made a complete recovery. However, an infection in the big toe of his right foot proved to be more serious. The toe had to be amputated, and there was some discussion among his doctors that they might have to remove the whole foot. The decision ultimately was to try to draw out the infection but spare the foot. His wife, Sally, believed that this is what led eventually to his death. "I just don't think they ever got all the infection out of that foot," she said.

Seriously ill or not, Pricer was determined to return to Baltimore in December 1998, for the fortieth anniversary of the

Billy Pricer

Colts first championship team, the team that won "The Greatest Game Ever Played." Sally remembered, "He was in really bad shape. He had just had the toe amputated, and he had to be in a wheelchair. It was a struggle getting him through the airports, but he really, really wanted to go, and we had a wonderful time."

It was a great testament to how much Pricer was loved that when he died on September 24, 1999, thirty-five of his former teammates, both college and pro, came to Oklahoma City to attend his funeral.

One of the last things that needs a press agent to extol its charms is autumn.

—*Herbert Warren Wind,* Sports Illustrated, *October 29, 1956*

Oklahoma City, Oklahoma, Monday, October 29, 1956

Wilkinson told the QB Club, "To talk about how good our team is when the season is only half over is foolish. Any athletic contest is always a matter of such delicate balance it can go either way."

New York City, New York, Tuesday, October 30, 1956

The Major League All-Star team for 1956 was announced today.

1956 Major League Baseball All-Star Team

Position	Player	Team
1B	Ted Kluszewski	Cin NL
2B	Nelson Fox	Chi AL
3B	Ken Boyer	St. L NL
SS	Harvey Kuenn	Det AL
OF	Mickey Mantle	NY AL
OF	Hank Aaron	Mil NL
OF	Ted Williams	Bos AL
C	Yogi Berra	NY AL
RHP	Don Newcombe	Brok NL
LHP	Billy Pierce	Chi AL

Oklahoma 27   Colorado 19

Boulder, Colorado, November 3, 1956

Colorado may have been the only Big Seven team that actually believed they could beat OU. Their single-wing attack always caused problems for the Sooners. The Buffaloes played several close games with the Sooners in this era, including a 7–7 tie in 1952. OU won in '53, 27–20, and in '54, 13–6, and in '57 only a blocked extra point by Bill Krisher allowed the Sooners to escape with a 14–13 victory.

The Colorado Buffaloes were a very good football team in 1956. By finishing second in the Big Seven, Colorado earned the right to go to the Orange Bowl where they defeated Clemson 27–21. The Buffs had several good athletes on their team. John "the Beast" Bayuk was an exceptionally large fullback (212 pounds) for those days. CU also had Eddie Dove and Boyd Dowler in their backfield.

Coming into the game Colorado had won five games in a row, and Bayuk was leading the Big Seven in rushing with 457 yards. Bayuk's yardage did not come exclusively on short plunges up the middle. His average per carry was 6.2.

There was much concern (apparently well founded) that the Sooners might suffer a letdown after their emotional victory over

Notre Dame. Doyle Jennings, the alternate-team right guard, believed this may have been the case. "We just didn't practice like we should have all week. We had the worst practices since two-a-day drills. I don't know whether it was because we had just played Notre Dame or because we just didn't figure Colorado was very tough because they had lost their first game to Oregon 35–0. We just weren't ready to play."

The game was played before a sellout crowd of 47,000 in what was decidedly not Wilkinson weather. It was thirty-three degrees in Boulder for the kickoff and getting colder. On the day before the game, five inches of snow had to be scraped from the field darkened by an overcast sky.

OU kicked off and stopped the Colorado drive, but a good punt by Dowler pinned the Sooners back on their own ten. From there Pricer tried a quick-kick with disastrous results. John Wooden blocked the kick, and Bayuk recovered in the end zone. Colorado led 7–0. Football coaches agree that there is nothing more demoralizing than suffering a blocked punt. A team that has a punt blocked seldom wins the game. This was the only kick Pricer ever had blocked while at OU. "I don't know where that son-of-a-gun came from either," he said.

The alternate team stopped the next CU drive, and the starters came back into the game. Jimmy Harris hit McDonald for thirty-five yards and a TD, but OU missed the conversion. Near the end of the first quarter, McDonald returned a punt seventy-five yards for a TD with good blocking by Billy Pricer, but the play was called back. Colorado also had a long TD run by their tailback Stranksy negated in this game.

Colorado led 7–6 at the end of the first quarter, but the second quarter was a debacle for the Sooners. Colorado drove 50 yards for a TD by Eddie Dove but missed the extra point.

A drive by the alternate unit stalled out at the CU thirty-four. Later the starters fumbled the ball away to CU on the Buffs twenty-nine. David Baker, years later, recalled that it was at this point that Jimmy Harris, his confidence unshaken, turned to the bench and gestured as if to say, "It's OK, we can get it back."

However, the day only grew darker for OU. Colorado marched decisively seventy-one yards in ten plays against the first team, to score with only thirty-six seconds left in the first half. Stransky crossed the goal line standing up. McDonald blocked the conversion, a very important play because it made the score 19–6, which meant OU could win by making two touchdowns and two extra points.

Even a one-point victory for the Sooners did not seem likely at this point, as anyone who was listening to the game on their radio will remember. OU had been thoroughly outplayed by the Buffs in the first half. Colorado had already rushed for 191 yards.

There are two versions of what Bud said to the team at half time. Doyle Jennings said, "The thing that got me was when Coach told us if we couldn't play better, then we'd better take off those Oklahoma jerseys." His is also the version Clendon Thomas recalled. David Baker said, "Bud told us he thought we could win. He didn't know if anyone else did, but he did." Baker himself was not quite so confident. "They had kind of controlled us. It wasn't a fluke. Players realize this. I've been in games when I know, given time, it's going to turn around. But this was one of those games where I didn't know."

OU received the second half kickoff and as Don Meredith would have said, "Ol' mo [momentum] started changin'." The Sooners came up with a fourth and two on their own twenty-eight yard line. Thirty years later Bud said, "It all came down to one play, and we simply weren't going to kick!"

Harris called a handoff to Clendon Thomas; Tubbs, Krisher, Emerson, and Bell provided the blocking; and the Sooners got the first down. No one can know for sure, but this may have been the point at which Colorado stopped believing they could win. Dandy Don probably would not have sung "Turn Out the Lights" yet, but he could have.

After this crucial first down, McDonald ran for eleven, then twenty-two, and ended the drive with a fourth-down, six-yard touchdown pass to Thomas. Harris kicked the extra point, and the score was now CU 19–OU 13.

> ### *The Upset Was not to Be*
>
> Colorado kicked off to open the third quarter, and Oklahoma, splitting linemen a little wider to loosen the defense, moved 80 yards in 14 plays with adroit, cool precision. Almost at once everyone knew the upset was not to be.
>
> Tex Maule
> *Sports Illustrated,* November 10, 1956

Colorado's offense faded into winter. After 191 yards rushing in the first half, they got only 51 in the second.

OU made the tying touchdown by going forty-eight yards in eight plays. This time McDonald faked a pass to Thomas and ran the ball in for the score. Jimmy Harris kicked the extra point, and the Sooners led for the first time 20–19.

Harris passed sixteen yards to Thomas for OU's fourth TD and then kicked the potentially important extra point to make the final score 27–19. After the game Harris said, "We stopped ourselves in the first half on most of our drives with fumbles and mistakes. Everything we ran moved well but we kept hurting ourselves."

Joe Oujesky said, "They were big and tough. I guess it's the toughest team we've ever played."

Gomer Jones gave his analysis of the game. "It takes a little time to adjust to the single-wing. They don't hit as fast as on the T, but there's more double-team blocking. We should have adjusted a little quicker, I guess, but the boys played a great second half."

In his alumni newsletter, Bud said, "It's easy to play good football when things are going in your favor. That has been the pattern in every game we've played so far this year—until Saturday.

Against Colorado our team had to play well when the chips were down and the going was tough. Our team made a magnificent comeback. I truly feel fortunate to be associated with so courageous a group of men. However, I hope we all learned that you can take nothing for granted in football. Each opponent is ready, capable and able, to defeat us. We must play our best football for 60 minutes if we are to win."

Clendon Thomas

Oklahoma City, Oklahoma, Thirty Years after the Game

Clendon Thomas never doubted that the Sooners would come back and defeat Colorado in the second half. "Yes I thought we

would win it at the half. We believed, and I don't know if Wilkinson had brainwashed us or not, but we believed that the fourth quarter was ours. We didn't care how big the other team was. We thought that by the fourth quarter they would not be able to breathe, and it was a fact. We knew that if we'd go out and nail 'em the fourth quarter would be ours."

Thomas did not specifically remember picking up a first down on the crucial fourth and two situation early in the third quarter. But he was not surprised that Harris would call the play even though the Sooners were behind and on their own twenty-eight yard line. "If the guys up front said they could make it, they could make it," Thomas said.

In 1956 Clendon Thomas was a junior right halfback on the OU Varsity. David Baker recalled Thomas's play that year: "Thomas was a perfect compliment to that kind of offense. They were so worried about containing McDonald to the outside that Clendon would hit the handoff and cut back, and before you knew it he would have run thirty yards. The safeties would have to chase him down."

Thomas led the nation in scoring in 1956 with 108 points on eighteen touchdowns. He recorded his eighteen touchdowns on only 105 carries. Thomas's yards per carry average in '56 was 7.78. In comparison, Herschel Walker scored sixteen touchdowns on 335 carries and had a 5.2 yards per carry average during his 1982 Heisman Trophy season. Despite having the ball in his hands three times as often, Walker produced two fewer touchdowns than Thomas.

In '56 Thomas and McDonald were the "Touchdown Twins" who fought for the scoring title all year long. With sixteen touchdowns each going into the last game against Oklahoma A&M, Thomas collected two TDs to win the individual scoring honors. McDonald, who scored once against A&M, ended up fourth in scoring. Thomas laughed heartily as he recalled Billy Pricer breaking into the clear for a long touchdown run with McDonald chasing behind him, trying to get Pricer to lateral the ball to him.

"Yes," Thomas said, "the rivalry was there. Whatever I did, he would duplicate. It was a good healthy situation. I used to tell Jimmy Harris, 'If you don't want to score, don't give it to me.' I didn't say, 'I want the ball.' That was my way of getting the ball, and a lot of times I scored too." Indeed, Thomas averaged one touchdown every 6.4 times he got his hands on the ball, either rushing or receiving. Obviously this is a tremendous tribute to his offensive line. "Tommy knew I would score if he didn't. Pricer just didn't have a prayer with both of us trying to get our hands on the ball every trip. The amount of times you could get your hands on the ball was limited. We played both ways, and we had to split our time with the alternate team. Thirteen to fifteen carries was about all you could get."

This rivalry notwithstanding, Thomas and McDonald teamed up on many a successful run-pass option with one throwing to the other. They were the two fastest Sooners in '56. "I know Tommy could run at least a 4.5 forty and that's exceptional," Thomas said. "That's even exceptional today. We were both very quick white boys. He could move. He was fast enough to play all those years of pro football as a receiver. And, of course, I had to cover all those guys that could run. I didn't last that long [twelve years, the same as McDonald] because I was big or whatever. You have to be quick. You have to have a certain amount of speed.

"We had an unbelievable team," Thomas said of his '56 Sooners. "We had two unbelievable teams. It wasn't like we ran just one football team. We ran two full teams, and they were both good. I think it's interesting that we ran two complete backfields, and two complete lines, quarterback and all. Today they think nothing about running a bunch of backs in and out in pro ball, but they've got this hang-up about running quarterbacks in and out. There is no difference."

Thomas was a consensus All-American in 1957. This edition of the Sooners won nine regular season games and defeated Duke 48–21 in the Orange Bowl, but Thomas remembers best the one 7–0 loss to Notre Dame that broke the forty-seven-game winning streak. "We should not have let Notre Dame beat us. It was a mental breakdown, one of those things that Bud warned us about. We knew it could happen. In '57 we didn't have the talent we had in '56. We couldn't throw the ball as well in '57 as we could in '56. We didn't have Jimmy Harris, and we didn't have Tommy McDonald. We couldn't throw the pass-run option as well in '57. That's how Notre Dame beat us. They stacked everybody on the line of scrimmage. We didn't have to throw much in '56, but when we did throw, we completed them."

The mention of Bud Wilkinson's name brought a quick and unequivocal response from Thomas. "The best coach I ever played for and that includes some pretty good coaches. He was brilliant. He was good with people. He was good with his coaching staff. I never saw him put down any of his coaches. I can't say that about the pro coaches I played for.

"When Bud took a player off to the side, he would either praise you or correct you or both. You never knew when he pulled a guy aside, if he was praising them or correcting them. Normally, when he pulled a guy aside, he was telling him what a good day he had had. He corrected people in private, away from the team. He didn't do it right there in front of everyone. He might call you to his office and about half the time he was building you up. But if he had to correct you, he would correct you in his office. There were a few guys he couldn't handle, but he handled most of them and handled them well.

"His focal point in going over the game films was to watch for second effort. He would always point to guys that were doing something extra. Jerry Tubbs would hit his man, block him, get him down, and then he would get up and go get another block, and Bud would look at that over and over again. One time Pricer blocked four guys on one play. Wilkinson must have run that play back about fifteen times. Pricer got the initial block, then he got right back up and got a couple more. They just happened to be right together so they fell over one another. How many guys get up and keep knocking people down? I remember Wilkinson was berserk that day. He kept running that play over and over. Bud made you have the attitude that you would be the one he pointed out next week."

Thomas then began to speculate about what ingredients separate good teams and good coaches from poor teams and poor coaches. "During my last five years of pro ball, they began to run IQ tests on all the teams. They ran IQ tests on the Packers in the years they were winning championships under Lombardi. They ran IQ tests on the Colts when they won the championship. Sure enough the teams that were winning championships were the teams with the highest average IQs. I think the Packers had an average IQ of about 125.

"When Lombardi went to Green Bay he had a bunch of guys nobody could handle. They were bright and they were good players but no one could handle them. A coach has to have enough IQ to deal with these guys that have a 125 IQ.

"Bud was dealing with bright players. He was bright and he had bright coaches. He made the comment after that ballgame in Stillwater [the Sooners final game in '56] that this was the best team he'd ever coached. In looking back on it, you have to be a little bit lucky to get that many great players together at one time."

Thomas continued to expound on coaching philosophy, "Players today are a little spoiled or they expect too much. I didn't really expect a great deal then. It is very easy today to spoil a guy or make a prima donna. I think from a coaching standpoint it is taking the easy way out to be one of the boys. I think historically the great coaches have been disciplinarians.

"When you have a boy who is not disciplined, that you cannot discipline, it will ultimately cost you at a critical time in a ballgame. He is going to jump offsides or do something to cost you a ballgame and possibly even a national championship.

"There is always a group of four or five players on every team who will challenge the coaches. If you give them an inch, they will take six miles. You must be able to handle those four or five troublemakers because you're not going to win without them. They have a certain type of personality. They're the aggressive kind of people it takes to win a ballgame. Doyle Jennings [alternate-team right guard in '56] came out of a tough background. He spent a little time in the jailhouse. Doyle was not easy to handle. Doyle was a big ol' bear. He might go out to Louie's [the tavern about a half mile south of the OU campus on Porter] and tie one on, but he had been raised that way. He grew up in a tough part of Lawton. Now he's a pillar of his community down in Louisiana somewhere." Thomas quickly added that he did not intend this remark to be taken facetiously. "John Bell [the starting right end in '56] was a tough guy. There were some rough ol' boys in those days, but there always are."

At the time of this interview, Clendon Thomas was president of Chemical Products Incorporated, an Oklahoma City firm that manufactured waterproofing for concrete. Thomas spoke very positively about his business dealings. "We sell out of state. I've got a distributor in Kansas City and one in Texas. We have some business in Pennsylvania and Ohio."

On one wall of his office Thomas had a huge map of the United States, which he used in keeping tabs on his various construction projects. On another wall of his spacious office he had several pictures and mementos from his playing days at OU, Los Angeles, and Pittsburgh. One such souvenir was a picture of the 1957 college All-American team. The chubby bespectacled visage of Alex Karras was easily recognizable in the picture.

Thomas looked not unlike what Bud Wilkinson looked when he was in his late forties. Thomas had the same commanding physical presence of Wilkinson. Many of his mannerisms, the way he folded his hands, sat in his chair, and gestured to emphasize a point, were reminiscent of Wilkinson, as was his gray hair. Thomas was perhaps just a little rougher around the edges than the urbane Wilkinson.

Thomas was one of the '56 Sooners who would have been big enough to have played decades after he actually did. At six-foot, three, 220 pounds, he was not much over his playing weight. Although Thomas achieved his fame at OU primarily because of his offensive prowess, he played defensive halfback throughout his professional career. "I played defense by choice," he said. "Les Richter [Ram's linebacker] took me to dinner when I was a rookie with the Rams. He told me, 'You're big, you're fast, and you'll hit people, but if you play offense, all I can tell you, Clendon, is that you'll last three years and they'll carry you off on a stretcher.'

"I began as an offensive running back. I'd scored once or twice in preseason. I'd gotten a taste of it. But Richter said, 'I've been here thirteen years. I know what I'm talking about. If you get over on defense you don't read your name in the paper as much, but you can play ten or twelve years and retire whenever you get ready to.' He told me, 'They never change the defensive teams.' To this day in professional football the defensive teams never change very much. The names on the defensive teams basically stay the same year after year. But offenses change constantly because they get hurt. Steve Owens, for example, lasted three or four years before his knee pain forced him to quit. Some players hang on and hang on. When Walter Peyton had his knee hurt he hung on but still he got beat up. Tommy Mason was beat up in his third year. He stayed a long time but he could never start after that. Billy Pricer couldn't start because of his knees. As long as Pricer could back up Ameche, he was great. But Ameche got his Achilles tendon hurt and Pricer had to play full time and he couldn't stand it."

Thomas stayed with the Rams four years before trying to be traded to Dallas so he could play close to home. "I wanted to get out of Los Angeles. They were having a lot of turmoil. They had a bunch of owners and they were all squabbling. They had three coaching changes in four years. Dallas was growing and I could see they were building a good team. I told Elroy ["Crazy Legs" Hirsch] to trade me if he had a chance. I know Dallas wanted me because I had picked up the phone and asked them. However, in those days, two teams that were desperate to get help were Pittsburgh and Green Bay. I wound up in Pittsburgh, which was a good deal. I loved it."

Despite playing defense exclusively, Thomas still accumulated his share of injuries, which he described as "little things." "Through the years, I broke my leg, I had fifteen stitches in my face, knocked my shoulder down, busted three ribs, dislocated all my fingers; every one of them got bent out of joint. I had a broken ring in my larynx. It's that kind of game. If you play long enough you get injuries. I was very fortunate I didn't get hurt bad. I had one knee worked on for cartilage. I didn't have any ligament damage. When I left pro ball I was pretty much as fast as I was when I started. I was just older and ready to get out. I was burned out between the ears."

Thomas thought the increased number of injuries in football over the years could be blamed on bigger players and artificial turf. "Part of it is that coaches are constantly looking for great big men and great big men have a tendency to wear down in the third and fourth quarter. If you wear down, you're not going wide open and you're going to get hurt. Our guys watched very carefully. They didn't want to just get big. They wanted to have a certain weight. Any extra weight can get you hurt.

"The artificial turf has caused some problems in this regard. I played one game on it in Houston and I thought I had been in a car wreck. I only played one half. I couldn't walk for two days. I had sore spots all over. They've improved it a lot, but I'm not sure artificial turf has been everything everyone had hoped for." Apparently several major universities, including Oklahoma, eventually came to agree with these remarks because they pulled up their artificial turf and went back to natural grass.

In his twelve seasons in the NFL, Thomas played with and against some great athletes. He seemed to enjoy reminiscing about the speed and power of these superstars. "Ollie Matson could outrun everybody on the Rams except Deacon Jones, and he lost a whole bunch of money one day to Jones. Deacon came in one day and said, 'I'll bet one hundred dollars I can outrun anybody at any distance.' Ollie Matson said, 'I'll take that bet.' Jones said, 'How far do you want to run, Ollie?' They ran a fifty-yard dash and Deacon Jones [six-foot, five inches, 240 pounds] won.

"Sammy Davis, a 250 pound guard [at Pittsburgh in the late sixties], could run a 4.4 or 4.5 forty," Thomas said. "Jimmy Brown could run 4.4. Few people realized that Brown was that fast, but you never saw him get caught from behind. He had his glide speed, then he would put on a little spurt and away he would go. You either had to hit him at the ankles or in the head. He was top heavy. He would go down real easy if you hit him in the helmet. It was easier to hit him in the helmet than in the feet. He was a big guy. He weighed 230 to 235.

"Bobby Mitchell [Washington wide receiver] won the Big Ten sprint championship, but Jimmy Brown outran him in a forty. Mitchell went berserk, so they ran a hundred and Brown beat him again, and I know this is true.

"Big Daddy Lipscomb was fast as lightning. He outran everyone on our team at Pittsburgh at 290. He outran all the backs.

"Sonny Jurgensen was the best quarterback. He was hard to intercept. Yet he was so ordinary—ordinary size, ordinary hands—but he could throw the ball eighty yards."

Thomas recalled a story that Art Rooney, the Pittsburgh owner, told on himself concerning another pretty good quarterback.

When Johnny Unitas tried out for the Steelers, Mr. Rooney took him aside and told him, "Son, you're just not going to be a player. I advise you to give this up and hunt another line of work."

The football career of Clendon Thomas got off to a rather slow start. His high school team lost eight games his senior year. "I had no idea OU would offer me a scholarship. I don't know how they found me," Thomas said. "[Oklahoma] A&M did not offer me a scholarship. They told me I could walk on, but they didn't recruit me. When I had a chance to go to OU, there was never any doubt about where I would go. A&M made only one contact. I always enjoyed having a good day against A&M."

As a freshman at OU, Thomas was not highly regarded by his coaches. "Jack Santee [a freshman coach in '54] just didn't think I was a player. I was a big long-legged gawky-looking kid and some of the freshman coaches didn't think I was putting out, but I was. There were three freshman teams and the AOs. I was an AO my entire freshman year."

In 1956 no one doubted Thomas's ability as a football player. He was one of several extremely talented players at OU that golden autumn season. "As I look back on all those people we had then—Jerry Tubbs, Tommy McDonald, and Billy Pricer—you have to have a little bit of luck to get those particular kids together at the same time. That's what I was always in awe of, that all those kids including those kids on the bench were all sitting there at one time. We had some good players sitting there waiting to play.

"We had a lot of guys that today would be considered average or small physically. They said that about Jerry Tubbs throughout his professional career. But they could never replace him. We had a group of kids that were terrific players, and we had great team speed. The whole team had good quickness. I think that's how we could beat some teams that were bigger physically. We played some teams that were as big as pro teams, but they didn't last long with us.

"These were big ol' rangy boys. We had some strong kids, too. I don't know how you would change that team around. I think some teams today might have a lot of trouble with that '56 Sooner team."

Oklahoma City, Oklahoma, January 2005

Clendon Thomas had sold the chemical company he operated for twenty-seven years so now he has more time to play golf. However, he had not completely retired. He and his current business partners have succeeded in doing what every occidental entrepreneur has wanted to do for the last five hundred years: they have gained access to the Chinese market.

"Because of the contacts we had made through the years," he explained, "we put together a deal to do wastewater cleanup in China. It has turned out to be a good deal and a long-term deal it looks like." Thomas had not yet made any trips to China at the time of this interview, but "My passport is in order and I can if I need to," he said.

Thomas pronounced himself to be in good health, and he certainly looked strong and well for a man of seventy autumns. The resemblance to Bud Wilkinson was still apparent, especially when he smiled, which was often.

He thought the toughest opponent the Sooners faced in his era was not Texas, Colorado, or Notre Dame, but OU . . . the OU alumni, that is. "Playin' the alumni was worse than any game we played all year," he said. "It was a rough game. Indian Jack Jacobs would come back and play and Plato and Dee Andros. These were tough, tough guys."

Thomas's teammate Byron Searcy agreed with this assessment. "There was this guy named Plato Andros," Searcy said. "He must have been about forty then, at least he seemed old to me. But blocking him was like hitting a post, and he had a vicious forearm. My whole college career I never ran into anybody like that. [Andros was probably in his mid-thirties at the time Searcy played against him. He lettered for the Sooners in 1941 and returned after four years in the Coast Guard to make All-American in 1946.]

"I remember Jim Weatherall would take the cardboard containers that the rolls of tape came in and strap them on his forearms, and just beat the tar out of people," Thomas said. "When we beat the alumni in the spring of '55 just before the '56 season, I knew then that we must have a pretty good team."

Had it not been for the efforts of one man, Clendon Thomas might not have played in these alumni games or any other games as a Sooner. "A guy named Hal Mix was a writer for the *Daily Oklahoman*," Thomas said. "He wasn't a sportswriter really, but every now and then he would fill in for Volney Meece when Volney could not get to a ballgame, and he saw some of my games at Southeast High School.

"He would pick up Bill Krisher at Midwest City and Benton Ladd at Capitol Hill, and then he would come by and get me and we would go down to Norman to the coaches' office. They wanted to see Benton Ladd, who was a high school All-American, and so was Bill Krisher. They were highly sought-after young men. But Mix would tell Port, Pete Elliott, Pop Ivy, and those guys, 'You need to take a serious look at this tall kid.' We did not have films of my high school games in those days, and the coaches couldn't go watch every kid play. There is no doubt in my mind that, had it not been for Hal, I would never have gotten a scholarship at OU."

Still, there was one man who was even more prescient in his assessment of Thomas's football prowess than Hal Mix and that was his high school coach George Franck. George "Sunny" Franck, as he was known, had played college football at the University of Minnesota for the redoubtable Bernie Bierman. He had also played professional football with the New York Giants, and had been a Marine Corps pilot.

After watching Thomas for only a couple of practices, Franck asked him, "Would you like to play professional football someday?"

"Sure," Thomas replied.

"If you don't get hurt," Franck said, "you will."

"What he saw in a six-foot-one, 155-pound high school freshman that made him think he could ever play professional football, I still haven't been able to figure out," Thomas recalled some fifty-five years later.

"I don't really dwell on my college days," Thomas said. "But when I look back on those times, I'm just so thankful that I was one of a hundred or so young men who had the opportunity to play for the best coach in America—Wilkinson—and that whole group of coaches who were such fine men: Pete Elliott, Pop Ivy, Port, and Gomer. I have such great memories."

Oklahoma City, Oklahoma, Monday, November 5, 1956

Wilkinson told the Quarterback Club, "There was nothing wrong with Oklahoma except Colorado." Former Sooner quarterback, Darrell Royal, if he were describing Colorado's team, might have said, "These boys didn't ride into town on a pile of wood."

Tuesday, November 6, 1956

Dwight Eisenhower won a landslide victory over Adlai Stevenson, and *Giant*, starring Elizabeth Taylor, James Dean, and Rock Hudson, opened in theaters across the country.

Norman, Oklahoma, Thursday, November 8, 1956

Prentice Gautt from Oklahoma City's Douglass High School, the first black athlete to play football at the University of Oklahoma, blasted in for a touchdown from two yards out to give the Sooner frosh a 7–7 tie with the Oklahoma A&M freshmen.

Tulsa, Oklahoma, Thursday, November 8, 1956

Mickey Mantle, who had just won the Triple Crown and the MVP awards by hitting .353 with 52 homers and 130 RBI, said he would seek an increase in his $30,000 salary for the 1957 season.

Friday, November 9, 1956

The 1957 Oldsmobile Golden Rocket with a 277 hp engine went on display at dealerships.

While Iowa State is a physically strong team they've
had a lot of injuries and lack speed. So with a little
more speed we were able to move past them.

—*Bud Wilkinson*

Oklahoma 44   Iowa State 0

Ames, Iowa, November 10, 1956

When trees begin to lose their leaves, the chlorophyll is broken down and chemically removed. This leaves the waste products of photosynthesis, which gives the dying leaves their brown, yellow, and red colors. The vessels that carry sap to the leaves become blocked at the base of the stalk, cutting the leaf off from its lifeblood. The stalks of the leaves become brittle and autumn's chill winds soon rob the trees of their beautiful fall foliage, as the days grow shorter and shorter.

The trees in Ames were barren, although the weather was forty degrees, mild for Iowa in late autumn. Despite the good weather, only thirteen thousand people found their way to Clyde Williams Field to watch the number-one team in the nation take on the Cyclones. Apparently the Iowans saw little hope of victory. It had been twenty-five years since Iowa State had beaten OU. They had tied OU 7–7 in '36 but had not won since '31. It was not until Clay Stapleton, a disciple of General Neyland's Tennessee balanced-line single-wing attack, took over at Iowa State, that the Cyclones were able to defeat the Sooners in 1960 and again in 1961 with Stapleton's famous "Dirty Thirty" team. ISU could not manage another victory over the Sooners until 1992.

The "Touchdown Terrors" McDonald and Thomas scored twice each, and OU was forced to punt to the Cyclones only once in this runaway. The entire traveling squad got to play, as OU was ahead 32–0 at the half.

On their first possession after a Cyclone punt, the Sooners went forty-six yards in seven plays. The longest play in this drive was a reverse in which McDonald took a pitchout from Harris, ran wide to his right, and handed off to Thomas, who ran for nineteen yards to the Iowa State twenty-two. Five plays later, McDonald got the TD on a one-yard plunge, and Pricer kicked the extra point.

After the alternate team stopped a Cyclone drive, the starters reentered the game and scored on the mirror image of the play that set up the first touchdown. This time Thomas took the pitch from Harris, ran left, and handed off to McDonald coming back to the right. Tubbs executed a good block, and McDonald, who made ninety-seven yards on ten carries, had a forty-five-yard touchdown.

Thomas got the third score of the day on a six-yard plunge, and Carl Dodd scored from the two for the fourth TD. The starting unit got the ball once more in the first half. They had only twenty-eight seconds to go forty-five yards, but that was all the time Jimmy Harris needed to complete two passes to his left end, Don Stiller from Shawnee, Oklahoma. The second completion to Stiller went for fifteen yards and the TD.

With the second and third units playing most of the second half, OU scored twice more, once on a short handoff to Thomas and once on a spectacular seventy-eight-yard pass interception return by center/linebacker Jerry Tubbs. On this long run Tubbs displayed the ball-carrying form that he had previously exhibited in his sophomore season when he had played fullback. John Cronley, of the *Daily Oklahoman,* said that Tubbs had "utilized good speed, deceptive footwork, and some plain old bulldozing which belted aside three would-be tacklers."

Tubbs was a football player.

—Port Robertson

Jerry Tubbs

Dallas, Texas, Thirty Years after the Game

"Tubbs was the man." This seemed to be the consensus of his former teammates. When the other Sooner alums spoke of Tubbs

they did so with a timbre of reverence. When an example was needed to illuminate the greatness of the '56 Oklahoma team, Tubbs's name was invoked.

Wilkinson said simply, "Jerry was a hell of an athlete." His longtime friend and former teammate both at OU and at Dallas, Jimmy Harris, said, "Jerry was probably our best athlete, really. Bob Harrison was a very good center, but he had to work like hell to do the things Jerry could do naturally."

Harrison himself said, "Jerry was my hero. He was a fine fellow. I was always just hopin' I could be like him."

In 1956 Tubbs, a center/linebacker, won the Walter Camp Award, which was given each year to the nation's outstanding player. He was also fourth in the balloting for the Heisman Trophy that year, an extremely high finish for a lineman. Tubbs played middle linebacker for the Dallas Cowboys for eight seasons ('61–'67), serving as a player-coach the last two. He was the

Cowboys' first All-Pro linebacker in 1962. At the time of this interview he was the Cowboys' linebacker coach.

Sitting in his Dallas office, Tubbs spoke in his characteristically modest way of the touchdown he scored against the Cyclones many autumns ago. "I remember I got a lot of blocking. I think I might have broken one tackle, but I had a lot of blocking. I remember all the players were excited for me. I remember this more than the details of it. I came off the field and they were all real happy. This shows the kind of esprit de corps we had on that team."

The pass interception was not the first time Tubbs ran with the ball as a Sooner. During his sophomore year he played eight games at fullback, even though he had been recruited as a center and had never been a back in high school. "This move came after the second game, as I remember," Tubbs said. "Back then they didn't ask you. They said, 'We need you at fullback.' I had never been a back. My freshman year I had been a center and linebacker. But in my sophomore year we were having some problems on defense. This was right before the Texas game. [The Sooners had an open date before Texas so Tubbs had an additional week to adjust to his new position.] They had moved Bob Burris from fullback to halfback because his defensive play had not been so good. [Moving Burris from fullback to halfback on offense meant he would also play halfback on defense rather than linebacker.] And they moved Billy Pricer from second-string fullback to first-string fullback.

"I was playing second-team fullback against Texas, but Pricer got hurt right off and I played more time in my first game as a fullback against Texas than I did in any other game I ever played. It was hot and I like to died." Defensive statistics were not kept in those days so it is not possible to report the number of tackles Tubbs made in this or any other game. Offensively, he was used primarily as a blocker. He carried the ball only three times but he gained thirty-two yards, and OU won 14–7.

Thirty-two years later, Bud Wilkinson explained this surprising move of Tubbs to fullback. "First, he was the best defensive player we had so he had to go somewhere. The fullback position in our offense was primarily a blocking position. Jerry was a great athlete and well equipped to handle the requirements of that position."

Port Robertson was at the coaches' meeting when Bud announced the switch for Tubbs. "It was Bud's idea and the rest of the staff didn't exactly jump up and down and clap their hands when he made the move," Port said. "Everyone thought of Jerry as a center and a linebacker. It was a little hard for people to think of him as a fullback, but he played a pretty dad-gum good year of football. He was a good athlete. He would have been a good defensive end. He didn't have the great quickness, although he could run fast. He was faster than Pricer."

At first Tubbs was perplexed by the move. "I knew I'd been playing pretty well at center, and I always told everybody I kind of thought he [Bud] was trying to run me off or something—moving me from what I knew. I didn't dream I'd start, but from that game [Texas] on I started every game at fullback the rest of the season. I always told them, if they would block me for ten yards, I'd run for six. I would never have made it in pro ball if I had stayed at fullback. I would never have been All-American if I'd stayed at fullback. They didn't pick an offensive and a defensive All-American team then. They just picked a team. I'd probably have gotten hurt, too. I was kind of clumsy as a fullback. I had pretty good speed and I had fun carrying the ball, and I had a lot more fun blocking the way we did from the fullback position than I did from the center position. At center you've got your head down. At fullback you run out there and, if the guy comes up, you cut him down. If he's floating you just keep running right over him. Bob Herndon and Buddy Leake were the halfbacks then ['54] and they would set up the blocks. The backs would fake the defensive man and make it an easy block. That's probably the best job of blocking I ever did because they set them up so well."

Despite Tubbs's protestations to the contrary, the record shows that he was a good ball carrier. In 1954 he carried the ball sixty-three times for 387 yards, which is an average of 6.1 yards per carry. Even though Tubbs did such an outstanding job at fullback in his sophomore year, Bud never really considered leaving him at this position. "He was a great center and if you're controlling the line of scrimmage it doesn't matter who the backs are," Bud said. And Bud had Billy Pricer to play fullback.

Tubbs was dressed casually in a polo shirt, double-knit slacks, and loafers. He was heavier than he was during his college days when he played at 208. "I weigh 240 now, but I weigh about 220 after training camp because I'm on the field a lot for two-a-days, plus I run. But I love to eat. God put people here on Earth for a lot of different reasons, and the thing I do best is eat. I just wish He hadn't given me such a good appetite." Even with the extra pounds, Tubbs did not look all that different from what he did in '56. He always looked older than his college teammates because he was already losing his hair back in the fifties. Thirty years later he and his boss Tom Landry had the same hairline.

Tubbs is a friendly and cordial person. He is simply Jerry Tubbs, not Jerry Tubbs, former All-American and All-Pro, or Jerry Tubbs, Dallas Cowboy coach. He seemed so relaxed and comfortable in his office, which was cluttered with paraphernalia of the coaching trade, films, projector, scouting reports, and so on, that one could almost forget what a ferocious tackler he had been for the Sooners.

Comfortable is very descriptive of Jerry Tubbs—comfortable clothes, comfortable office, comfortable lifestyle. "I sort of like to stay in the background," he said. "I'd hate to be one who couldn't go into a restaurant. Things are just about the way I like them now. A lot of people will know me and once in a while someone will say, 'I remember you,' or something, so I still get a stroke or two here and there."

Jimmy Harris said of Tubbs, "He's got everything lined up. His ducks are in a row. He's got what he wants. He doesn't like to make waves. I've told him he's just dull."

When Tubbs came out of Breckenridge High School in 1953,

he signed a letter of intent with Baylor, which was only binding within the Southwest Conference. Tubbs later changed his mind and enrolled at OU. A disappointed Baylor alum claimed that OU had put twelve thousand dollars in a bank account in Tubbs's name. The NCAA investigated the charge but found no such account.

Tubbs said that he knew, in '56, that the Sooners had a team far superior to their opposition, but he did not then think that they would be remembered as one of the greatest teams ever. "We had very good talent," Tubbs said. "Today they have more talent than we did back then. But relative to the time, we had a lot of talent. We had so many guys who played pro football."

In '56 Paul Hornung of Notre Dame won the Heisman Trophy, with Tubbs finishing fourth in the balloting, just behind his teammate Tommy McDonald. "I had no idea I could win the Heisman," Tubbs said. "I heard they [OU Sports Information Department and some local sportswriters] were pushing me for the Heisman at the first of the year, but McDonald was having such a good year that it was obvious he had a chance to win it. I think Hornung had fifteen hundred votes. McDonald had over nine hundred, and I had over eight hundred, so together we had more than Hornung."

David Baker's understandably biased observation on the '56 Heisman balloting was: "Either Tubbs or McDonald should have won the Heisman, no doubt about it, but they split the votes so Hornung wound up winning it. But one of those guys [Tubbs or McDonald] should have won it because they had far better years than Hornung. Hornung only won it because he was at Notre Dame. Notre Dame was 2–8 that year. They were terrible."

Tubbs was able to exact some degree of revenge on Hornung that year with his now-famous bone-crushing tackle in the early moments of the Notre Dame contest. In typical fashion Tubbs downplayed the incident. "I think he was playing tailback on this particular play and he came out to his left, and I guess he didn't see me or something. I hit him pretty good as he cut up the field. Undoubtedly he didn't see me too well because I stopped him dead. Usually there has been a mistake when something like this happens. Somebody has not done his job blocking." Mistake or not, because of the teams and the individuals involved in this play, "Tubbs's tackle" may be the single most memorable tackle in OU football history. Most of those who saw it live and in person or on national TV have never forgotten it.

Although Tubbs downplayed this individual effort on his part, he took great pride in the sound thrashing the Sooners gave the Irish on that day. "When I was in grade school in the forties, and all through my junior high and high school years, Notre Dame had been good. We really wanted to beat Notre Dame. I'd say it was probably the game I enjoyed the most."

Tubbs played for two of the most successful coaches ever, Bud Wilkinson and Tom Landry. "They were both great coaches and good teachers," Tubbs said. "I think Tom was more into the technical aspect of football, that's his forte. Bud was more into the psychological aspect. They both crossed over into the other's specialty. Bud knew the technical aspect but Bud was more into motivation. And Tom—nobody's ever known more football than Tom. He knows offense, defense, kicking. He's phenomenal."

At the time of this interview (1986), Tubbs was the only member of his OU team who was still coaching on either the college or professional level, but as a young man he never aspired to be a coach. "I always thought I'd go into business and get rich," he said with a laugh. "Coaching just happened. I became a player/coach because that's the way the Cowboys could pay me the most money. Then, I just kind of evolved into a full-time coach. I've been here ever since. I have no desire to be a head coach, although anybody who says he wouldn't like certain parts of it would be crazy. But I've never liked the idea of being a head coach because they've got too many problems. I'm sure if someone had said, 'we want you to be our head coach,' it would have been hard to turn down, but I've never really aspired to be a head coach." Tubbs had absolutely no desire to be a college coach. "The recruiting would be terrible. I couldn't handle that," he said.

Harris thought Tubbs could have been a head coach long ago had this been his desire. "Tubbs is a clone of Landry. He even looks like him. He's got the mental capacity to be a head coach. He could have been a head coach years ago—easily."

Tubbs's duties with the Cowboys required him to be in the press box during the games. Thus he never appeared on camera when NBC panned the Cowboy sidelines or when ABC moved in for a close-up of Landry on *Monday Night Football*. This lack of TV exposure was undoubtedly to Tubbs's liking and very much in keeping with his low-profile personality. Even though he was not shown on television and almost never mentioned by the media, he nonetheless performed an indispensable role in Cowboy operations. From his press box position Tubbs watched the opponents' blocking schemes against the Cowboy defense. He tried to see where the defense was breaking down and made suggestions as to what to do. "Sometimes my suggestions were taken and sometimes they weren't," he said. Tubbs relayed what he saw to Ernie Stautner, who then called the defensive signals.

In his eight years as a player and twenty as a coach in professional football, Tubbs has obviously seen many changes in the game. "The offenses have really changed," he said. "The idea behind Tom's philosophy was to put the strength of the defense against the strength of the offense. That's the basic premise. Everything is recognition [recognizing the offensive formation]. You know the offense will run certain plays from certain formations, so you set your defense. Teams used to not use that many offensive formations, maybe three or four. But now you've got thirty-seven thousand offenses. Consequently, defense has become vastly more complicated. All the different offensive formations with all the men in motion and everything else destroy your ability to set defense the way you want it without tremendous problems.

"A defensive player must adjust to what he sees the offense do, and there are so many variables and so many different situations. Consequently, the players have so much more to think about than they used to that they can't be as aggressive. It [coaching] has gotten vastly more difficult and vastly more complicated."

As a coach Tubbs produced four Pro-Bowl linebackers: Chuck Howley, Lee Roy Jordan, Thomas Henderson, and Bob Breunig. "Howley was a guy who could miss an assignment and end up making a good play out of it. If he was supposed to cover a guy, he might all of a sudden decide to blitz the quarterback. He'd end up trappin' the quarterback but his man would be wide open. He did that a lot. He got beat some and he missed some assignments, but if he went to Las Vegas, he'd break the bank because he won a lot more than he lost.

"He had great coordination. The two guys I've seen with the best coordination were Howley and Bob Lilly. They were both into gymnastics, and I've often thought this is why they have such great body control. They were both great natural athletes."

Another of Tubbs's linebacker pupils who was also a great natural athlete was Thomas Henderson from Langston University, but Thomas tragically never realized his potential. "Thomas had tremendous natural ability," Tubbs said. "He could run and cover pass receivers. It was so unfortunate that Thomas got into the drug scene. I think probably had it not been for drugs he would have been fine. He was a very likable guy but he lacked discipline, and I'm sure that was attributable to the drugs. He did a lot of good things, but he screwed up a lot, too. That's what the fans don't see—the missed plays. We have a statistical category we call big plays against us, plays which gain over twenty yards. In the first game he started for us Thomas made a couple of good plays, and Tex Schramm said, 'Thomas really played well, didn't he?' I said, 'Yes, but he cost us four big plays.'

"I remember I could make one good hit in a game and play very mediocre or even poor the rest of the game and people would tell me I played a great game. Then maybe the next game I'd play

well, do my job, make a lot of tackles but not do anything spectacular, and people would say, 'I didn't see you much out there.'"

A Big Hunting Cat

Jerry Tubbs played adroitly, intelligently, moving behind
the Oklahoma line with the graceful speed of a big hunting cat, so strong that the firm grip of one hand on a
shoulder pad was enough for him to upend a Texas ball
carrier.

Tex Maule
Sports Illustrated, October 22, 1956

Tubbs's pro career began in 1957 as the number-one draft pick
of the Chicago Cardinals, who used him as an outside linebacker,
a position he had never played before. "I didn't do well in
Chicago," Tubbs said. "But it wasn't because I didn't try. I wanted
to play in the middle and they wouldn't let me. I just couldn't play
very well on the outside."

After one and one-half seasons, Chicago traded Tubbs to San
Francisco, where he finished out that year at outside linebacker,
but the following year he moved into the middle linebacker spot.

After the '59 season with the Forty-Niners, Tubbs planned to
retire. "I never did go into pro ball with the idea of playing forever. I was planning on retiring and getting into business, and I
told them that." The San Francisco management, thinking Tubbs
would retire, left him off their list of players who were exempt
from the expansion draft. Seeing that Tubbs was available for their
first NFL season, the Dallas Cowboys drafted him and signed him
to play. Had the Forty-Niners thought Tubbs wanted to play for
another team they would never have let him get away.

Tubbs's first year with Dallas was one he would like to forget.
The hapless Cowboys lost eleven games and tied one in their first
season. "That was awful," he said. "We had some guys who
wanted to win, but we had some other guys who were old-timers

Jerry Tubbs

and they just wanted to finish out their careers. We didn't have very good athletes really. We just didn't have enough good-quality people."

But the Cowboys began to add quality people such as Bob Lilly, George Andre, Lee Roy Jordan, Bob Hayes, Mel Renfro, and others. When Tubbs became a player-coach in 1965, the Cowboys qualified for the playoff bowl by finishing second in the Eastern Division of the NFL. "You would have thought we had won the Super Bowl," Tubbs said.

In 1966 Tubbs retired and was working for the Dallas Federal Savings and Loan Association, but he was lured back for one more year by Landry. "I was getting bored," Tubbs said. "I played quite a bit in the first two or three games then I got my back hurt."

The following year, Landry, sensing that the Cowboys had a real chance at a championship, wanted to have Tubbs as insurance in the event Lee Roy Jordan should be injured. "Coach, my back just can't take it," Tubbs told Landry. But Tom persisted and Tubbs came back again. "I was on the roster that whole year, and I never went into a single game. I'm probably the only linebacker in the history of the NFL that was on the active roster one whole year and never played a down," Tubbs said.

Tubbs felt lucky to have survived so many years of professional football with his body still intact. "Oh, my back bothers me some," he said. "I do exercises all the time to strengthen it. Part of the problem is congenital. In fact, my son, Alan, has a worse case of it than I do. I had some injuries to my elbows and knees but I'm pretty lucky. The human body is not made for running into people at full speed."

Returning to the subject of the '56 Sooners, Tubbs explained that there were factors other than physical talent that made this club so good. "I think the big thing about it was that we were a team. Guys want to do well, but there are egos involved whether anyone admits it or not. Another guy may not wish you bad, but he doesn't wish you quite as good as he wishes himself. But I thought we probably had about as good an esprit de corps as you could have."

Norman, Oklahoma, January 2005

Jerry Tubbs's twenty-nine-year career with the Dallas Cowboys ended abruptly one February day in 1989 when Jerry Jones purchased the club. "I heard it on the radio," Tubbs said. "My wife, Maurine, and I were on our way to Breckenridge and I heard, on the radio, that Jerry Jones had bought the Cowboys. Then Jimmy Johnson called me and talked to me a few days later. So, I thought, well . . . that's the way it is. I was about ready to retire anyway, so it didn't cause any great concern on my part.

"Twenty-one years of coaching, that's sufficient. I had some good runs. It was good. It was interesting, but it was long hours at times. I had some opportunities to stay in coaching. I got a call from San Diego. A guy named Dickey Daniels, who I had played with and coached at Dallas, called me, but I wasn't interested."

Tubbs still lives in Dallas, but he spends a lot of time driving up and down Highway 75 to his farm in northeast Texas. "It's about an hour's drive each way," he said. "I go up every day, seven days a week. Sometimes I might stay home but usually I go every day."

Although he has several head of cattle, he was careful to point out that this is a farm and not a ranch. "In west Texas, where I came from," he explained, "if you say you've got a ranch and it's less than a thousand acres, you'd be braggin', so I say it's a farm.

"I've bought four or five different little patches of land. I bought my first one in 1963 and sold it in '67. I got a smaller place and added on to that. I've kind of dabbled in land. The last land I bought was twenty-five years ago, and I've sold land the last five years."

Today, Tubbs's investments in land, cattle, and oil allow him to live a comfortable lifestyle, but this was not always the case. Like many of his Sooner teammates he remembers the days of the Great Depression quite well. "I remember the WPA. I remember people talking about getting government jobs back in the thirties. We didn't get electricity until I was in the seventh grade. We burned wood in the fireplace and we had butane and propane.

"When I was in the ninth grade we moved into town. Before that we did not have indoor plumbing; we had an outhouse but we were not unusual. We were just like everyone else."

Given this background it is not hard to understand why Tubbs was impressed when Texas multimillionaire Eddie Chiles picked him up in his private plane and flew him up to Norman for his first look at the OU campus. "Eddie was a good guy," Tubbs said.

"He bought my football tickets. Nobody got any big money then. We would sell our football tickets then but that was about it."

Tubbs survived all his autumns on the gridiron without having to undergo any surgeries. This is in marked contrast to his OU teammate Billy Pricer, who had seventy-two inches of scars from surgeries.

Fifty years after his playing days with the Sooners and forty years after he took off his Cowboy uniform for the last time, Tubbs finds there are still some people who remember him. "I really kind of did not like to sign autographs. I'd be in a restaurant or something and somebody would come up and I never did really care for it. But now I kind of like it. It's nice now because so many people who saw me play are dead, or if they are alive they don't remember. It's nice to be remembered."

New York City, New York, Tuesday, November 13, 1956

Tennessee replaced OU as the nation's number-one college football team in this week's AP poll. The Vols, led by the running and passing of tailback Johnny Majors, finished ahead of OU by two votes because one sportswriter refused to rank the Sooners in his top-ten teams.

Sooner fans received a strong indication of just who this culprit was when Ed Danforth's article appeared in the *Atlanta Constitution*. Danforth wrote, "Unless the voters in football polls are hypnotized by heavy scoring at the expense of weak opponents, there is no way to rank Oklahoma ahead of either Princeton or Wyoming, who have gone through unbeaten schedules of equal caliber." Princeton???

New York, Friday, November 16, 1956

Elvis Presley's first movie, *Love Me Tender*, opened today.

This is Bud's best team, or certainly the best team we have ever played against. After a game like this there is not much to say except that they're the greatest.

—*Don Faurot, coach, University of Missouri*

Oklahoma 67   Missouri 14

Norman, Oklahoma, Saturday, November 17, 1956

This was Don Faurot's last game against OU. He had already announced that he would retire at the end of the season. Faurot, the inventor of the T-offense, had never defeated a Wilkinson-coached team.

Coach Dorothy

Dr. Dorothy Truex, who, in 1956, was OU's Dean of Women, believed it was she and not Faurot who first conceived the idea of the T-formation. As a coed at the University of Missouri, Ms. Truex enrolled in a course entitled Theory of Football. While the instructor, Coach Faurot, was explaining how the single-wing tailback must line up five yards deep behind the center to receive the snap, Ms. Truex raised her hand and asked why one would not simply move this man directly behind the center to exchange a handoff rather than the more difficult long snap. Ms. Truex explained that such an alignment would not only reduce fumbles but it also would allow the offense to initiate their plays more quickly, giv-

---

ing the defense less time to react. Faurot merely chuck-
led at the young girl's suggestion, but in the next gridiron season, the T-formation was born.

Whether it was Don Faurot or Dr. Dorothy Truex who
invented the T-formation, there is no doubt that it was Bud
Wilkinson who perfected it. OU ran up 602 yards of total offense
against Missouri. Eight different Sooner backs scored touchdowns. Oklahoma had ten scoring drives: 58 yards in seven plays,
74 yards in eleven plays, 40 yards in three plays, 69 yards in four
plays, 60 yards in seven plays, 83 yards in six plays, 8 yards in two
plays, 16 yards in three plays, 55 yards in four plays, and finally
the fourth team put together an eight-play 51-yard touchdown
drive. The Sooners accomplished all this despite losing five of
seven fumbles.

Missouri showed some offense of their own as they compiled
323 total yards and the same twenty first downs as OU, but they
lost three fumbles, had three passes intercepted, and did not manage to score until the fourth quarter. In fact, their second touchdown came on the last play of the game. The Sooners scored
twenty-seven points in the second quarter to dissolve any hopes
Faurot may have had of a victory.

Wilkinson was apparently pleased with the play of his team
but not with the behavior of some fans. In his newsletter to the
alumni he observed, "I was distressed at something that happened
before the game. Missouri was practicing extra points at the south
end of the field. Each time they kicked, the ball sailed into the
south bleachers, which were filled with visiting high school football squads. The high school boys kept two of the Missouri foot-
balls despite all our efforts to recover them. We regretted this very
much since we were the host team. The actions reflected not only
upon the high school players and the schools they represent but
also our university."

This was OU's first home game in six weeks. The temperature
was sixty degrees at game time, nearly thirty degrees cooler than

it had been the last time the Sooners had played in Memorial Stadium.

Clendon Thomas got OU's first two TDs on an eleven-yard pass from McDonald and a six-yard run. The Sooners' third touchdown of the day was scored by Carl Dodd, an alternate-team right halfback, after taking a pitchout from Jay O'Neal at the nine yard line. McDonald capped a sixty-nine-yard drive with a twenty-three-yard scamper on a reverse. The Sooners' fifth and last touchdown of the half was a forty-one-yard pass from Harris to Don Stiller.

The Sooner onslaught continued in the second half as Tommy McDonald, who gained 136 yards on only eleven carries, ran 58 yards with a pitchout for a TD. Carl Dodd set up the Sooners' next TD with a 33-yard punt return to the Missouri nine yard line. Two plays later Jakie Sandefer got the score.

Missouri's bad luck continued as Byron Searcy knocked the ball away from their receiver following OU's ninth kickoff of the day. Steve Jennings recovered the fumble on the Tigers' sixteen yard line, and the Sooners' third-team quarterback, Dale Sherrod, took the ball into the end zone.

After Missouri's first TD, David Baker scored for the Big Red on a twenty-yard run. The tenth and final Sooner TD was scored by fourth-team halfback Ron Pillow from one yard out. In addition to the eight Sooners who recorded TDs, Harris, O'Neal, and David Rolle kicked extra points to make a total of eleven different players to score for OU in this game. One Sooner who missed a chance to score was Ed Gray, the left tackle from Odessa, Texas, who was given an opportunity to kick an extra point but missed. After the game Harris commented, "We've been trying to get him [Gray] to score all year. He had his chance. He won't get another one."

"Oh yes, I will," Gray responded. "I'm going to carry the ball in the A&M game."

*We had a simple existence. We went to class. We
worked out. It wasn't all that complicated. If Bud said
something, we believed him. We did it. We didn't question him.*

—*Byron Searcy*

Byron Searcy

Fort Worth, Texas, Thirty Years after the Game

"The headlines said, 'OU waves goodbye to Faurot sixty-seven
times.' I remember that headline, but I really don't remember any
of the details of the game," Byron
Searcy said.

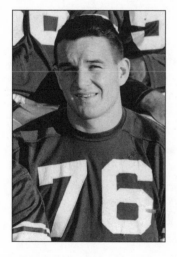

"The games that stand out in
my mind that year are the Notre
Dame game because we were so
keyed up, the Colorado game
because we fooled around and
nearly lost it, and I remember the
A&M game because we had such
a good time. We just buried 'em.
It was a fun kind of game. I
remember that Bud let Ed Gray
score a touchdown, and everybody
got a kick out of that because they
all loved Ed so much."

Byron Searcy, alternate-team left tackle in 1956, looked quite
distinguished in his neatly tailored shirt and tie as he spoke in his
Fort Worth real estate office. His gray hair and aristocratic bear-
ing evoked images of yacht parties, polo ponies, and mint juleps
on the veranda of Fort Worth's River Oaks Country Club. This
"old money" metaphor is somewhat deceiving, however. Searcy's

father was a brakeman on the railroad. "I'd say my family was in the low-middle income bracket," he said. "I never was conscious of social strata or money because I got the basic things I needed at home as far as care and shelter. I never worried about not having anything.

"I'm the only one in my family to get a college degree. That was very important to my folks and it was important to me, and I think that's true of a lot of the guys on that team. All our parents had gone through the depression. They knew what it meant to go through hard times. Most of us had worked. Most of us had come from middle-income or below families and a scholarship was very important to us. If I were to set down and look at a roster, I bet I couldn't name two or three guys who had a bad attitude toward school."

Academic Stats

None of the first thirty-three players among OU's Grantland Rice Award winners as the 1955 national champions flunked a single hour during the fall semester. In fact, tackle Cal Woodworth, end Bob Timberlake, halfback Tommy McDonald, and quarterback Jay O'Neal were named among the nation's thirty-three star football players who were also top scholastically. Ten OU players carded all As and Bs and another eight approximated a straight B average. Statistics show that players take solid major courses and that better than ninety percent graduate.

Tim Cohane
Look, November 13, 1956

Searcy continued to muse, in his Texas drawl, about the sociological and psychological factors of the fifties that affected him and his teammates. "That was just a bunch of guys and that was a special period. As I look back on it now in perspective, I'd say we typified the fifties. Life was pretty simple then. Eisenhower was president. He was a kind of grandfather image. The whole country was happy. It was basically a content time in the history of our country, and the guys that were there were basically content. We had a simple existence. We went to class. We worked out. It wasn't all that complicated. If Bud said something, we believed him. We did it. We didn't question him.

"It's funny. I saw in '57 an entirely different bunch of guys, and it began a whole new era for Bud in dealing with boys. There were guys on that team who questioned. They didn't see the importance of discipline.

"We had a lot of little things that we would do—like when we got on the bus on Friday afternoon to go to Oklahoma City, that was a time when nobody opened his mouth. That was the time when you did some mental preparation, and when you got on the bus to go to the stadium on Saturday morning that was a time when nobody opened his mouth. It was a time when you thought about the game and mentally got ready to play. It was just an example of the discipline we had. If you didn't want to think about the game you might sit there and daydream, but you didn't open your mouth or raise hell or anything like that. My senior year ['57] was kind of frustrating because I saw a lot of guys that just didn't want to get ready mentally or to do the extra things you have to do to have a quality team."

A Study in Contrast

The 1982 edition of the OU Sooners boarded a plane en route to Tempe, Arizona, where they were to meet Arizona State in the Fiesta Bowl. During the flight, senior offensive guard Steve "Dr. Death" Williams told the stewardess to bring him a bourbon and Coke, which she did. The 270-pound Williams earned his nickname through his prowess as a heavyweight wrestler at OU. In fact Williams had already made his debut the

---

previous summer on the pro wrestling circuit, where he earned his livelihood for several years.

One of the assistant coaches did not think it was a good idea for Williams to be drinking on a team trip. The coach made his way to the back of the plane and told Williams to pour the drink out.

The truculent Williams told the coach that he was twenty-one years old and that he would damn sure have a drink any time he wanted one. The coach shook his head and meekly returned to his seat. Williams played in the Fiesta Bowl game, which the Sooners lost 32–21 despite 239 rushing yards by Marcus Dupree.

"In '56," Searcy said, "it was the personality of the guys and it was the leadership of guys like Tubbs that made us so good. Before him there had been guys like Max Boydston, Kurt Burris, Gene Mears, Gene Calame, and J. D. Roberts. Regardless of how great a coaching staff you have, you've got to have team leadership and the kind of kids who are willing to do what you're asking them to do."

The Wilkinson era was an era of dignity in college football. In the fifties players did not taunt their opponents with words and gestures. They praised them, always finding something good to say about an opponent. In Wilkinson's time players never boasted that they would easily beat another team. They never spoke disrespectfully of an opponent.

When players such as Brian Bosworth came along and called other teams "doormats" and said they wanted to deliberately injure, kick, and spit on opponents, this inflammatory rhetoric stuck in the craw of older fans who remembered when Wilkinson's Sooners won with dignity.

The University of Oklahoma was not Searcy's first choice of colleges. He had grown up in Fort Worth and originally had planned to stay close to home and attend Southern Methodist

University in Dallas. In fact he signed a Southwest Conference letter of intent with SMU. Shortly after his signing, Searcy met Jerry Tubbs at a high school track meet (both were discus throwers). Although Tubbs, like Searcy, had already signed a Southwest Conference letter of intent (with Baylor), he told Byron that he had not ruled out the possibility of attending OU. Both young men understood their letters were only binding within the Southwest Conference. OU was still recruiting Searcy, and this meeting with Tubbs piqued his interest in the Sooners. However, it was ultimately an incident that occurred at a softball game that made Searcy decide for OU. He explained, "There was this guy pitching for our softball team, who at that time I thought was older than God. He must have been twenty-seven or twenty-eight years old. He asked me if I'd decided where I was going to school. I said I've decided to go to SMU, but I'm kind of thinking about OU. By this time I knew Tubbs was going to OU because I had read it in the paper.

"So this pitcher said, 'Isn't it a football scholarship that you're going to get?'

"I said, 'Yeah.'

"Then he said, 'How in the world could you go to SMU if you want to play football?' He said, 'It's a great school, but if you're going to play football and you're going to work your butt off in college, why not do it in a place where you've got a chance to accomplish something?'

"I hardly knew the guy, but a light came on for me and I went home and called [OU assistant coach] Bill Jennings and said, 'Do you all still have a place for me?' He said, 'Yes,' and I said, 'I'll be there.'"

Searcy's football career at OU almost ended prematurely due to a serious back injury he suffered as a sophomore. After his surgery Searcy lay in his infirmary bed for three weeks. His weight dropped from 210 to 178 pounds. After the injury Searcy literally had to work his way back on to the team. He was given a job at the student union serving food to pay for his scholarship. Searcy said that there was a point at which he seriously considered leaving OU but he decided not to.

"I needed the scholarship," he said. "I wanted a college degree and I just felt like I could compete with those guys and I had to find out. I had to see if I could do it. When I went back to practice that spring, [assistant coach] Ted Youngling took an interest in me and encouraged me. When two-a-days began the next fall I started out on the forty-fifty team with the walk-ons, but I had an intuitive feeling that I could make it if I got a break. By that time I had my weight back up to 210 [which was the same as he weighed at the time of this interview in 1986] and Youngling continued to encourage me and that really made a difference to have one guy pattin' you on the back. Then I started to get some breaks. It seems like one guy who was a pretty good player quit and I was getting close to making the traveling squad, so I really turned it on. After the last scrimmage, before the season started, Gomer came over and put his arm around me. I'll never forget it and it was all downhill after that.

"As I look back on this experience now, I don't think it was a hardship. I think it probably was one of the best things that ever happened as far as my own personal growth was concerned."

Jerry Tubbs, a man with back problems himself, said, "It was really something for Byron to come back from that injury the way he did."

Searcy's position, left tackle, was a key element in OU's one-platoon system. On defense, the offensive left tackle was called upon to play defensive end. This meant that in certain defensive situations Searcy would have to drop off the line to cover pass receivers. This position required great athletic ability. The left tackle had to have the strength to block big bulky linemen on offense and the quickness and mobility to cover pass receivers on defense. The demands of this position were to Searcy's liking, however. "I liked to have more room to move around. I probably fit that position [at six-foot-three, 210 pounds] a little better than some interior linemen who were built low to the ground. I'm glad I played in an era where you could play both ways. If we had had two-platoon football, I would probably have played offense."

The Oklahoma Defense

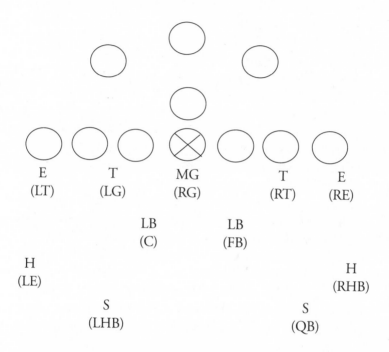

Offensive positions are listed in parentheses.

"I played against bigger guys," Searcy said, "but we were just so much quicker and smarter and better coached that I never felt, even one time, that I couldn't beat my man. I don't mean to sound cocky, but there was just never a time I thought I couldn't beat the guy I was playing against."

Searcy's roommate in his sophomore year was Tommy McDonald, whom Searcy credits with starting OU's fast-break or quick-huddle offense. He explained, "We were getting ready for the '56 Orange Bowl. When we ran our offense against blocking dummies Bud was trying to build conditioning into this as well as timing, and he liked for everybody to really make an effort to get back to the huddle as quick as we could. Tommy was a guy who, whether he was faking or had the ball, would run thirty or forty yards downfield and turn around and run back to the huddle. He just had this great energy level, and he'd get back to the huddle and kid the linemen, saying things like, 'Where have you guys been?' So everybody started to hurry to try to beat him back to the huddle and that's how the fast break actually started. Bud just picked up on it and had Harris call the plays at the line or call three plays in the huddle.

"In the Orange Bowl [when OU defeated Maryland 20–6] Harris would call three plays at once, and we'd run three plays without a huddle. If he needed to change a play, he'd change at the line. We were in such good shape that this wasn't that hard really. It was so funny to see the looks on the faces of the other team when we did this. It really got them rattled. It took a certain rhythm to be able to do that and keep your concentration. I thought that was one of the unique things we did.

"When you do the same thing over and over again, it gets kind of boring, but one good thing Bud did was put in eight or ten new plays each week. We probably wouldn't use them in the game, but he did this just to take some of the boredom out of it and occasionally we'd use them."

Searcy remembered that many unheralded freshmen became good players while some other kids who arrived at OU with great press clippings never made it. "Tom Emerson, the first-team right tackle in '56, was from Wilson, Oklahoma. He was probably the most country guy you'll ever see in your life. He had never been out of the state of Oklahoma. Our freshman year he was probably on the third or fourth team, but he was one of those guys who got better and better. He was a hard worker. He went on to get a Ph.D. in entomology and teach at Berkeley. He's a very bright guy.

"On our freshman team there was a big ol' boy from Pampa, Texas, named Buddy Cockrel. Everybody thought he was going to be the next Jim Weatherall [an All-American tackle at OU in '50 and '51]. He had the talent and the size, but he missed his ropin' and doggin' and rodeoin' so he went off to Hardin Simmons, back to the rodeo country of Abilene, Texas. He was a great player, but you can just never tell about kids as a freshman.

"There was very little jealousy if any among the players. There was some but it didn't surface much. The only two guys who used to gig one another a little bit were Harris and McDonald. They were two of the key guys who used to get most of the press anyway. I think maybe Harris thought he didn't get his share of the recognition and he may have been right, but overall it was a very unselfish family-type situation.

"I think this was just the personality of the players. I don't think you can coach that. I think the coaches can influence it and take it and build on it, but I think it was just that the players who were there at that time had such a good attitude.

"That's not to say that everybody was absolutely happy. I'm sure that there were some guys who thought they should have been playing more or felt like they were better than the other guy. If you're a competitive person you've got to think like that. I know that must have been in the minds of some of the guys, but it didn't surface in such a way that it created any negative feelings.

"I just can't imagine there being another situation like that ['56] again because kids today are too independent. They're going to do their own thing. They want it now. They're not patient. It's a whole new situation today. I'm not being critical of it. I'm just saying that coaching today is a lot more complicated than it was in our era. There was a big difference."

The precise cultural and economic conditions that existed in the postwar, post-depression fifties of west Texas and Oklahoma that produced a group of young men capable of winning all their college football games will never exist again. If a coach is to break Wilkinson's record of forty-seven consecutive victories, he will have to do it with a much more heterogeneous group of players: heterogeneous in terms of race, religion, politics, cultural and economic background, goals, and values.

"Maybe it was magic or something," Searcy said, "but it seemed there were just certain ingredients that complemented one another so well that brought out the good things. That's not to say that bunch in '56 couldn't raise hell—or be mischievous. But that bunch had very little dissipation from the standpoint of drinking and carousing or anything like that. Now there were some times out of season when there was some beer drinkin' and hell raisin' but I honestly can't remember it happening during the '56 season. I can remember coming back on the plane from Kansas State in '57 after we had played so poorly [defeating lowly K-State only 13–0], and Gomer came up to me and said, 'Go out and have a beer tonight.' I nearly fell over. I never thought a coach would say that to you. I think they were trying to loosen us up a little bit. The coaches thought maybe we had been playing tight because of the winning streak. I think it was a matter of attitude. The irony of it was that a few days before that '57 Notre Dame game, *Sports Illustrated* came out with an article entitled 'Why Oklahoma Is Unbeatable.'"

That feature article was illustrated by a cover picturing several Oklahoma players cheering their teammates on from the sidelines. *SI* was then twenty-five cents an issue or $7.50 a year. Tex Maule wrote in this piece that the combination of talent, spirit, coaching, and weak competition that existed at the University of Oklahoma produced invincible Sooner teams.

A Perfect Expression of Their Way of Life

The red clay of Oklahoma and the sands of the west Texas desert country produce scrubby crops, oil and football players. For the hardy, lean, tough people who inhabit this country, the crops are a last resort; oil a hopeful dream and football a religion. Football is the

---

> perfect expression of their way of life—hit harder than
> you are hit, don't cry when you're hurt, win. The ulti-
> mate expression of this rather Spartan philosophy is at
> the state university, where the sixty-odd young men who
> make up the football squad hit superlatively hard, bear
> the bruises of the game stoically and above all else win.
> Tex Maule
> *Sports Illustrated,* November 8, 1957

Maule also quoted Clendon Thomas as saying, "You can't pin-point it [the Oklahoma winning spirit]. The guys way back started it. Then it rubs off on you. We go out to win and we play to win. None of us wants to be on the team that ends this streak. I guess no matter what else you ever did, people would remember you were on the team that lost the game that ended the streak."

The next week, after the loss which Maule had argued was impossible, he wrote a sequel to his "Why Oklahoma Is Unbeatable" piece, entitled "Reason Takes a Holiday," in which he had to explain how Notre Dame beat the Sooners. Maule cred-ited Notre Dame with doing a great job of scouting and simply outlasting the Sooners. Searcy believed it was more a case of OU losing the game than Notre Dame winning it.

"When we beat them up there in '56, I'd never seen such an intense bunch of boys. We remembered the '52 game [which Notre Dame won 28–21]. We were all in high school then but we'd heard about it. We knew Bud had never beaten them, and we saw the intensity Bud had and we were ready to play.

"The damn thing about it was the next year it was completely reversed and we were flat as could be. We had cinched the Big Seven championship the week before [with a 39–14 victory over Missouri], and we were going to the Orange Bowl. We'd had an up-and-down year. We just barely beat Kansas State. We beat Colorado 14–13. We were struggling. We were still rated number one then and we had the talent. I'm not going to name any names, but we had some guys who became well-known players at Oklahoma—

but I'm just glad I didn't have to play with them but one year." Searcy did not make this charge frivolously, nor did he intend to sensationalize; nonetheless, in giving an opinion, his speech and gestures revealed that this was an emotionally laden subject for him.

"I've seen in the *Football News* that they've had our '56 team rated up there with the top three or four teams in history, which is a neat thing to look back on. I think we could have an off day and win a lot easier than good teams today could because I think we were so far ahead of everyone else. I think it would be easier for someone to slip up on, say, Nebraska's '82 or '83 teams or even their great '71 team than it was for somebody to slip up on us because we were just that much farther ahead of our competition."

Several of his former teammates said they thought Byron Searcy had been the most "successful" of them all in his post-college days. "Successful in terms of what?" he asked. "There are all kinds of definitions of success. I think if a person finds the right niche, where he's happy and he's in good health and has a good family, he's successful. I have no idea how to evaluate that. I know that Jim Harris has done well in the oil business. Jakie Sandefer [unlike most of his teammates] was wealthy when he got to OU. There are a lot of guys who have done well—look at a guy like Tubbs. He's done well. Most of the guys have the basic fiber from the standpoint of character to do whatever they want to do."

Fort Worth, Texas, January 2005

Byron Searcy still looked very much the patrician southern gentleman as he spoke in his well-appointed real estate office. "I've slowed down some, but I'm still active in the business," he said. "I've been on this bank board since 1975, so I think that when I go off of it in about two or three years I'll probably retire. My son Jay pretty much runs the business now, and it's enjoyable working with him."

Searcy first met many of the men who would become valuable business contacts for him some sixty years ago on the meticulously

Byron Searcy

manicured fairways of the Colonial Country Club. But he was not a member. He was a caddy.

"When I was about ten or twelve, I would ride my bike over to Colonial. It took about fifteen minutes," he said. "I would carry two bags and get $1.40 per bag, and usually most guys would give me a dollar tip. On Saturdays I'd get out there and do thirty-six holes a lot of times. It was a great way to make money in those days." Of course, these days there are no caddies. They have gone the way of passenger trains and pool halls.

When he wasn't caddying, Searcy would often shag balls for the great Ben Hogan. "That was easy," he said. "He would hit them right at my feet. When he changed clubs he'd just wave for me to back up a little bit. I'd stand out there for two or three hours while he practiced."

"I got to know a lot of rich people at Colonial. It was a great experience for me because with a few rare exceptions they treated me great. When I got back to Fort Worth after college, I called on some of these men I had caddied for. I didn't know if they'd remember me or not. But several of them helped me get started in the real estate business."

Searcy, now seventy years old, still enjoys his autumn rituals of returning to Norman for the football games. "I feel some nostalgia sitting there in the stadium," Searcy explained. "I look around and think about how much things have changed: the changes in the stadium, the size of the crowds, and the size of the players. But I can't help but look up and see that 'National Champions '55 and '56' painted on the press box and that's a nice thing to think about."

Before the games Searcy likes to visit the O Club where he typically meets some of his old teammates. "I will often see Clendon Thomas, Bill Krisher, once in a while Jimmy Harris, and I sit close to Benton Ladd so I see him frequently, but really I'm surprised that I don't see more of the guys."

One person Searcy always made a special attempt to see was his old coach Port Robertson. "Fortunately I was able to keep in touch with Port, over the years, right up until he died. If nothin' else I'd just pick up the phone and call him. I still have the most positive feelings of respect and admiration for him, and like everyone else I've got a lot of Port stories." Searcy then proceeded to relate the following Port story, concerning his son Jay, a former OU baseball player.

"They were in about the fourth or fifth inning of a game out at Dale Mitchell Park when the phone rings in the dugout. [Assistant coach] Butch Roberts answered the phone and it was Port. Roberts listened for a minute and then called out, 'Jay, it's for you.'

"Jay picked up the phone, and Port said, 'Mr. Searcy, do you know that you have several outstanding parking tickets with the city of Norman?'

"'Oh, yes sir,' Jay said. 'I will take care of those real soon.'

"'You need to take care of that right now,' Port replied.

"Jay said, 'Well, we're in the middle of a game right now.'

"'I don't care,' Port said. 'You need to just get right on down there and pay those tickets.'

"So Jay left the game and went down and paid his tickets."

Obviously Byron Searcy retains many treasured memories of his time at OU. "If I were to come up with a metaphor for that '56 season," he said, "it would be a diamond. There may have been some imperfections, but if so I don't know where they were."

New York City, New York, Tuesday, November 20, 1956

Collier's magazine revealed its College Football All-American team today. Jerry Tubbs and Tommy McDonald of OU were named to the team.

Tubbs was named Player of the Year and as such would receive the Walter Camp Memorial Trophy. Tubbs, cited for his "bulldozing, blocking, and terrific tackling," was virtually a unanimous choice among the 503 coaches who voted for this award. Jim Tatum said, "Tubbs is just too rugged to play with college boys." Wilkinson said of Tubbs, "Jerry's contribution to our team has been just as great in the area of attitude and desire as in football playing ability."

Collier's All-Americans, 1956

Position	Player	School
QB	John Brodie	Stanford
HB	Tommy McDonald	Oklahoma
HB	Johnny Majors	Tennessee
FB	Jimmy Brown	Syracuse
E	Ron Kramer	Michigan
E	Joe Walton	Pittsburgh
T	John Witte	Oregon State
T	Lou Michael	Kentucky
G	Jim Parker	Ohio State
G	Bill Glass	Baylor
C	Jerry Tubbs*	Oklahoma

* Player of the Year

Not chosen to this team was the eventual Heisman Trophy winner Paul Hornung.

Melbourne, Australia, Wednesday, November 21, 1956

The Duke of Edinburgh declared the Sixteenth Modern Olympiad open. Hungary sought to have Russia barred from the games. Avery Brundage, president of the International Olympic Committee, refused this request. Brundage said that political considerations cannot be permitted to strain the games, which are contests between individuals and not nations.

We came down here to win. Not to try to keep the score down or be satisfied with a credible showing. It just didn't work. All you can say is that Oklahoma has a great football team. One of the really great teams I have ever seen.

—Pete Elliott, coach, University of Nebraska

Oklahoma 54 Nebraska 6

Norman, Oklahoma, Saturday, November 24, 1956

Pete Elliott had been one of Wilkinson's assistant coaches the year before. Elliott's assistants, Bill Jennings and Dee Andros, were both former Sooner players and coaches, so the Nebraska Big Red had a decided Oklahoma hue for this game.

Bud liked having Elliott as an assistant, not just for his coaching ability but because he was a good man to have as a partner in a golf match. Elliott, a fine player and an extremely long hitter, was known to blast many a 300-yard drive on the long Perry Maxwell designed OU golf course. One of Elliott's most memorable accomplishments while at OU was the sound thrashing he gave Labron Harris Sr., the Oklahoma A&M golf coach. Harris had brought his golfers to Norman for a match with the Sooners and thought he might pick up some walking-around money while he was there, but he proved to be no match for the powerful Elliott.

On this day Elliott's Cornhuskers were no match for his mentor's Sooners. OU gained 565 total yards (506 rushing). All fifty-five Sooners who suited out played in the game, including the sixteen seniors who were playing before the home fans for the last time: Tommy McDonald, Jerry Tubbs, Ed Gray, Jimmy Harris, Billy Pricer, Tom Emerson, John Bell, Jay O'Neal, Bill Brown, Bob Timberlake, Delbert Long, Bob Derrick, Hugh Ballard, Dale Depue, Bill Harris, and Henry Broyles. Seniors Wayne Greenlee and Ken Northcutt were not able to play due to injuries they had suffered in the North Carolina game.

This was the last opportunity for Sooner fans to see these seniors play on their home turf, yet only forty-six thousand showed up despite the mild fifty-six-degree temperature. There would not have been nearly this many people in Memorial Stadium had it not been Band Day. Over one hundred high school bands were present for this annual affair.

Tommy McDonald, Carl Dodd, and Jimmy Harris scored two touchdowns each, but Clendon Thomas, who gained 100 yards on only six carries, was shut out for the only time all year.

The Sooners began by taking the opening kickoff and going seventy-eight yards in nine plays. The key to this drive was Thomas's fifty-four-yard run to the Nebraska nine yard line. Four plays later, McDonald, with ninety-one yards on eleven carries, took a pitchout from Harris into the end zone for the TD.

The next touchdown was scored by the alternate team when Dodd got loose for a thirty-two-yard score. After Nebraska put together their seventy-four-yard touchdown drive early in the second quarter, the Sooners recorded twenty points and led 34–6 at half time.

Jimmy Harris got OU's first TD of the second quarter from the six, and after Steve Jennings blocked a Nebraska kick, David Baker passed eleven yards to Carl Dodd for the next TD. Then, just before half time, Harris and McDonald hooked up on a forty-six-yard touchdown pass.

The first team started the second half scoring by marching sixty-nine yards in five plays. Pricer had runs of fourteen and ten yards in the drive, and Harris got the TD on a thirty-one-yard run. Next, the alternates took the ball seventy-two yards in five plays with fullback Bill Brown going fifty yards for the score.

When the Sooners stopped Nebraska's scoring threat at the two yard line, the starters moved the ball to the Cornhusker twenty-three. From there the third team took over, and quarterback Dale Sherrod scored on a two-yard keeper to make the final score 54–6.

After the game, Nebraska captain Jim Murphy said, "Their whole team just flew past us, and Tubbs is terrific defensively. Bill Glass of Baylor and Jim Parker of Ohio State don't belong on the same field with Tubbs. It's not so much his hitting. It's his quickness."

With OU's thirty-ninth straight victory, the Sooners equaled the University of Washington's record for consecutive wins. Washington established this streak during the seasons of 1908–1914. Wilkinson was mindful of this as he spoke of the Sooners' next opponent: "Our sixteen seniors play their final game for Oklahoma against the Aggies at Stillwater Saturday. In this game they can do something no other team in the history of college football has ever done—win forty consecutive games. Coach Cliff Speegle's Aggies had an open date last Saturday and came to Norman as a group to see us play Nebraska. The Aggies are tough. Kansas's twenty-one points and Arkansas's nineteen are the most points scored against them all season. Our coaching staff hopes our boys realize what is at stake and that our team will play their best football of the year. We must do this if we expect to win our final game."

Bob Harrison is really one of the great all-time OU players.

—Benton Ladd

Bob Harrison

Stamford, Texas, Thirty Years after the Game

Woody Guthrie said, "Texas is where you can see farther, see less, walk farther and travel less, see more cows and less milk, more trees and less shade, more rivers and less water, and have more fun on less money than anywhere else." He had to be talking about Stamford.

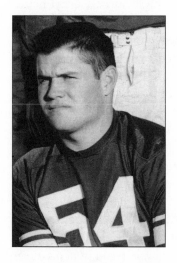

Stamford is a one-stoplight town about fifty miles north of Abilene. Farmers in this hard-scrabble country try to beat back the mesquite trees and pray for rain.

Stamford, like most small Texas towns, is built around the courthouse square. The neighborhood near the square is comprised of pre–World War II frame houses, but farther north and away from the stoplight are several modern houses. Bob Harrison's large two-story brick home looked more like one you would expect to find in Dallas's Preston Trail addition rather than in Stamford. The fourth tee of the Stamford Country Club Golf Course (which would never be confused with the Preston Trail course) was just behind Harrison's patio.

Upon entering Harrison's house, one first sees a large framed color portrait of number 54 in his Oklahoma uniform, which hangs in his foyer. This portrait was given to Harrison in recognition of his feat of playing in twenty-five OU Varsity-Alumni football games, from 1956 through 1980. It is obviously one of the paintings done by Tommy McDonald's company.

Harrison played nine years of professional football, retiring in 1967. Then, he played in thirteen more alumni games even though OU had made a rule that no alum could play in the game if he had been out of football (college or pro) for more than five years. But who was going to tell Harrison he couldn't play? Toward the end of this amazing streak, Harrison was playing against young men who were not even born when he played in his first varsity-alumni game—men such as Elvis Peacock, Daryl Hunt, Greg Roberts, Thomas Lott, Billy Sims, J. C. Watts, and the late David Overstreet. "What was unreal is that the last time I went up there [at age forty-three] was that I was only going to play a little bit," Harrison said. "But we didn't have many linebackers to start with and a couple of 'em got hurt and I ended up havin' to play 'bout three quarters."

The United States had six different presidents during the twenty-five years Harrison played in these alumni games. Harrison played on through the New Frontier, the Great Society, moon walks (both Neil Armstrong's and Michael Jackson's), Vietnam, and Watergate. His career spanned the administrations from Eisenhower to Carter, from Wilkinson to Switzer.

Harrison's scrapbook, yellowed with age, nearly covered his entire kitchen table. In it were pictures and accounts of his career with the Sooners and also his professional career with San Francisco '59–'61, Philadelphia '62–'63, Pittsburgh '64, and finally San Francisco again from '65–'67. In this scrapbook there was only one mention of the '56 Nebraska game, a small excerpt from an article told how Harrison had intercepted a pass in the third quarter. "My mother put this scrapbook together," Harrison explained. "She probably just cut out that part because it had my name in it."

"Yon Sooners have a lean and hungry look. Such men are dangerous." This was the thought that struck my mind as the sun sizzled down on an early morning practice session at Norman a few days ago. How Bud Wilkinson keeps them cavorting like kittens and hungry as lions no one knows. This is a select group of veterans, but somehow you get the impression they are not very large until scrimmage is called, and then they look BIG. Speed is the backbone of this squad, supplemented by superior coaching technique. Wilkinson threatens to create more problems for his foes by additions to his attack.

Herman Hickman
Sports Illustrated, September 24, 1956

Thirty years after they played their last game in the crimson and cream Harrison was the most youthful looking and appeared to be in the best physical condition of all the former Sooners. He said, "I'll be forty-nine on my next birthday, and I could probably pass for thirty-nine." He was probably right. He had thick black hair with no traces of gray and stayed in shape by lifting weights and jogging. His fitness routine consisted of one-hour weight-lifting sessions on Mondays, Wednesdays, and Fridays. On Tuesdays, Thursdays, and Saturdays he jogged for one hour.

Weight training was something Harrison started after his football career. While at OU he was introduced to weight lifting by Mike Lindsey, a shot-putter from England. "Mike was a weight lifter," Harrison said. "We had some weights down in the basement of Jeff House [the athletic dorm] in the laundry room. That's the first time I ever lifted weights." Now, the Sooners, like all other big-time football programs, lift weights year-round in a state-of-the-art training facility under the supervision of full-time strength coaches.

College teams may soon have to add a chemical coach to their staffs. The apparently widespread use of steroids, pain killers, and stimulants by today's athletes is enough to make one speculate that the best football team will soon be produced by the school with the best chemistry department. Perhaps schools will begin to recruit chemistry professors as zealously as running backs.

Harrison was a very highly regarded high school footballer. He was recruited by all the Southwest Conference teams as well as Colorado and Notre Dame. Apparently the recruiters found a plethora of talent in the west Texas area. Two years earlier Jerry Tubbs had graduated from Breckenridge High School, which is fifty miles east of Stamford.

"You go anywhere in the state of Texas and mention Stamford and people will say one of two things. They either mention the big rodeo we have here every year, or they talk about Stamford football. One year Abilene, Breckenridge, and Stamford all won state championships in different divisions. There were three state champions within fifty miles of one another," Harrison said.

After meeting Wilkinson, Harrison had no trouble making up his mind about where he wanted to go to school. "I was talking to SMU and I could have gone to lots of schools, but Coach Wilkinson came down here and I said, 'I want to play for that man.'

"I remember the first time I ever saw OU play. We were down at the State Fair of Texas. I walked into this room and I guess I knew Oklahoma and Texas were playing, and they had this little ol' bitty TV set there. Billy Vessels was playing so it must have been in the early fifties.

"I went up there to Norman to visit, and Byron Searcy was the guy who showed me around. He and Buddy Oujesky [first-team right guard in '56] treated me like I was an equal. They didn't treat me like I was a high school kid. Even when you were a fresh-man up there people treated you the same. There was no hazin'.

No one was looked down on. Everyone was treated as a person, and I really liked it after I got to visit."

As a co-captain in 1958, Harrison was named UPI Lineman of the Year. David Baker recalled that a pro scout had predicted great things for Harrison in his sophomore year of 1956. "This pro scout came in to look at films of Tubbs, McDonald, Harris, people like that, to get ready for the draft. He said, 'I can already see who your next All-American center is.' We had had several All-American centers, Tom Catlin, Kurt Burris, and Tubbs. So we kinda had a string of 'em. The scout said, 'Number 54 will be your All-American center.' Harrison was my roommate in college and in pro ball too. A lot of people think he may have been as good a center and linebacker as OU ever had. I don't know that you could prove it or disprove it. He may have been as good as Tubbs."

Benton Ladd also praised Bob Harrison's football skills: "Harrison was a sophomore when Tubbs was a senior. Both of those guys were great players. Tubbs had all the ability in the world, but he was a little bit lazy—well, that's really too strong a word to say that he was lazy, but if you'd take it a little bit easy on him in practice, he'd appreciate it. Bob Harrison was totally different. He thought you ought to hit the field runnin' and never stop. He and Tommy McDonald probably were the only two guys I ever knew who really and truly enjoyed practice. They thought practice was great. I don't mean to depreciate Tubbs, but Harrison was a little bit more fanatical, I guess is the way to put it."

Harrison loved to reminisce about his career as a Sooner. "In 1956 I was a sophomore and comin' from a small town like this and getting to play on a team like that was just awesome. I guess, really, the greatest thrill I've ever had in football is the first time I got to step on the field as an Oklahoma Sooner. When I stepped out on that field for the first time and those sixty thousand fans were screamin' and hollerin' the way they were—it was a feelin' you just can't describe.

"The thing we had was quickness. We were not a big team. In fact, in 1958 when I was a senior, I weighed 212 pounds and there was only one guy on the team bigger than me. In '56 we had a great football team, but every week you had to go out and prove it again because that would be the game of the year for your opponents. If they beat us, their season would be complete. We were trying to win ten ball games to be national champions. Our opponents knew they weren't as good as us, and beating us would make their season. So every week we had to go out and compete against teams that were fired up like that."

Like all his former teammates, Harrison credits the Sooner coaches for the team's success. "I think the reason Wilkinson was so successful was that he got people to play at a higher level than other coaches probably could have. Wilkinson's players thought they were better. Especially in the spring or in the off-season, you'd walk out of his office thinking you were the greatest thing on earth. I don't care if you were on the first team or the fifth team, Bud made you think that if you continued to work as hard as you could, there was nothing you couldn't do.

"I guess I've been fortunate to have had such good coaches. In high school I played for Gordon Wood. He won two state championships here at Stamford, and he won six or eight down at Brownwood. He won more football games than Bear Bryant. Coach Wood won over four hundred games. I was very fortunate to play for two positive people who were winners. Most guys are a little bit negative.

"It might have been different if we were losing, but Bud would never call a name out and embarrass anyone. When we were going over the films, Bud would say, 'Well, I see the center didn't get his block this time, but I know that he wanted to get it.' He'd never say, 'Harrison, you didn't get your man.' I think this was a plus for him. I've always believed that you can get more out of a guy by pattin' him on the back than by kickin' him in the butt, and I think that was Bud's philosophy. In pro ball it certainly was not that way. But even in pro ball if a guy's not tryin' he needs his butt kicked, but if he's doin' the best he can and he gets beat . . . so what?

"We had this guy who was a good player but not a good guy. In fact we caught him stealing some things from the other players. He didn't last very long, but after he was gone Bud said, 'Basically he was not a bad guy.' This was the worst thing Bud ever said about anyone."

Gomer Jones was a significant figure in Harrison's football career. "If Gomer liked you, he'd go to the moon for you and he was an excellent teacher. He was so patient. He took it step by step. We would walk through everything before we would run. He and Bud were a positive force that created a winner.

"I enjoyed OU more than the pros," Harrison said. "For one reason at OU we won all the time. In the pros we didn't always win. In college there is not the pressure of playing for money, and in the pros I just never played for a real good team or a real good coach. If I had played for someone who was a real winner, I would have gotten into that, but the pro coaches I played for would put us out there when we weren't really prepared, mentally, to play. At OU we were always prepared. We went over things so many times."

In Harrison's day one did not get rich playing pro football. "The most I ever made in pro ball was fifteen thousand dollars," Harrison said. "Even the quarterbacks didn't make fifty thousand. Once I was in the weight room at OU and Jackie Shipp [OU linebacker '80–'83] was in there. He was talkin' about gettin' drafted, and I said, 'You should sign for at least what I got.' He said, 'What's that?' I said, a nine-thousand-dollar contract and a two-thousand-dollar bonus."

Twenty years after his last pro season, Harrison had no financial worries. "We live comfortably, let's put it that way," he said. "I'm a farmer, cotton and wheat, and I've invested in oil. I farm about fifteen hundred acres. I've got some land east of town and some land over by Tuxedo [a small hamlet west of Stamford, which the locals pronounce TUXIE-dough]. I enjoy farmin'. It's not only my livelihood, it's my hobby." Indeed several of Harrison's former teammates had warned that he might not want to get off his tractor even to talk about OU football.

"I do all the farming myself, except I hire my wheat to be harvested. I keep pretty busy around here, so I don't get back to see too many OU football games any more. My sister [Mrs. Alan Grubb] lives in Norman, and I've always let her have my tickets."

Harrison remarkably came through his college and nine-year pro career relatively injury free. "I'm probably the luckiest guy in the world," he said. "I separated my shoulder once and it aches sometimes and I've got some bursitis, but to play as long as I played and not have more wrong with me than I've got is really lucky."

There are not many OU fans in Stamford, Texas, so few of Harrison's neighbors recall his college football days, but in Oklahoma people remember the name Bob Harrison. "I've got a friend who sells cotton seed up in Oklahoma," Harrison said. "He kids me all the time. He says, 'I've got the key to anything I want in Oklahoma, all I've got to do is tell them I know Harrison.'"

Harrison remembered his teammates, too. "That '56 team was a great football team," he said, "but the best part of it is the friendships you form with guys like Tubbs, Searcy, and McDonald."

Stamford, Texas, March 2005

It is in ruins now—the once proud mansion that Bob Harrison's father built almost one hundred years ago. The Harrison family sold the old place long ago and along with it six sections of land, but it was beautiful once, strong and stately with fifty-foot tall Roman columns glistening alabaster in the intense west Texas sun. Now the windows of the old homestead are boarded up. The roof is collapsing and the paint is gone. One wonders how much longer it can stand against the fierce northwest winds that drive the tumbleweeds mercilessly across the prairie.

The same could be said for the rest of Stamford. The town square is practically deserted. The independent shopkeepers, the life's blood of small towns, have pulled their shades, locked their doors for the last time, and moved away. If they haven't already shown *The Last Picture Show* in Stamford, they will soon.

"Wal-Mart," Harrison said. "It's just killed us. We had a square full of stores. Now it's just dwindled down to nothin'. All we have is farmin' here. There's no industry and no jobs for anybody. When I was goin' to school here, there was probably six thousand people here. Now we'd be lucky to have twenty-five hundred."

In 2005, Bob Harrison was still living in the same spacious ranch-style home adjacent to the Stamford golf course, but he wasn't farming anymore. "I loved to drive a tractor," he said. "But I was driven out of the farmin' business because of no rain, insects, and low cotton prices. I just couldn't stay, so I sold my land and got out. I worked my butt off farmin' for thirty years for nothin'."

Now Harrison works two jobs. "I work at the high school from 7:30 A.M. to 12:30 P.M. every day. I have these three kids that I sit with. They were kicked out of school and now I do this study hall for them. They study sometimes. Sometimes they're asleep. There are all kinds of problems. There is stress you wouldn't believe."

Fortunately, Harrison's other job is much more tranquil. "I work at the prison from two P.M. until ten P.M. every day," he said. The Rolling Plains Regional County Jail and Detention Center, in Haskell, just fifteen miles north of Stamford, is a privately owned prison. "We have county prisoners, DWI'ers, drug addicts, and the like. We also have these so-called detainees, which the government has sent here while they decide what to do with them. This is a result of 9–11. They're guys that have no citizenship papers, mostly Mexicans, but we also have Middle Easterners, Russians, Chinese, and we have about fifty women. There's a bunch of 'em that don't need to be here, at least not for what they are charged with.

"The kids at the high school are much worse than the prisoners. If you treat the prisoners halfway decent, you'll get treated back the same way. But them kids, they run their mouth. They're likely to say anything. They're about to drive me crazy."

Despite this tough schedule Harrison remained positive about the future. "Barbra, my wife [of forty-two years], has been the high school librarian for thirty-six years. She'll retire in four more

Bob Harrison

years, and then we're planning to move to Lubbock where our children live. I plan to get a job out there drivin' an armored car, and I'll make about two and a half times what I'm makin' now. I've got some money saved in case of emergency and I'm still strong. I work out all the time. I can bench press three hundred pounds." Harrison certainly looked strong. The only concession to his sixty-seven years seemed to be the two hearing aids he wore.

When Bob Harrison was a senior in high school, his family was still living in the large two-story house just north of the courthouse square on Highway 277. In those days, there was not a finer home in either Jones or Haskell Counties. It was in the living room of this grand estate, in the spring of 1955, that Bob Harrison first met Bud Wilkinson. "I still remember the first time I saw him walk through the door," Harrison said. "We talked like good friends, relaxed and comfortable. I was very impressed.

"Bear Bryant also came up here to Stamford to try to recruit me to go to Texas A&M, but Bryant was a gruff old gripey guy. I just liked Coach Wilkinson a lot better."

So Bob Harrison made the decision to venture north of the Red River to play for Wilkinson's Sooners, and he has never regretted it. "We had some great, great guys on that team," he said, "Tubbs, Harris, Thomas, Pricer, Krisher, McDonald, et cetera, et cetera. There was not a bad guy in the whole bunch, and everybody played just as hard as they could. We were the greatest college football team that's ever been. We won forty-seven games in a row. Who else has done it?"

Melbourne, Australia, Wednesday, November 28, 1956

Perry O'Brien broke the Olympic shot-put record with a toss of 60 feet, 7 1/2 inches, and Bobby Morrow recorded a time of 20.6 in the 200-meter dash to break the twenty-year-old record of Jessie Owens.

Lawrence, Kansas, Wednesday, November 28, 1956

Wilt Chamberlin, who was about to make his debut in college basketball, said in an interview for the *Saturday Evening Post,* "I want to do my race some good. If I get Jim Crowed, I'll pack my bags and leave. I'm part of the Kansas team and I go wherever it goes. They agree with me. That's why we don't make a trip to Texas this year."

Melbourne, Australia, Thursday, November 29, 1956

Led by Bill Russell of San Francisco University, the U.S. Olympic basketball team defeated the Russians 85–55. The coach of the U.S. team was former University of Oklahoma All-American Gerald Tucker.

Chicago, Illinois, Friday, November 30, 1956

Floyd Patterson (age twenty-one) became the youngest heavyweight boxing champion in history when he knocked out thirty-nine-year-old Archie Moore in the fifth round. Moore retained his light-heavyweight title.

What you lose as you age are witnesses; the ones who watched you from early on and cared. Like your own little grandstand, Mom, Pop, etc.

—*John Updike,* Rabbit Is Rich

Oklahoma 53   Oklahoma A&M 0

Stillwater, Oklahoma, Saturday, December 1, 1956

After this A&M game the fans' memories of the 1956 team would begin to fade as the Indian summer would inevitably dissolve into winter, slowly but certainly, irreversibly. The future autumns would bring many other great athletes to the University of Oklahoma campus—young men like Steve Owens, Jack Mildren, Greg Pruitt, Joe Washington, Lucious Selmon, Billy Sims, Marcus Dupree, Brian Bosworth, Keith Jackson, Rocky Calmus, Josh Heupel, Roy Williams, and Jason White. Their football feats would obscure the memory of Tubbs, Harris, McDonald, Pricer, Gray, etc. But on the first day of December in 1956 OU's greatest team was given one last perfect day of autumn. The skies were clear and the temperature rose to seventy-two degrees.

OU took the opening kickoff and scored in three plays. Billy Pricer ran 37 yards for the TD. Clendon Thomas, who gained 123 yards on fifteen carries, got the next two Sooner scores, first on a one-yard plunge and then on an eight-yard pass reception.

Thomas's second touchdown was, ironically, a pass from McDonald. Coming into this game, Thomas and McDonald were tied for the national scoring title, each having scored 96 points on sixteen touchdowns. McDonald scored once in this game and finished fourth nationally in scoring with 102 points. Thomas, with two TDs, won the national scoring honors. The "winning" TD, although neither man knew it at the time, was this pass from McDonald.

David Baker recorded the next score for the Sooners when he took a pitchout from Jay O'Neal and stepped over from the three yard line. O'Neal got the next TD when he picked off an Aggie pass and sprinted sixty-three yards to make the score OU 33–A&M 0 at the half.

The alternates scored OU's only TD in the third quarter and once again it was O'Neal pitching to Baker for the score, which capped a sixty-five-yard, fourteen-play drive.

The Sooners recorded two more scores in the fourth quarter. For the first of these the starters drove sixty-eight yards in five plays with Thomas getting loose for forty-one yards. On the next play McDonald scored his last touchdown as a Sooner (the thirty-sixth of his illustrious career) when he made a weaving seventeen-yard run.

OU's last touchdown of the season was scored by an all-senior team that marched seventy-seven yards in nine plays. From the two yard line, co-captain Ed Gray moved from his left tackle position into the backfield and, with Hugh Ballard, Tom Emerson, and John Bell providing the blocking, scored the TD. Billy Pricer recalled that Gray, still clutching the football, walked directly up to Wilkinson and told him, "See, Coach, you've been playing me at the wrong position all these years."

Thus it was over: the perfect season for the team, 10–0–0, and the perfect career for the seniors, 31–0–0. In his final newsletter of the season, Bud said, "I hope Gomer and I will be coaching for a number of years, but I doubt if we will ever be associated with a group of seniors or a squad with a finer balance of personalities or a more wholesome attitude towards the game than those who played for Oklahoma in 1956."

In this same newsletter, Bud thanked his coaching staff, Gomer

Jones, Eddie Crowder, Sam Lyle, Ted Youngling, and Bill Canfield, as well as trainer Ken Rawlinson, for "loyalty and service to the team."

Bud also wrote, "Football is a squad game. If you don't have several real good boys to help you, you cannot have a good team. We have been very fortunate in this respect this year, and I should like to thank these players for giving us this priceless preparation that meant so much to our successful season: Carl Buck, George Talbott, Chuck Newman, Lyle Burris, Kenny Crossland, Dick Means, Ken Fitch, Victor Hayes, Mickey Johnson, Bob Martin, Don Nelson, Benton O'Neal, and Cloyd Shilling.

The Last Lineup

No.	Name	Class	Weight	Position
89	Don Stiller	SR	200	LE
73	Ed Gray	SR	208	LT
68	Joe Oujesky	SR	193	LG
53	Jerry Tubbs	SR	206	C
65	Bill Krisher	JR	213	RG
69	Tom Emerson	SR	214	RT
83	John Bell	SR	191	RE
15	Jim Harris	SR	173	QB
25	Tommy McDonald	SR	170	LH
35	Clendon Thomas	JR	188	RH
43	Billy Pricer	SR	197	FB

"It is always a melancholy thing to see a fine group of seniors play their final game. I believe strongly that in order to be a good football player, you must first of all be a fine man. This quality far outranks athletic ability. When you have several boys who are both fine men and outstanding athletes you have the ingredients of a great team. I feel most fortunate to have been associated with so many boys possessing both these qualities."

After this game, quarterback Jimmy Harris told reporters,

"How do I feel about being through? It's kind of a funny feeling really. It doesn't seem possible that it's over. It doesn't seem like we've been playing that long."

Nobody gets to be a cowboy forever.

—*From the movie* Monty Walsh

Jimmy Harris

Shreveport, Louisiana, Thirty Years after the Game

"We didn't realize it was all about to end," Jimmy Harris said. "I didn't really appreciate it at the time. I do now. It was an emo-

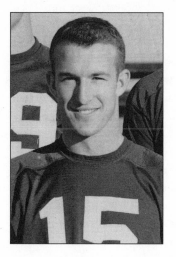

tional thing, to a degree, at that time, but it was not anywhere near as emotional as it is thinking about it now.

"I knew I was going to try to achieve another goal—pro football. It was just another step for me, and I think a lot of our guys were thinking that way. A lot of 'em didn't play in the pros, of course, but several of us were going to all-star games. McDonald, Bell, Tubbs, Gray, and I were all going to the North-South game. I think it was prob-

ably ten years later before I looked back and said, gosh, that was an emotional thing. But in some sense we were aware of it. We let Ed Gray score a touchdown at the end of the game. We were havin' fun.

"College football was fun the whole time. I really felt like it was a game the whole way. It was not really work other than running the stadium steps and a few things like that. If you asked Wilkinson he'd tell you that I hated to practice in the spring. I was not a very good spring player. I think Jay O'Neal may have started the spring games because that was Bud's way of punishing me but I had enough confidence that I thought I would be number one in the fall."

Egotistical, cocky, and confident were terms used by Harris's former teammates in describing him. They also mentioned talented and underrated. David Baker recalled, "Harris was a real cocky guy, but no one took offense at it. Everyone liked Jimmy. At a banquet after the season they gave Jimmy an award for being OU's best quarterback ever, and he said, 'It's about time I got something I deserve.'" Harris, of course, said this in jest, but some may not have taken it that way.

Baker, who quarterbacked OU in 1958, was very impressed with Harris's athletic skills. "Jimmy Harris would have been the greatest wishbone quarterback they ever had at OU if they had had the wishbone in 1956. He had great speed. He was tough. He never got hurt. He could throw the ball much, much better than people realized. If Harris had come along in 1970, Jack Mildren would have never played. I think Harris was the most underrated player on that team."

Billy Pricer said, "Jimmy was an excellent option quarterback. They said Jimmy couldn't throw the ball well, but he was probably one of the better-throwing quarterbacks that we ever had at OU, where we never had to throw the ball. He could sure run the option. He was a skinny guy [six-foot-one, 171 pounds]. We called him 'Hairy' because he could turn sideways and you couldn't see him. He was an underrated quarterback."

Whether Harris is cocky or confident is arguable and depends on one's perspective. What is not arguable is Harris's candor. He was much less guarded in his comments than his teammates. He was this way in '56, and he remained so thirty years later. Perhaps this outspokenness is better understood if one realizes that Harris's perspective on football, particularly OU football, may have been quite different than some of his teammates' at the outset.

Harris explained, "Just before my sophomore year I was talking to a guy who was an All-American at OU. He told me he had achieved the 'ultimate in life.' Now, maybe I've got more intelligence than that, but I thought, making All-American at OU is the ultimate in life? Really, from then on I did not have that as a priority. I thought, there are a hell of a lot of things more important than makin' All-American at OU. This made me realize the importance of Wilkinson saying, 'You're here to get a college education, not just to play football.' And he meant it. He expected everyone to graduate."

Such a philosophy is reminiscent of former Dallas Cowboy running back Duane Thomas's question about the Super Bowl, "If this is the ultimate game, why are they going to play it again next year?"

Harris's perspective on football is similar to the philosophy espoused publicly by Don Meredith, who is Harris's friend. In fact, it is easy for one to think he is listening to Meredith when he is talking to Harris; even the voices are similar. Meredith once called into question the "gung-ho" coaching philosophy of George Allen when he said, "If George Allen would give a year of his life to win the Super Bowl, just think what he'd do with your life."

Perhaps it is because both Meredith (Mount Vernon) and Harris (Terrell) grew up in east Texas at about the same time, or maybe it is simply that both quarterbacks take a philosophical approach to the game, but each thinks football should, above all, be fun. Harris, in college at least, was able to have fun and win.

Going into the A&M game, the only issue in doubt for the Sooners was whether Thomas or McDonald would be the national scoring leader. As things turned out it was Thomas.

"I gave the ball to Thomas because he was a much better short-yardage straight-ahead type runner. I didn't care about who won the scoring title. My objective was to win the game, so I called the play that gave us the best chance to score right then.

"Thomas was very low key. He was not a ball hog at all. Tommy wanted the ball every play. He was the same when he played basketball. He wanted to shoot the ball every time. If you passed the ball to Tommy he shot it. In football he felt like he could carry the ball every time and he wanted to carry it every time, and of course he did a hell of a job whenever he did get the ball."

Harris did not think there was as much emphasis on statistics in '56 as there is in today's game, by the media, the fans, or the players. "This is something that I think has changed more than anything else. I never thought about my statistics at all." Harris did not have very many stats, at least not by today's standards, because he had to play defense and split his time with alternate-team quarterback Jay O'Neal. Harris attempted only thirty-nine passes in '56, but he completed twenty-three for 482 yards and eight TDs. He also rushed the ball seventy-eight times for 362 yards and three TDs.

"The stats were just not as publicized as they are today. McDonald was the only guy I knew who kept his statistics. He had scored in every game in his junior year. In 1956 against Kansas State he didn't score and he came to me crying. This was the second half and we weren't going to go back in. He said it was all my fault. Well, hell, everything we had scored had been from the twenty or twenty-five. This was something I clearly had no control over, but to Tommy his stats were the big thing. To me winning was the thing and it took a team effort all the way, and I never even thought about personal stats, except one time. This was against Notre Dame, and Tubbs will remember this. I had not scored at all and I think everybody else had scored. I said, 'I'm going to score.' It was in the second half, and I knew the first team wouldn't get to play a lot more. It took about three plays for me to plunge in from about the two yard line.

"For us, whoever scored was usually whoever got away for a long run or whatever. I know a number of times I possibly could have made it in but I'd flip it to Thomas or McDonald. I really don't think anyone else knew about their stats. I really don't. I think they were all just playing to win.

"You don't want to knock Tommy too much because he had that drive that very few people had," Harris said. "He was enthusiastic as hell. He was a hot dog before hot dogs were popular. But he was also a spark that kept everyone else going.

"Tommy was such an achiever. Everything went so well for him in high school, college, and the pros. He and I went to the Eagles together, and he didn't play much until the last three games of the season. As a 165-pound running back he was about to be killed. He was really down, but once they put him at split end he took off. He was a tremendous athlete. He had a lot of ability. He was fast and quick. He had tremendous hands. His hand-eye coordination was fantastic. He certainly deserves to be in the pro football hall of fame.

"Tommy made a tremendous impact on Oklahoma. McDonald's name is a name people remember. When I tell people I played in the mid-fifties they ask who played then and I say McDonald, Thomas, and Tubbs. They remember McDonald. I don't like to tell people I played that long ago. I don't feel like I'm that old."

Harris, at age fifty-one, still had the quick movements and quick mind of a quarterback and remained the consummate competitor. "I'm into tennis right now," he said. "I took it up about five years ago and I just love it. I'll probably drop dead doin' something, but I kind of like to be number one at whatever I do or at least be good at it. I don't have to be the greatest, but I damn sure like to be respected by my peers at anything I do. In the last fifteen years the biggest goal I've had is to be respected by my peers in the oil business. Rich doesn't mean a hell of a lot. Being successful is a lot more than being rich."

Harris apparently has been successful. He completed his geology degree at OU and, after his retirement from pro football in 1961, went to work for the Roy Guffey Oil Company in Abilene, Texas. Guffey was a Sooner footballer in the 1920s, and Harris had roughnecked for him during his college days.

Many ex-OU footballers work in the oil business. Their names are often well known because of their athletic exploits and they can be assets to the company as salesmen, even if they know very little about the oil business. This is not the case with Jimmy Harris. As a geologist, Harris is a valuable man in the petroleum industry. He is the one who finds the oil.

In 1964 Harris and a partner moved to Shreveport, Louisiana, and formed Midroc Operating Company. He now has a large suite of offices in the Commercial National Bank of Shreveport and lunches at the Shreveport Petroleum Club.

Oil Ball

To an Oklahoma football player, a successful football career can do much to relieve financial cares during his undergraduate days and simultaneously furnish a springboard toward truly impressive financial achievements in later life. This is oil country, and to provide the petroleum industry with the geologists and engineers it needs, the University of Oklahoma claims it has the world's largest petroleum geology school and says it has turned out over 2400 of the nation's geologists—one fourth of all those in the petroleum industry and one fifth of all the geologists in the Western Hemisphere. The football player who studies geology at Oklahoma has summer jobs open to him with the big petroleum companies like Kerr-McGee Oil Co. and Philips Petroleum, for whom he can work on drilling rigs as a roughneck. While the hourly pay ($1.32) is not high, the rigs work around the clock and overtime is available in nearly unlimited amounts, so that an average weekly paycheck is around $100. The work is hard and physically demanding and semi-dangerous (but not so dangerous that OU has ever lost a player) but the rewards are big enough so that a football player is expected to return to the campus in September with at least $500 saved from this summer work to cushion him against the financial burdens he must carry while occupied with both football and studies.

Tex Maule

Sports Illustrated, September 28, 1957

As the Sooners' quarterback, Harris was closer to Coach Wilkinson than any of the other players, so he had a chance to learn Bud's football philosophy first hand. Because of the limited substitution rule, the quarterback's role was much different in the fifties. Since the coaches could not send in a play or give hand signals, the quarterback had to be thoroughly schooled in the fine art of play selection before the game.

"I worked with Bud on play selection," Harris said. "Crowder worked with the quarterbacks on technique, but as far as play selection and things like that it was all Bud.

"To prepare for games we would select certain plays we wanted to run. We would talk about our basic plays. Then we would talk about play selection. Bud would say, 'OK, you've received the kickoff and you've got the ball on the twenty on the right hash mark. What are you going to call?' You'd call the play and he'd say, 'OK, you made six yards. It's second and four. What are you going to call now?'

"When we were playing Texas that year, I'd dropped back to pass and I'd had the ball knocked out of my hand. We lost several yards and it was third and thirty or something like that. I'd called a play in the huddle, and he called a timeout and sent in exactly the same play I'd already called [a fake quick-kick that gained forty-four yards].

"You just got to where you thought like him after working with him for three years. By that time I thought I knew what he was thinking."

The execution of the '56 Sooners was so good that it made Bud's and Harris's job of play selection easy. Harris had only one critical call all year, so complete was the Sooners' domination of their opponents. This was, of course, in the Colorado game when

OU was behind 19–6. They had received the second half kickoff and were facing a fourth and two from their own twenty-eight, which they boldly went for and made.

"I really don't remember for sure, but I think I called it on my own," Harris said. "The way I remember it, it was a 'short' two. I think one of the linemen said, 'We can make it, or I can block my man.' Thomas carried the ball, I'm sure.

"We had a two-minute drill in those days. People don't realize how much we worked on that. We seldom got to use it because we were so far ahead usually. We had a tremendous passing attack, also, that we just didn't use. One out of every three plays called was a run-pass option. Almost every play that was designed to go wide was an option, but Bud's philosophy was to run if you could make four yards. Even if a man was wide open, if you could make four yards, you ran. It was gospel. You just did it."

The Norman banker Brewster Hobby scrimmaged against Harris, Thomas, McDonald, and company many times as a freshman in 1956. Hobby was impressed with their passing ability. "Their best play was a run-pass option. I still think that's a good offensive weapon, but nobody uses it much anymore. Some teams go through the motions, but they don't run it the way the '56 Sooners ran it. It was truly a run until they were forced to pass and they could execute it perfectly. I thought Jimmy Harris was a great quarterback."

Harris in the mid-1980s still saw his coach frequently. "I still stay in pretty close contact with him. The last visit I had with him was when he came down to the Independence Bowl here in Shreveport to broadcast the game for ESPN. We got together and had dinner. I talk to him maybe three or four times a year. He calls me sometimes to talk about the oil business.

"Bud is very definitely the reason I went to OU. I wanted to go to either SMU or Texas, but Bud was such a charismatic personality and so much more sincere than anyone I'd met. It was unusual for someone from east Texas to go to OU in those days.

The man has really been a father figure to me. My own father died when I was ten years old, so I really didn't know him.

"Wilkinson always made these big speeches to the squad saying, 'You're going to have to give your best effort.' Even if we were playing Kansas State he made it sound like the Super Bowl. That year when we played Notre Dame at South Bend, we had prepared for that game all spring and we had never showed the formation that we ended up using, which was a kind of spread offense. It was the first time we had really used flankers and such. He had just given a big pep talk to the squad, and we went back to the quarterback meeting, O'Neal, Sherrod, and I, and Bud told us, "We are going to beat 'em into the ground. We can beat 'em as bad as we want to. All you have to do is execute like you're supposed to and we won't have any trouble.' That's the only time I've ever seen him when he knew he had it under control.

"Bud would talk with the quarterbacks one-to-one, two or three times a week. You'd go over your game plan, and you'd play the game with those 'little men' he had."

Harris spent one year with Bud as an assistant coach in 1959. "I learned a hell of a lot coaching with Bud that one year," he said. "I learned more than I did in all the years I played college or pro ball. I didn't realize it until I coached with him that one year, but Bud was a one-man coaching staff. He rotated his coaching staff all the time. He brought in new blood, new ideas, and Bud wanted to know everyone's ideas. He assimilated everything he heard about football. After I came back from playing with the Eagles and Rams he wanted to know everything I knew about playing defensive halfback. He wanted to know what the pros were doing.

"Landry was the only other coach I played for who was like this. Now almost every head coach has an offensive coordinator who runs the offense and a defensive coordinator who runs the defense. Wilkinson did it all. But there are only a few Landrys and a few Wilkinsons and they are way above the rest.

"Football is like the oil business or geology or anything else. You've got to have new ideas. You've got to get input. There is no such thing as an original idea. It's a composite of two or three things that makes a new idea."

Jimmy Harris has always maintained a rather critical reserve in evaluating coaches. Harris is critical in the sense that he exercises careful judgment and judicious evaluation. In the fifties, Oklahomans assumed that when Bud resigned, his top assistant, Gomer Jones, would get the position. When Harris was asked (in 1956) if he thought Jones would do a good job as head coach, he replied, "Gomer is a good assistant coach." Gomer Jones, of course, became the head man at Oklahoma in 1964 and compiled a two-year record of 9–11–1.

Playing quarterback was only 50 percent of Harris's responsibility as a Sooner footballer. He was required to play defense just like his teammates. "It is not really tough to play both offense and defense," Harris said. "But if you play both ways you can only learn half as much about each phase so you couldn't be quite the quarterback you could be if you only went one way. Players from my era don't hold any of the records any more because we only played part time." Harris still has the third longest touchdown run from scrimmage, ninety-one yards versus Kansas in 1954.

"I think playing both ways is still the most fulfilling. I don't know that I'd like to see college football go back to this, but it might eliminate a lot of the problems we have today in the area of scholastic cheating. It would make a player a more well rounded athlete. It would take away the 240-pound running back because what's he going to play on defense? He's going to have to play linebacker because he's not going to be a defensive back. It would change the game completely." Bud, of course, was of the same opinion.

Quarterback was a new position for Harris when he came to OU. He had been a halfback at Terrell High School, which lost only one game during Harris's stint on the varsity. "When Bud recruited me, he said, 'You'll either be a great player or you won't play at all, but I'm probably going to change you to another position.' I went up there and played behind McDonald at halfback the first few weeks. Then they moved me to quarterback. We had seven teams and I started off on number seven, but by the last of our two freshman games, I ended up playing about as much as O'Neal, who had played quarterback in high school for four years [for the legendary Elvin George at Ada, Oklahoma, on undefeated state championship teams]. I enjoyed playing defense and I really never disagreed with Bud about play selection, but I always thought the easiest way to move the ball down the field was by passing. I probably wouldn't have made a good coach for that reason." Or, perhaps he was just ahead of his time.

After his career at OU Harris was picked to play in the College All-Star Game. He has a picture of his All-Star team hanging in his office. This team included Jimmy Brown, Johnny Majors, Lenny Dawson, Paul Hornung, John Brodie, Jerry Tubbs, and Tommy McDonald. Harris had many other football pictures in his office. He had a picture of himself wearing the crimson and cream of OU taking a snap from center as the Sooner line fires out low and hard in perfect form. He had pictures of himself with Wilkinson, Landry, and Meredith. "My wife, Angie, put up all those photos," Harris said.

Harris was drafted by the Eagles and spent one year in Philadelphia before being traded to Los Angeles. "The Eagles, in those days, were like a bunch of vagabonds compared to OU in terms of discipline and organization," Harris said. "Wilkinson was so much more organized at that time. He was way ahead of any other coach then.

"Bud was completely against going to the pros. I told him I wanted to try pro ball and he said, 'You can make it. There is no doubt in my mind that you will play, but it's a waste of time.' In those days it damn near was because there was no money in it. You might sign out of college for six, seven, or eight thousand dollars. [Nonetheless, there were many professors at the University of Oklahoma who were not making this much money in the late fifties.] Bud recommended that I finish my geology degree, which I ultimately did."

After one year in Philadelphia, Harris and two other players were traded to the Rams for Norm Van Brocklin. Harris played cornerback for the Rams in 1958, but because of a contract dispute with general manager/coach Sid Gilman (the Rams offered eighty-five hundred dollars and Harris wanted ten thousand), he returned to OU to work on his geology degree and to assist Wilkinson.

Harris finished his geology degree in the spring of 1960. He had already earned one bachelor's degree in education, apparently thinking he might want to coach one day. In the meantime Gilman had been fired from the Rams ("I always told him it was because I didn't play," Harris said.) and had moved to San Diego to build their franchise in the American Football League. Gilman called Harris and offered him thirteen thousand dollars to play for the Chargers in 1960.

"You wouldn't give me ten thousand dollars before. What's the big deal now?" Harris asked.

Gilman said, "Things have changed. This is a new league."

Harris said, "If you'll give me thirteen thousand dollars, I'm going to Lamar Hunt [then the owner of the Dallas Texans] and see what he'll pay."

At this point, the Rams, who still held the playing rights to Harris, traded him to the Dallas Cowboys. Hunt, who wanted Harris, took the Cowboys to court and Harris played half a season for the Texans. The next year, 1961, he became a Cowboy and got acquainted with Coach Landry.

"Landry may have known more about football than anybody I've ever known," Harris said, echoing Tubbs's thoughts. "He may have the most brilliant football mind I've ever seen. If he could have motivated his players like Wilkinson he would have been unbeatable. Wilkinson, in his heyday, had as good a football mind as anybody, but he got bored with it. I asked Landry how he kept

Jimmy Harris

his desire for the game and he said, 'It's a challenge. It's kind of like a chess game.'

"I questioned a hell of a lot in Landry's system, and we argued a lot," Harris said. "But I got along with him and had great respect for him. With him there was a right way, a wrong way, and the Landry way. He didn't give a damn if it was right or wrong, you were going to do it his way. He had a lot of quirks that I didn't think were important. In other words, if you've got the man covered, you've got him covered, but Landry wanted him covered his way, and it paid off for him. He was like a computer before the computer age. His mind just worked that way."

Harris played only one season with the Cowboys before retiring from pro football. "Both shoulders were hurt. I had an ankle hurt. It was the first time football had not been fun."

Harris coached the OU alumni games for several years, and he still regularly attends the spring games. Because of this he has seen his former teammates often. "Our whole group has been successful, and I think because of the winning we're closer than some of the other teams. Losers don't like to come back and talk to each other. I played with the Eagles, Rams, and Cowboys, and the Cowboys are the only team that has a reunion every year. I went to Oklahoma only because they were winners. Of course, thirty or forty other guys did, too, and some of them didn't make it. I think it has to do with whether or not you feel you have to make it. I knew I had to play football.

"My mother was very strong-willed, and I was lucky to have grown up in a small town where you didn't have a lot of problems. The best thing that happened to me was Wilkinson coming down and recruiting me to go to the University of Oklahoma. Now I'm trying to pay some of that back with contributions to the energy center and things like that."

Harris said he didn't realize how good the Sooner talent really was in '56 until he played in some of the All-Star games. "Johnny Majors was an All-American at Tennessee that year. [He also finished second in the Heisman voting.] He couldn't have played for us. Our linemen would be too small for today's game, but they were quick. We used quickness to beat the big guys. John Bell [first team right end in '56] weighed only 190 pounds, but he was so tightly packed. He was a real tough guy and a good receiver. He's another guy who's never come back. They say he's in Houston and doesn't keep up with the university at all. He's one of the few guys I have not kept up with."

Despite the fact that the Sooners won every game Harris quarterbacked, Wilkinson told him many times that he was not playing up to his full potential. One might ask: "What more could he have done?" But then one must recall Bud's criterion: "The real opponent is yourself. You must play the best you can play regardless of your opposition."

"Bud always said I wasted a lot of my ability. He told me many times I was lazy. I really was. Now, to a degree, I regret it, but not too much. Hell, I was havin' fun," Harris said.

"I never thought of myself. I just thought of the team. I probably could have set more goals for myself. I don't think we realized how good we were in '56. Bud gave you confidence. We just thought we were a well-balanced team that was supposed to go out and win 50–0 and have a lot of fun.

"What '56 did was, it gave you a philosophy of life. You won 'em all, and you expected to win 'em all the rest of your life. I think most of us thought that was what you were supposed to do. I know one thing. It's a team effort. It takes a team to win."

Norman, Oklahoma, January 2005

"Bud was my idol," Jimmy Harris said.

"As a quarterback you spent so much more time with Bud. You spent a hundred times more time with him than a guard or tackle would. He was the quarterback coach in those days. You didn't have the offensive co-coordinators and all the other coaches like they do now. Bud knew his quarterbacks better than his other players and you knew him better.

"I was at a celebration for Bud over in Tulsa. They had given him this large picture of himself in a big frame. After everyone had left, I could tell that Bud was not feeling just right, so I said, 'Let me help you with that picture.'

"He said, 'Jim, I just have no strength.' So I helped him carry it up to his room and we visited a little after that. That was one of the last times I got to be with him one-on-one. He was quite aware, then, that his health was not going well.

"Then a little later, when they had the dinner for him in Oklahoma City in 1991, I walked into his room and I said, 'Hello, Coach!' He couldn't see. I tear up when I think about this. I can't help it. He just meant so much to me. He said, 'Jimmy!' He recognized my voice. That was the last time I saw him alive. At that time we knew he was not going to last very much longer."

➢

"Nineteen fifty-six . . . I can remember certain things out of certain games, but I'd have to go back and look at some of the film to remember a lot of the things. I've got the highlights of the '55 and '56 seasons, but I don't know that I've ever watched them all completely. It's of interest to me. I'm very proud of it and the winning streak we had but you do other things.

"I love what I do right now as a geologist in the oil business. You envision how the sea was depositing the limestone and sandstone at that time. Everybody's got different ideas about seeing three dimensionally or two dimensionally. You have success and you have failures, but I've been fortunate to have had a lot more successes than failures.

"I'd like to go out a winner. I'll never retire. I want to be drillin' wells right to the day I die. The financial rewards are nice, but it's not just about the money. It's the hunt. It's not the kill. It's the hunt that's fun."

Or as the Buddhists would say, "Success is the quality of your journey."

➢

In 2000, Jimmy Harris noticed that Hunt Oil Company had put a well up for sale in southeastern Alabama. It was only a thirty-barrel per day well (30 bbl/day) but the ever-optimistic Harris saw the potential for much more. However, his partner at Midroc, Don Clark, was not as enthusiastic. "Why would you want to buy a well in the middle of nowhere?" he asked.

"Thirty barrels a day is a good show," Harris replied. Which, in oil field lingo, means, "There may be more oil down there."

Fortunately for both of them, Harris prevailed. Midroc acquired title to that well and Hunt's surrounding leases and started drilling. After one poor performing well and one dry hole, they drilled a northeast offset well that came in at 400 bbl/day. And this was just the beginning. In fact, this has proven to be the largest oil field found in Alabama in the last twenty years.

The count now stands at thirty-one big producing wells in a row (the same number of games Harris won as a quarterback at OU). "Now I'm going for forty-seven straight," he said.

. . . and the times, they are a changin'

—Bob Dylan

*We may have a lot of people who have won more
awards and honors, but no one made a greater impact
on the University of Oklahoma than Prentice Gautt.
Sooners everywhere will forever honor and celebrate his
life.*

*—Joe Castiglione, athletics director, University of
Oklahoma, March 17, 2005*

Dr. Prentice Gautt

Kansas City, Missouri, Tuesday, March 27, 1986

In the fall of 1956 a shy, soft-spoken young black man from Oklahoma City's Douglass High School stood in line with his freshmen teammates, all of whom were white, to check out his football equipment. Prentice Gautt, OU's first black football player, put on his pads and went out to scrimmage against the OU varsity, the number-one team in college football.

While Prentice Gautt was the first black athlete to ever receive a scholarship at OU, and the first black to ever play in a game for the Sooners, he was not the first black to try out for the OU team. In the autumn of 1955, four young black men tried out for the OU team as walk-ons. None of the four was offered scholarships, and they attended practice only for a few days. Billy Pricer said he thought these young men were not really serious about making the team. "I think they just came out so they could say they had tried out for football at OU," Pricer said.

There were no blacks on Wilkinson's championship teams of the fifties. OU did not win another national championship until 1974. The Sooners were number one again in 1975 to give them back-to-back titles almost twenty years after the '55–'56 powerhouse teams. By '74 and '75 the racial composition of the Sooner team had changed dramatically. Black players such as All-Americans Joe Washington, Greg Roberts, and Dewey and Lee Roy Selmon were stalwarts on these teams along with such other outstanding black athletes as Elvis Peacock, Thomas Lott, George Cumby, Kenny King, Horace Ivory, Glen Comeaux, Terry Webb, Chez Evans, Victor Hicks, Billy Brooks, and Daryl Hunt. The 1978 Heisman Trophy winner, Billy Sims, was a freshman on the 1975 championship team. Of the fifty-four players pictured in the 1975 *Sooner Press Guide,* twenty-seven were black. At least some of this credit should go to Prentice Gautt.

Gautt arrived on the OU campus just two years after the landmark *Brown vs. Board of Education* Supreme Court decision that struck down segregation in public education. Norman, Oklahoma, was not exactly Selma, Alabama, but neither was it a bastion of liberalism. The University of Oklahoma had not permitted a black student to enroll until October 13, 1948, when George W. McLaurin was allowed to enter the College of Education's graduate school. Mr. McLaurin's admission to OU was made possible by the long court battle involving Ada Lois Sipuel Fisher, a black woman who first petitioned the University of Oklahoma for admission to its law school in January 1946.

The denial of admission to blacks by OU had been based upon the "separate but equal" doctrine, which was the way the political powers in Oklahoma chose to interpret the Fourteenth Amendment, with respect to public education. The OU Board of Regents and the State Board of Regents for Higher Education contended that, since Langston University had been established solely for black students, the state of Oklahoma was not depriving blacks of their right to pursue higher education, and the opportunity for a post-secondary education for blacks did exist on a "separate but equal" basis.

Ms. Fisher and her legal counselors—Amos T. Hall, resident council for the NAACP; Dr. H. W. Williamson, state president of the NAACP; and Thurgood Marshall, attorney from the New York office of the NAACP—argued that since there was no law school for blacks at Langston, Ms. Fisher must be allowed to enroll at the University of Oklahoma.

After several court battles Ms. Fisher was finally allowed to enroll at OU on June 18, 1949, three and one-half years after she first made application. The Oklahoma regents for higher education did their best to keep Ms. Fisher from attending OU. The regents established, in one week's time, the Langston University School of Law, which consisted of rooms 426, 427, and 428 of the state capitol building and the Oklahoma State Library. The new "school" had a faculty of three, and yet district judge Justin Hinshaw held that the hastily constructed school was "fully qualified," the library "equal in all respects" to the law library at OU, and that the physical conditions at the new school compared favorably to the "overcrowded" conditions that existed on the Norman campus. Since this new "school" had no students at all, it certainly was not overcrowded.

When Mr. McLaurin was finally allowed to attend classes at OU, the university still attempted to segregate him from white students by requiring him to sit in a roped-off portion of the classroom away from the whites. McLaurin was permitted in the Student Union only at specified times, and even then he had to eat at a specially designated table. He was also required to study at a specially designated table in the OU library.

> ### *Reserved for Negroes*
>
> A plywood barrier was erected in the northeastern por-
> tion of the football stadium, which separated a small sec-
> tion reserved for Negroes. Both Negroes and whites
> accepted this solution, and the only complaint I received
> came from negroes who reported that the white students
> sitting in front of it used the barrier as a back rest and
> pushed it into their laps.
>
> There were various suggestions as to what might be
> done; perhaps a rope or chain should be used instead of
> plywood. Vice President Franklin thought that we could
> "get by" if the barrier was removed and the seats were
> marked "Reserved for Negroes." After discussing this
> possibility informally with the members of the govern-
> ing board, it was decided not to experiment with the
> state laws in such a highly visible manner; the plywood
> barrier was braced and left for the remainder of the sea-
> son.
>
> > George L. Cross
> > *Blacks in White Colleges*

Seven years after the McLaurin–Fisher legal battles, when
Prentice Gautt enrolled at OU, there were still very few black students. "You could count them on one hand," Gautt said. "I don't
remember being in a class with another black student."

Norman, Oklahoma, in 1956 was a content little college town
of about twenty-eight thousand. Few if any of these residents were
black. Some black families who lived in small communities east of
Norman, such as Little Axe and Stella, sent their children into town
to attend Norman High School, but it was not until the mid-sixties
that any black children attended Norman elementary schools.

Virtually the only black man to be seen in the city of Norman
was "Old Amos," a very Uncle Tom-like man who shined shoes

at one of the barbershops on the campus corner. Amos lived in Seminole and drove the forty miles to and from Norman each day. This was the environment Prentice Gautt entered in 1956. Gautt had grown up in segregated schools. He had never had a white classmate, teacher, or coach in his life.

Gautt was not recruited to OU in the same manner as other members of his class. No coach came to him, scholarship in hand, and said, "We want you to play for the University of Oklahoma." Rather, a group of black doctors and pharmacists had made a scholarship available to Prentice, who was interested in being a pre-med major at that time. "But after I was there a brief period of time, Bud gave the money back to that group and quietly and discreetly put me on athletic aid."

Wilkinson confirmed this story. "We did not give him a scholarship his freshman year. There was a group of black doctors in Oklahoma City who were willing to give the money. It went through normal channels, but we did not spend our scholarship money. But I had an agreement with Prentice that if he made our team we would use our regular scholarship funds and that took just one semester. I think the first kickoff he handled in a freshman game, he ran back for a touchdown. He was an exceptional athlete."

Ironically, Oklahoma A&M did offer Gautt a scholarship. OU's first contact with Gautt came after the high school All-State game in his senior year when he was the first black player in the All-State game. "I had a pretty good game," Gautt said with characteristic modesty.

Norman banker Brewster Hobby, a former teammate of Gautt's at OU, recalled that game. "I met Prentice at the All-State game in 1956. He was not picked to the team originally. I think the North squad had a couple of injuries, and I think they picked him up. I know he had a ninety-yard kickoff return for a TD, and I think he scored from about sixty yards out on a couple of runs. He was named the Most Valuable Player in the game."

After this game Kurt Burris, OU assistant coach and a former

All-American center, talked to Gautt about coming to OU. This was Gautt's first contact with any representative from the University of Oklahoma.

"My first contact with Bud came after I had gotten to school," Gautt said. "Some of the doctors who had provided the scholarship for me accompanied me to talk to Bud about the possibility of my playing there. I had made up my mind that I wanted to go to OU, but this was before I had actually enrolled. At one time I thought I was going to wind up at Ohio State, which had offered me a scholarship."

Gautt, like so many other young men in Oklahoma, had wanted to play for Wilkinson's Sooners for a long time. "I had always been in awe of Bud. The team used to come to Oklahoma City and stay in a hotel on Friday night before the home games. I used to walk downtown from my home when I was a kid and get their autographs. I used to get [1952 Heisman Trophy winner] Billy Vessels's autograph. At that time I didn't think there was any way I could play at Oklahoma.

"I didn't even know anybody who had tried out at OU. There were two or three guys who had come from Dungee High School to try out the year before I went. There was one of these that I thought could possibly make it—his name was Farmer—but he didn't, and I was wondering if anyone could make it, so I began looking north. A guy by the name of Merrill Green who was coaching at Wichita State had come to recruit me. He came in and talked to my parents and told them I probably could not make it at Oklahoma and that I should go to Wichita State where I could play. People began telling me, 'Even if you go to OU, we don't expect you to make it,' and that challenged me."

Disappearin' Pool Hall Blues

The mention of the name Merrill Green revives memories of stories told in Norman pool halls, apocryphal vignettes recited over the banging and clanking of dominoes and the clicking of snooker balls. In 1956 Norman had no less than seven pool halls. There were four on the campus corner: the Union Pool Hall, Rickners, the Campus Sport Shop, and the Boomer Snooker. Downtown, there were the H&H, where the serious gamblers hung out, the Play-More, and the enigmatic Pass Time, which displayed Rose rocks (a curious geological phenomenon indigenous to the Norman area) in the front window. If you lived in Norman in the fifties, regardless of your station in life, there was a pool hall for you—if you were male, that is.

Fifty years later none of these survives. The old pool halls, not the antiseptic "Family Recreation Centers," were an important but misunderstood sociological phenomenon. They were a place where males could escape the wife/mother.

The feminist psychologist Karen Horney recognized the need for these all-male sanctuaries when she wrote, "We see how happily relieved men are when they are among themselves, whether it be on the basis of sports, clubs, science, or even war, they look like relieved schoolboys who have escaped supervision." No wonder young men today are turning to drugs; they don't have the pool halls to hang out in anymore.

The Merrill Green story that was often heard in the Campus Sport Shop and even in the H&H concerns Green's game-winning touchdown run against Colorado in 1953. With only forty-four seconds left in the game, the score was tied 20–20. Green took a handoff and ran fifty-one yards for the TD. The pool hall intelligentsia said, just as Green broke through the line of scrimmage, a referee, detecting a clip by one of the OU players, reached into his pocket for his flag. However, this pusillanimous zebra, seeing that Green was sure to score on the play, quickly stuffed the flag back into his pocket.

Wilkinson got a lot of hate mail about Gautt being at OU. "Even though there were states like Kansas and Iowa that had integrated schools, it was just kind of an unwritten law that no blacks played in the Big Seven," Bud said. "Even when Prentice was a junior and a senior, I would still get hate mail. We lost a couple of games. We had good teams, but the general feeling was, 'If you didn't have that black SOB on your team, you'd be winning all your games.' If Prentice had not been the caliber of person that he was, he could not have handled it." OU's record was 27 and 5 during Gautt's three years of eligibility.

Gautt was not the first black to play in the Big Seven. Verl Switzer (pronounced as if it were Schweitzer), an All-Conference halfback at Kansas State in '51–'53, was the first to break the color barrier in the Big Seven. Kansas, Iowa State, Colorado, and Nebraska also had black players before the "southern" schools of OU and Oklahoma A&M.

Unlike 1956, all major athletic conferences recruit black players today, although the Southeastern and Southwestern Conferences were slow to start recruiting blacks. "The thing that really hurt the Big Ten," Wilkinson said, "was that the great black athletes used to go north to play. A few played at Florida A&M or Grambling, but most of the blacks would leave the south. Then the day that blacks were recruited at Texas and Alabama, the world changed. The black kids all stayed home and played where they should have been able to play before. This all happened in six or seven years.

"When Alabama played Southern Cal in 1970 at Birmingham and got chewed up 42–21 because Sam 'Bam' Cunningham and all the other black players for Southern Cal blew them right out of the box, the Bear said—and Bryant and I were good friends— 'Now I think I can recruit some black players even though this is Alabama.' [The Bear's exact words in reference to the swift 230-pound tailback Cunningham were reported to have been, "I gotta get me one of them."] But it represents quite a change when you have George Wallace standing in the schoolhouse door and then five years later you have blacks competing for Alabama and every-one is proud of the blacks."

An apocryphal story that made its way around the campuses of southern schools in the fifties when it was still unusual to see blacks on major college football teams tells of the woman who, caught up in the excitement of the game, rose to her feet and yelled, "Look at our colored boy tackle their nigger."

Given the social climate of the times, it is very easy to imagine Bud Wilkinson playing Branch Rickey to Prentice Gautt's Jackie Robinson, and to think that Bud must have been very careful to have selected just the right person to be the first black football player at OU. One could easily envision Bud counseling Gautt about problems he would face, the way Mr. Rickey did with Robinson. This was apparently not the case, however. Prentice remembered, "Bud never said that to me. It would have been good for me to think that way. I've heard that [that he had been screened and selected by Bud as carefully as Robinson had been screened by Mr. Rickey], but Bud never said that to me."

Prentice Gautt had none of Jackie Robinson's combativeness. Gautt's personality was more like the quiet, amicable demeanor of Robinson's teammate, Roy Campanella, whom Red Smith called "the colored gentleman." While Robinson fought the big-otry and racism openly and fiercely, Gautt would avoid con-frontation. Gautt did not acquiesce to bigotry, but he would ignore it whenever he could.

There is really no evidence to suggest that Wilkinson, in 1956, was particularly interested in social reform, as say Branch Rickey apparently was when Jackie Robinson broke into Major League Baseball in 1947. If integration had been the issue, it seems that Wilkinson would have visited Gautt and his parents in person to offer the scholarship instead of waiting for the black doctors and pharmacists to take the initiative. While Wilkinson was certainly not a bigot, he could not be called a liberal, either. Politically he was very conservative, having been allied with Barry Goldwater and Richard Nixon ideologically.

Although Wilkinson apparently did not actively attack the integration controversy, he did not run from it, either. He could have refused Gautt a scholarship, which would have been in keeping with the university's foot dragging on desegregation. In Cross's book, *Blacks in White Colleges,* there is not one instance of a single representative of the University of Oklahoma going on record as favoring integration of the OU campus, although it is possible some ideological liberals were cowed by practical and financial considerations, such as the possibility of losing their jobs.

Port Robertson, Gautt's freshman coach, said, "They looked at Prentice as a football prospect rather than a black football prospect. He had very good credentials. He was a good student. He came with very good recommendations, which he verified. We could have recruited a black player sooner or later if he had the same credentials as Prentice. When you have a chance to get a Prentice Gautt, you better take him."

Wilkinson said simply, "Our relationship was like that of any other player and coach." Prentice said of his relationship with Wilkinson, "I felt like I could go in and talk with Bud if there was anything wrong. Our talks were more in the nature of a 'What's going on today?' type thing. He was almost like a therapist for me. I found a real source of strength in some people. I came to realize that there were some very legit, genuine people there, and from my standpoint, Bud was one of them. I know he took a lot of guff having me down there and having me playing first team. There were some guys who really hated this, some players and some alums. He stuck his neck out for me. But there were times . . ." Gautt said, exhaling slowly and emphasizing the last word.

Billy Pricer, Clendon Thomas, and David Baker, all members of the 1956 varsity, were apparently very impressed with Gautt. Each said he did not know of any problems or resentments among the white players during Gautt's freshman season. However, some ill feeling and prejudices did surface later when Gautt was playing varsity ball.

Billy Pricer said of Gautt, "Prentice and I became very good friends. He'd come over and get me and we'd go down under the big cottonwood tree on the south end of the practice field and I'd try to help him with his blocking. In high school he had primarily been a ball carrier and he never had to learn to block. He often came to my house to study with me. He was a very intelligent person."

Clendon Thomas could not recall any white players expressing resentment toward Gautt. "If there were problems, there were very few. I was not aware of any," Thomas said. "Basically we had a whole team that accepted him. He was a good guy. They couldn't have picked a better person to be the first black player because of his personality, his ability as a student, and his ability as a player. However, when I went out to play in the Senior Bowl, there were some guys from some of the southern teams who went out of their way to make it a point to say such things as 'Why did you let him on your team?'"

David Baker recalled, "I gave it no thought. It wasn't a black-white issue. I feel badly that I didn't say, 'Hey, Prentice, you're probably a little bit uncomfortable. Is there anything I can do to help?' But I didn't have the maturity to do that. As I look back on it now, I'm sorry I didn't."

Prentice credited Pricer, Baker, and Thomas as being "very significant" in his adjustment process as a freshman, along with Dick Carpenter, who was a member of his own class. "They facilitated the acclamation process," Gautt said. He also recalled that ticket managers Ken Farris and Red Reid helped him a great deal. "If I ever needed any tickets for my family, they made sure I got them," Gautt said.

The person Prentice recalled as being the most helpful to him while he was at OU was Brewster Hobby. Why did Hobby, a white boy from Midwest City, Oklahoma, become a special friend to Gautt? Hobby responded, "I was born in Arkansas. During the early part of my life, a lot of my friends were black kids. Also, we scrimmaged against Douglass when I was at Midwest City, and I had read a lot about Prentice. Then we came down to OU. He was married and I soon got married. We lived near one another [in the old Quonset huts that were built after World War II to accommodate the veterans and their families] and we often walked to class together. I took the time to get to know the guy and I got to like him. We would jokingly kid him about being black. I kind of initiated the kidding, and I think that made him relax and allowed all of us to become closer friends and to understand his plight. Had he not been the gentleman he was and the caliber player that he was—in my opinion—Wilkinson might not have recruited another black player."

As a freshman, Gautt often scrimmaged against the varsity. He was lavish in his praise of the '56 championship team. "I was in awe of the entire squad. They were national champions. They didn't think anybody could beat them. I can remember that I held Tommy McDonald in esteem. I can remember listening to that game in '56 with Colorado. Colorado and Oklahoma often had big battles, and OU was behind in that game 19–6 at the half. I didn't even worry about it because I knew they were going to come back that way, and sure enough they did. They beat them 27–19. That was the image I always had of Oklahoma, plus the fact that I believed Bud could walk on water. If we were going to have a practice or a football game, he could part the clouds and the sun would come out. It wasn't going to rain on his football game.

"That '56 team had so much talent. To be on the fifth team would be like being on someone else's first team. They set a lot of records, which fit the quality of the team. They could be serious when they had to be on the field, yet when they left the field they could joke around and have a good time together as friends.

"I think the '57 and '58 teams tried to ride in on the shirttails of that '55–'56 team. Because we were a part of OU's football team, we thought we would have the same success without really going out there and doing it. Bud really tried to make us understand that in order to win, you first had to prepare to win."

Gautt certainly did not think he was the first black athlete in Oklahoma with the ability to be a successful player at OU. "There were some players at my high school that I think could have made it, had they been given the opportunity. There were some players before my time that could have made it at Oklahoma. They went to Langston or perhaps Maryland State. There was a guy by the name of J. W. Lockett from Tulsa Washington, a great athlete. He played basketball. He was a pitcher in baseball and a great football player who went to Langston. But I think he could have easily made it at OU."

Making the adjustment from high school to college is difficult for anyone, but as virtually the only black student on a campus that is situated in a town that is all white, the adjustment is incredibly tough. Prentice gave a wry smile as he recalled his freshman year at OU. "I don't know if I looked at it as being tough or not. I had a lot of confidence when I went to OU. Of course, I was shaken a little bit by the size of the place and being away from home and stepping onto that campus not knowing anyone at that time."

Hobby remarked, "He did have a tough time, although Prentice was a very mentally tough person. He handled it, most of the time, very well."

Gautt is not the type of person to dwell on the negative, but he did have some very unpleasant episodes while at OU. "I had several experiences there at Oklahoma, in Norman, that I just blocked out. I think I've tried to mask a lot of it, too. I don't know what good it would do to get into it at this point. I tried to emphasize the positive aspects, because, as I look back on my career at OU, I think there were more positive things than negative. Yet the negatives were so significant that they were embossed on my mind. For instance, I can recall going into a drugstore there on the campus corner and being served in a paper cup while everyone else was being served in a glass. The only reason that I was allowed to go in there in the first place was that I was with some of the other athletes. Yet, when I think of Norman, I choose not to think of that aspect of it."

In his freshman year, an incident occurred which had a very

profound impact on Gautt and his teammates. The Sooner frosh had traveled to Tulsa to play the TU freshman team. After the game, the team went to a local restaurant to have dinner. The restaurant manager refused to serve Gautt. Port Robertson explained, "I took the freshman team over to play Tulsa. A couple of days ahead of time I had called the owner of the restaurant and explained the situation. He said there was no problem. He told us to come on over. We pulled up in front of the restaurant. I let the kids out but stayed on the bus while the driver was finding a place to park. When I got back they were comin' out the door just a cussin'. Brewster Hobby, a very volatile young man, said, 'Those sons-of-bitches won't let Prentice eat here.' The whole team got up and walked out."

Hobby gave his version of the incident. "Jim Davis, Bennit Watts, and I were sitting at the table with Prentice when this happened. It embarrassed all of us, but it humiliated Prentice and made me committed to being a good friend and to giving him a fair shake, which the restaurant owner definitely did not."

Three years later, Hobby was involved in another, now infamous, restaurant incident as a member of the OU football team. This was the food-poisoning episode at the Chez Paris in Chicago. Gautt, also a member of the team at that time, had, luckily, as it turned out, decided to stay in his hotel room and not go to the Chez Paris with the other players.

This incident occurred on a Thursday night before OU's opening game of the 1959 season. The Sooners were in Chicago to play Northwestern and, while dining at the Chez Paris, several members of the team became extremely ill with food poisoning. Everyone suspected the local gamblers of sabotaging the OU team. Gautt thought this was probably the case. "Based upon the certain people who got the food poisoning—basically those players on the first two teams—it certainly was a possibility. I'm glad I didn't go. My roommate was Ronnie Hartline, and he came home looking just horrible."

Hobby, who was at the Chez Paris that night, was absolutely

certain the gamblers were involved. "When we went into the restaurant, the waitress took us to meet this older gentleman who was sitting with a very good lookin' young girl. She wanted to meet all the Oklahoma players, and she asked us what positions we played. Well, being young guys, this was very good for our egos. When we were finally seated, they began serving the food to particular individuals instead of serving straight down the line. So, these people knew their stuff. They poisoned us with a drug called Alphamorphine, which was something they used in the late thirties and early forties for treating hangovers. If a person took the right amount of Alphamorphine after he had been on a drunk, it would supposedly cure the hangover. But, they gave us an over-dose, because, within about thirty minutes, we were all in the bathroom vomiting our guts out. It made you very weak." Weak enough to lose to Ara Parseghian's Northwestern team 45–13. Apparently the gamblers were happy.

As Gautt talked about his experiences at OU, his psychology background was very evident. He obviously thought very deeply about issues. He certainly had the demeanor of a clinical psychologist, which he was. Gautt had what the psychologist Herman Witkin described as a reflective cognitive tempo. Reflective types are long-pausers, slow and steady, very deliberate in their speech. They think before they speak, as opposed to the cognitively impulsive types who are quick off the mark and blurt out their words. Witkin would likely also describe Gautt as being cognitively complex (as opposed to the cognitively simple type) in his approach to resolving problems. Cognitively complex types consider many variables when confronted with a question. They tend to see complicated relationships among these variables. The cognitively simple types prefer neat, tidy solutions and function best when situations are clear and uncomplicated.

"I knew there would be some people who would have some problems with my being there at OU," Gautt said. "I would have been very naïve if I hadn't thought something negative was going to happen. But whether or not I could handle something when it did happen was the issue before me. I think outwardly people perceived me as handling it extremely well, but inwardly I had a difficult time, a very difficult time."

Brewster Hobby was aware of several incidents that were obviously tough for Gautt to handle. "Some guys would poke him or kick him in pileups. They went out of their way to administer punishment that he didn't need to be taking." This was physical punishment, but some players also administered other types of psychological and emotional punishment, which Gautt also did not need to take. Hobby continued, "A lot of times during two-a-days guys would gather up in rooms and have discussions. I know there were two or three times when Prentice walked up on those discussions but did not enter the room, although he heard what was going on—such things as 'the nigger this . . . and the nigger that.' That kind of stuff hurt him very much."

In college, Prentice did not often discuss his problems with others. He did not have a mentor from the black community from whom he could seek advice or even talk to about his troubles. To do this would be perceived as "weakness," Gautt said. He also never got into discussions of this sort with his white teammates. He felt that the less said about differences the better. "We talked about class, practice, things like that. There were a lot of people who would say, 'Hey, how are you doing?' I guess I saw that as social amenities more than anything else. To talk to somebody who has never experienced what prejudice is would not be very meaningful. He wouldn't understand it. It's kind of difficult to talk of these experiences when you're an eighteen- or nineteen-year-old kid. I think it would have been very difficult for somebody to really understand."

Despite the obvious problems Gautt faced while at OU, he was able to make very good grades. He was named to the Academic All-American Football Team. "As far as my class activities," Gautt said, "I had some teachers that I probably projected some negative things onto in terms of what I thought they were doing. I had an English teacher who was very demanding. As I look at it now,

I don't think that the guy was prejudiced. I think he probably pushed me more than the other students; maybe it was for my own benefit. I remember him more than anyone else."

The University of Oklahoma and the University of Texas began their rivalry in the year 1900. From 1900 through 1928 the two teams played twenty games. Ten of these contests were held in Austin, six in Dallas, two in Oklahoma City, and one each in Houston and Norman. Since 1929 the game has been played in Dallas every year on the second Saturday in October. Prentice Gautt was the first black player to participate in this series. It was fifteen years later before any blacks played for the University of Texas. In the late fifties Texas still had Jim Crow laws. This meant Prentice could not stay in the Worth Hotel in Fort Worth with his white Sooner teammates. Instead he had to stay at a black hotel in another area of Fort Worth. Brewster Hobby did not realize this until years later. "They kept it a secret," Hobby said. "I never knew this until long after we graduated. He was there for the group meetings and the meals and everything, but they didn't allow him to sleep there. I guess none of us were smart enough to realize what was going on."

Prentice said this is one of the experiences he tried to block out of his memory. He could not remember the name of either hotel, the white or the black. Wilkinson recalled, "After the movie on Friday night, I used to have to take him to his hotel and then go over and pick him up in the morning and bring him back for breakfast with the team."

Wilkinson recalled an incident involving Prentice and another hotel, the Skirvin, in Oklahoma City. On Friday nights before home games, the Sooners would travel to Oklahoma City to watch a movie and stay in the Skirvin Hotel. On Saturday morning, they would eat breakfast in Oklahoma City and then ride the bus back to Norman for the game. The routine was for the players to come to the hotel, pick up their room keys, take their personal effects to their rooms, and then go to the movie. Wilkinson said, "Dan James was the president of the Skirvin Corporation then and he said, 'Sure, we'll take the chance [and let Gautt stay at the Skirvin].' The black press in Oklahoma City found out Prentice was going to come in and pick up his hotel key at the Skirvin [the same hotel he had waited outside of years earlier to get Billy Vessels's autograph], and they were all there to photograph Prentice picking up his key. The next day Dan James was besieged by phone calls from black groups since the hotel was now integrated, wanting the ballroom for parties, church groups, organizations, and educational meetings. He had so many calls that he finally had to tell us, 'You can't stay with us anymore!' We only stayed at the Skirvin for that one game, then we had to move over to the Biltmore. The Biltmore was not a very socially attractive hotel at that time and they were willing to let us stay there."

In Prentice's senior year, which got off to a rather rocky start with the humiliating loss to Northwestern and a subsequent loss to Texas, some ill feelings toward Prentice began to surface among some of his teammates. Although this apparently involved only the small group of players competing with Prentice for his position, it escalated to the point where Bud had to call a halt to practice one day and settle the issue.

"Prentice was getting a lot of publicity," Wilkinson said. "This made some of the players mad because he was black and they were rednecks. They had grown up that way. I had a meeting with the entire squad and said we were not going to allow this to continue."

The Sooners were having a terrible practice that day because of the squabbling and backbiting on the part of some of the players. "Bud called the practice to a halt," Prentice said, "marched everyone into the dressing room and said, 'If you're men you will get up and tell Prentice to his face what you've been saying to him behind his back.' Then he left the dressing room. That was a weird kind of thing. People started jumping up but the ones I thought had been talking about me didn't say a word."

Hobby remembered that session. "Several people spoke. I kicked it off. We talked over petty jealousies, petty resentments. When it was all over, Prentice got up—it was kind of an emotional thing—and apologized for anything he might have done to offend anyone. Really, he didn't do a damn thing.

"He had a tough time. He was not given the same opportunity that I or some other white players were given. Most of us had never played with black players and many people felt that if he were given anything, it would be because he was the first black player. But Prentice overcame all that. He proved he was a fine gentleman, a hell of a fine intelligent man, and an excellent athlete."

Before he left OU, Gautt established one more "first," his last first. On January 1, 1959, Prentice Gautt became the first black player to score in the Orange Bowl when he broke away on a forty-six-yard run in OU's 21–6 victory over Syracuse. Gautt averaged 15.7 yards per carry in this game, which is still an Orange Bowl record. On Christmas Eve of 1985, Gautt was inducted into the Orange Bowl Hall of Fame, joining other Oklahomans Bud Wilkinson, Tommy McDonald, and Lee Roy Selmon.

After leaving OU, Gautt played eight years in the National Football League. His first year in the NFL was spent with the Cleveland Browns, where he was a backup to both Jimmy Brown and Bobby Mitchell. "Mitchell and Brown didn't get hurt very much so I spent the major portion of my time watching them play," Gautt said. He spent his last seven years in the NFL as a running back with the St. Louis Cardinals. Gautt, like most professional players, suffered his share of injuries. "I had a kidney injury, and midway through one season I broke my arm, so I missed about one and one-half seasons."

Although Gautt played long and well, he never intended to make a career of professional football. "My intent was to go to medical school. Oklahoma had a medical program for minorities, and my intent was to play one year of professional ball and then go back to medical school. But, they kept offering me what, at that time, was more money than I'd ever seen. As I look at today's salaries, I think I was born too soon. But they kept offering me opportunities to play and to gain some financial stability, so I continued to play. Then I decided it was time to get on with my life.

At the time I retired, playing had gotten quite boring. You'd go to work at nine o'clock and practice and watch films and sometimes you would take the films home. But, if you'd played four or five years you began to know what to expect from the people you played against. I don't think it was as scientific as it is now."

While playing professional football, Gautt worked part time for Pepsi Cola, and he conducted an educational class for children, which was televised. Gautt's TV class was a biology course that was geared to the elementary grades. He also worked for the Oklahoma City Board of Education from 1963 through 1967 in the off-season.

After his retirement from pro ball, Gautt joined the faculty of the University of Missouri, where he remained from 1968 through 1979. "The year before I retired, Dan Devine asked me to go to Missouri and coach," Gautt said. "Devine also told me I could go to school as long as I wanted."

Prentice Gautt

While at Missouri, Gautt coached football, did some counseling with athletes, taught a basic psychology course ("I avoided teaching student-athletes. I didn't want that pressure."), and completed his Ph.D. in psychology in 1975.

While at the University of Missouri during the late sixties and early seventies, Gautt once again became embroiled in the black-white controversy when several black athletes presented a list of grievances to coaches at several institutions around the country, including Missouri. Hearing protests of the mistreatment of black athletes, Gautt was in a difficult position. As a coach, he was a member of the power structure, but as a black person he could empathize with the athletes.

"I saw a list of grievances," Gautt said. "I was just getting out of pro ball and into coaching at that time. I had mixed emotions about this. I wanted to identify with some of these [stated grievances] and say some of this needs to be addressed by coaches. At Missouri the athletes got a chance to talk about it and have group discussions.

"However, it is very difficult to attribute a motive to people's behavior. I thought some of the grievances were right on but on other issues I was saying, 'Well, that's kind of hard to say.'

"I met with many of the black athletes and the coaches knew it. Some of the coaches were probably wondering what I was telling the athletes. The athletes knew I was going back to the coaching staff and having meetings with them so they were suspicious of what I was telling the coaches. I was walking a kind of tightrope but still trying to maintain my integrity, which I think I was able to do. Many of the grievances, such as the issue of stacking [the practice of allowing black players to play only certain positions, therefore competing only among themselves for a position rather than against the white players at other positions] were right on target. I had mixed emotions about scholarship limitations, but this ironically has eliminated a lot of stacking."

In his late forties, Prentice Gautt still had the trim athletic body of a much younger man. He worked out for an hour each morning on a jogging trampoline before going to work as associate commissioner of the Big Eight Conference where he presided over the three Es—Education, Eligibility, and Enforcement. "I make sure that student athletes are eligible academically, and I make sure that coaches, students, and anyone on campus connected with athletics is apprised of the rules and regulations of the Big Eight and the NCAA. After stating the rules on financial and academic eligibility, someone must enforce these rules. So, I wear these three hats, plus the things I do here in the Big Eight office, which is most often anything the commissioner doesn't want to do," Gautt said with a laugh.

"I think intercollegiate athletics has a problem. It has an image problem. As I look at the people in my class at Oklahoma, the majority of them graduated and went into business and are doing well. If you go back thirty years before my college days, you'd find the same thing. I don't know whether time, or society, or the kinds of things we enforce and reinforce are to blame?

"More pressure on coaches to win is part of the problem. You still have a school like Notre Dame which says, 'We won't recruit that person. Even though he is a good athlete, he would not fit into our program.' Of course, when you have a program like Notre Dame's you can do that kind of thing. This was true with Bud. He could recruit anyone he wanted. He had his pick."

Prentice Gautt has apparently been able to handle all the pressures he faced very well. But, one would think perhaps he would rather have come along thirty years later when he could have been just a football player and a student rather than "the first black player."

"When I was going through college, I couldn't objectively view it at all," Gautt said. "Somehow college helps one make the transition from adolescence to adulthood, or at least can facilitate this transition. I think that the University of Oklahoma was a kind of a training ground for some of the experiences I was to face later. If I had gone to OU always thinking that everybody I ran across had it in for me, or didn't want me to make it, I don't think I would have made it. I assumed that people did want me to make it. I saw, and it may have been a part of my denial process, but I think I saw people honestly saying, 'You can make it.' I think my experience was more positive than negative."

Nevertheless, young black athletes entering college today have a much easier adjustment process than Prentice Gautt faced in 1956 because the first wave of blacks to test the written and unwritten laws of discrimination preformed so well.

"There was a combination of things involved in my making it," Gautt explained. "It was one thing to make it on the athletic field, but there was also the classroom and other extraneous factors, such things as wondering, 'Where can I go? And how do I socialize?'" Obviously there was no social life for Gautt at OU or in Norman, so on weekends he would go back to the black community of Oklahoma City.

"I think these problems are almost eliminated now for a black kid going to Oklahoma or to any other school for that matter. But I had my boundaries. There were many places where I just wouldn't go. Guys would say, 'Come on, let's go get a soda,' or something. I guess they might forget or maybe they were just not sensitive to the issue. My first thought was, I'd like to go but . . . I didn't know whether I'd be served. It was easier for me to say, thanks, but I've got to study. I have vestiges of those thoughts today. Sometimes when I go places I catch myself saying, 'how will I be treated?' I used to wonder who would accept me, who will reject me. I think that a black kid going in today wouldn't have any boundaries. He can just go in and say, 'Here I am.' And if he's got the ability, he's going to play."

Prentice Gautt seems to have attained the level of personality development the psychologist Erik Erikson labeled as Integrity. Erikson said that as one approaches his fiftieth autumn, he encounters the crisis of Integrity versus Despair. Simply stated, having integrity means acceptance of one's place and one's past. If a person can look back upon his/her life with a sense of fulfillment and satisfaction, and if they can adjust to life's achievements and disappointments, then they have achieved Integrity. The opposite is Despair, to view one's life with a sense of regret over opportunities missed or mistakes made. The person who falls into despair is disgusted with life and bitter over what might have been. Prentice Gautt is obviously the former type.

"If I had it to do over again starting in 1956 in Norman, Oklahoma, I think basically I would do the same thing I did. I certainly kept college athletics in the proper perspective. I really had no intention of going into professional football. I didn't think I was good enough. To tell the truth, I might have gone to medical school. But life has been good. I don't think I've regretted anything I've done to this point."

Norman, Oklahoma, December 2005

Forty-nine years after he matriculated to the University of Oklahoma, Prentice Gautt was still involved with college athletics as the associate commissioner of the Big Twelve Conference. Gautt was first a student-athlete, but always with the emphasis on student. After his playing time on the green fields had passed, he quite literally devoted his life to helping other student athletes.

Thus it was most fitting for his alma mater to dedicate the Prentice Gautt Academic Center in his honor. And this is not the only honor the University of Oklahoma has bestowed upon him. In 1987 he was awarded the Distinguished Service Citation for ". . . conducting himself with dignity and integrity, touching and changing men and women far beyond the playing fields . . . for his advice and council which have benefited countless individuals, and for the profound impact which he had upon his alma mater."

In the spring of 2002, Gautt received an honorary doctorate in Human Letters for his lifetime achievement in student-athlete welfare.

In September 1999, at the formal dedication of the Prentice Gautt Academic Center, OU president David Boren said, "It is appropriate that this center be named after Prentice Gautt. His personal values and character, along with his leadership as associate commissioner of the Big Twelve Conference, continue to bring pride to his alma mater. His personal example of quiet courage, grace under pressure, and dedication to the university helped open the doors of opportunity for countless numbers of African American and minority student-athletes who have followed him into collegiate athletics."

On Monday, March 14, 2005, suffering from flu-like symptoms Dr. Prentice Gautt was admitted to a hospital near his home in Lawrence, Kansas. He died three days later. He was sixty-seven. On December 6, 2005, the College Football Hall of Fame honored Dr. Prentice Gautt (posthumously) with their Outstanding Contribution to Amateur Football Award.

Each perfect day, I know, is going to be the last beautiful day of autumn.
　　—John Nichols, The Last Beautiful Days of Autumn

EPILOGUE

Game Day, circa 1956

My father was shaking me gently. "Wake up," he said. "We've got to go park the car."

I knew what he meant of course. It was a part of our game-day ritual to drive one car over to the stadium hours before the game to get a choice parking spot. Then we would walk the mile or so back home to wait for our guests to arrive. At game time, my mother, who never went to the games, would drive me, my father, assorted aunts, and uncles or whoever had come that particular Saturday, back to the stadium. After the game, my father, aunts, uncles, et cetera would pile into the car, which had been strategically parked, and drive home. I would usually meet my friends and play touch football. Had it been only my father and myself, we would simply have walked to the game. This somewhat convoluted procedure was done for the benefit of the relatives. One parking spot that was a favorite of ours was on the west side of the stadium near the old varsity tennis courts, which were torn down when the stadium was expanded and the new press box was built.

I got out of bed and dressed quickly, being careful not to awaken my younger brother and my mother, who liked to sleep late on Saturday. I ate my breakfast of eggs, bacon, toast, and orange juice, which my father had made. My father drank coffee and read the paper while I ate.

Our kitchen was small. We had a red Formica-top table with aluminum legs. One thing I remember about eating on this table is that, then, before any teams had moved to the West Coast, it was still possible to get all the baseball scores from the previous day in the morning newspaper. But this morning I wasn't interested in baseball. Baseball season was over and I was anxious to get on with the events of the day.

We left the breakfast table and stepped outside. The weather was sunny and cool. It was one of those perfect mornings that come perhaps once or twice each fall, when the slight chill, the sunlight, and the mild breeze are unmistakable harbingers of an imminent football game.

We drove to a DX station where I bought a Grapette and my dad filled the tank with ethyl for twenty-seven cents a gallon. We talked about the game and tried to guess the score. We were certain of an OU victory. Since it was homecoming, we drove by the fraternity and sorority houses to look at the decorations. In the fifties, all the Greek houses were confined to an area of about four square blocks just west of the stadium. In the seventies most of the fraternities and sororities built newer, larger houses far to the south of this area away from the main campus.

Even though it was still early, about nine o'clock, a few fans were already beginning to come into town and some were driving around to look at the decorations. Finally we parked the car, a brown '54 Pontiac, and started walking home. My dad was a fast walker. He was only about five-seven or five-eight, but he moved his short legs very fast. I had to almost run to keep up, and he would not slow down to wait for me. As we passed McKinley grade school, where the day before I had struggled with long division in my sixth-grade classroom, we noticed several cars already parked in the schoolyard. We continued down a hill to the small creek that runs between Pickard and Berry and finally up a hill to our house. Today, these many years later, there are numerous large shade trees in this neighborhood. As a boy I remember pulling that hill either on foot or on my bicycle and looking directly into the sun.

When we got home, my father went inside to help my mother

prepare the food for our lunch. I got my football and kicking tee and went out to practice kickoffs.

Eric Feaver, a boy my age, came by on his bicycle and stopped to play. We took turns kicking the ball across neighbors' yards.

"Are we going to play after the game?" Eric asked.

"I think so," I replied. "You and Ed [Eric's older brother] will play, won't you?"

"Yeah," Eric said as he sailed a pass over my head.

My Uncle Ralph, Aunt Dorothy, and their daughter Linda arrived from Oklahoma City. Linda, who was a year younger than I, and Dorothy went into the house, but Ralph stayed outside to throw some passes to Eric and me.

A little later Uncle Jack Thornton and Aunt Jane from Blanchard, a small town about twenty miles west of Norman, drove up and we went inside to eat.

We always had good food. My dad loved to host these little parties, and he made sure we had good food and plenty of it. We got out plates and went through a buffet line that was arranged on the dining-room table. We had ham and chicken for sandwiches, chips, dips, potato salad, baked beans, green olives, black olives, and salad. I always made at least two trips through the line and piled my plate as high as I could. The leftovers, if there were any, would be eaten after the game.

The relatives envied us for living in Norman, so close to the Big Red. Ironically, it was my mother who was perhaps envied most of all, although she cared nothing about the games per se. She was one of only a handful of people in Norman who didn't even listen to the radio broadcasts, but as a professor at OU, she often had many athletes in her classes. The aunts and uncles asked her questions about the players. "What are they like?" "Are they good students?" "Did they think we could beat Colorado or Notre Dame or Texas?"

(She always said the athletes of that era were far better and more conscientious students than athletes of later years. She always remembered Jerry Tubbs hobbling to class on crutches.)

Soon the food was gone and we left for the game. On our way we saw people parking cars in their yards, charging one dollar per car. On game days there were many ways to make money. If you were lucky enough to live near the campus and had a big back yard or better still a vacant lot, you could park cars. Some people also sold hot dogs, hamburgers, and Cokes in their yards.

Near the stadium were the ticket scalpers, many of whom made money by buying the tickets for one or two dollars and selling them for the full price of four dollars each.

One could sell Cokes or hot dogs at the game, of course, but the best strategy of all was to carry a "flag" into the game. This "flag" was actually a pennant of one of the Big Seven schools. These pennants (there must have been three or four sets of them) were stationed around the top of the stadium. The pennants were given out at the field house (where OU played its basketball games in those days), which is just north of the stadium, at about 10:00 A.M. Along with your pennant, you received a free pass to the game. The usual procedure was to get your "flag," take it over to the stadium and put it up, then go scalp tickets until kickoff. After the game started, you returned and stayed by your pennant, which you had to return to the field house after the game.

My father and I took our seats and watched the score mount against the helpless opponent. I had not yet reached the stage in life when it becomes so important to a boy that he not, under any circumstances, ever be seen in public with his parents. I sat with my dad, just as I had since he started taking me to games when I was five or six years old. We always sat on the east side of the field across from the OU bench. By having their bench on the west side, OU had the advantage of being in the shade of the press box on hot days, thus making the visiting team look into the sun. The OU band was stationed right behind the visiting team playing "Boomer Sooner," the OU fight song about ten thousand times each game. Some time in the late seventies or early eighties the Big Eight passed a rule that stated that the home team's band must be behind the home team. The administration did not dare move the donors out of their shady seats, so the team had to move to the east side rather than the band to the west side. This was a move that may have cost the Sooners about three and one-half points a game against a good opponent.

As we watched the game my father pointed out the particularly good backs and tackles. In the fourth quarter, with the Sooners way ahead, as usual, I left our seats to meet Dwain. Our plan was to rendezvous behind the goal posts in the north end zone.

I found Dwain and we watched a few more plays together.

"OK, are you ready to go? The game's over. Bud's got the fifth team in there now," Dwain said.

I looked around at the emptying stadium. Some younger boys had already made their way down behind OU's bench to try to get a helmet chinstrap from one of their heroes. The field was now entirely in shadows as the sun was well below the top of the press box.

"Yeah, let's go," I said.

"Where are we going to play?" Dwain asked.

"At Massey's lot," I answered as I started to weave my way through the crowd, looking for the nearest exit.

Dwain and I made our way out of the north end zone, down the exit ramp, and into the darkness of the innards of Memorial Stadium. We began to break into a fast jog as soon as we had cleared the stadium gate. We hurried past the reflecting pool in front of the stadium. The pool was filling up with fallen leaves.

We began to pick up our pace a little, feeling a rush of adrenaline in anticipation of our upcoming game of touch football. We dodged the slower-moving fans, pretending we were making a long open-field run and they were potential tacklers.

"Who's going to play?" Dwain asked.

"The Masseys, the Feavers, Brookins, Huff, Locket, and Fertig, I think," I answered.

"What about Updegraph?" I asked Dwain. "Is he coming?"

"Yeah," Dwain said.

We headed down Brooks Street past the library and the infirmary. As we reached Chautaquah we were beginning to break away from the crowd, and we needed to go only another five or six blocks.

We were getting a little winded, so we slowed to a fast walk, kicking at red-and-white streamers in our path. When we reached Flood Street, my dad, along with the two sets of aunts and uncles, on their way home from the game, pulled up in the Pontiac. They waved at us, knowing where we were going, and pulled away.

When we reached Pickard, it was downhill, literally to Massey's lot. We began to sprint. We knew we didn't have much daylight left, and we wanted to start the game as soon as possible.

The other boys soon arrived and we decided on the rules. "Three out of four complete for a first down, and two hands below the belt," someone proposed. "No," countered another, "we better say only one hand, because there's too much bitchin' and arguin' about two." We agreed, and the teams were chosen.

The ball was snapped back to me. Dwain burst off the line and ran straight ahead six or seven yards. He made a quick head-and-shoulders fake as though he were going to run a sideline pattern, then he sprinted back across the middle on a post route, out-distancing the defender by a couple of steps.

I sidestepped the rusher and threw the ball as far as I could, about twenty yards. Dwain caught it over his shoulder for a touch-down.

APPENDIX

BOX SCORES

OKLAHOMA 36   NORTH CAROLINA 0

OU		NC
20	First Downs	5
17	Rushing	3
3	Passing	2
4–11	Passes Completed	2–12
61	Passing Yards	47
369	Rushing Yards	93
411	Total Yards	140
2–68	Pass Interceptions	0–0
7–43.7	Punting	9–40.9
2 of 4	Fumbles Lost	1 of 1
10–90	Penalties	4–29

INDIVIDUAL STATISTICS
Rushing

Baker 11–64, Thomas 7–57, Morris 8–35, Dodd 7–34, J. O'Neal 6–32, McDonald 9–19, Carpenter 3–19, Evans 1–16, Day 2–18, Pricer 4–26, J. Harris 4–12, Brown 1–11, Derrick 2–10, Holland 2–6, Rolle 1–6, Sherrod 1–4, B. O'Neal 1–4, Pellow 1–2

Passing

J. Harris 2–2–0 = 21, McDonald 1–1–0 = 20, Dodd 2–1–0 = 20, Baker 3–0–0 = 0, J. O'Neal 1–0–0 = 0, B. O'Neal 1–0–0 = 0, Evans 1–0–0 = 0

Receiving

McDonald 2–21, Thomas 1–20, Baker 1–20

251

SOONERS WHO PLAYED (59)

LE: Stiller, Long, Coyle, Hood, B. Harris, Buck

RE: Bell, Timberlake, Rector, Bowman, Martin

LT: Greenlee, Searcy, Ballard, S. Jennings, Nelson

QB: J. Harris, J. O'Neal, Holland, Sherrod, Crossland, B. O'Neal

LG: Northcutt, Oujesky, Powell, Broyles, Hayes

LH: McDonald, Baker, Pellow, Lewallen

C: Tubbs, Harrison, Lynn Burris, Scott, Johnson, Talbott

RH: Thomas, Dodd, Carpenter, Derrick, Evans, Lyle Burris

RG: Krisher, D. Jennings, Gwinn, Fitch, Shilling

FB: Pricer, Morris, Brown, Rolle, Depue

RT: Emerson, Gray, Ladd, Lawrence, Corbitt

SCORING

Touchdowns: McDonald 2, J. O'Neal, Thomas, Holland

Conversions: Dodd, Pricer 3

Safety: S. Jennings

Officials: Cliff Shaw (Arkansas), Harwood T. Smith (Duke), John Lloyd, James W. Gray (Davidson)

North Carolina:	0	0	0	0 = 0
Oklahoma:	0	21	0	15 = 36

OKLAHOMA 66　　　　KANSAS STATE 0

OU		KS
20	First Downs	5
1–6	Passes Completed	2–12
18	Passing Yards	19
479	Rushing Yards	172
497	Total Yards	191
3–13	Pass Interceptions	0–0
4–36.5	Punting	12–27.6
2 of 7	Fumbles Lost	2 of 6
9–83	Penalties	11–85

INDIVIDUAL STATISTICS
Rushing
Thomas 7–82, McDonald 6–79, Dodd 10–73, J. O'neal 2–31, Derrick 5–30, J. Harris 2–24, Baker 6–24, Morris 2–20, Day 4–15, Pellow 3–13, Pricer 3–12, Brown 4–11, B. O'Neal 1–5, Evans 1–3, Lewallen 2–2, Holland 6–0, Crossland 1–(–1), Sherrod 3–(–2)

Passing
J. Harris 1–1–0 = 18, Sherrod 2–0–0 = 0, Dodd 1–0–0 = 0, J. O'Neal 1–0–0 = 0, Day 1–0–0 = 0

Receiving
Thomas 1–18

SOONERS WHO PLAYED (56)
LE: Stiller, Long, Coyle, B. Harris, Buck
RE: Bell, Hood, Rector, Bowman, Martin
LT: Gray, Searcy, Ballard, Fitch, Nelson
QB: J. Harris, J. O'Neal, Holland, Sherrod, Crossland
LG: Oujesky, Powell, S. Jennings, Corbitt, Broyles
LH: McDonald, Baker, Pellow, Sandefer, Lewallen, Day
C: Tubbs, Harrison, Lynn Burris, Scott, Talbott
RH: Thomas, Dodd, B. O'Neal, Derrick, Lyle Burris
RG: Krisher, D. Jennings, Gwinn, Depue, Evans
FB: Pricer, Morris, Brown, Shilling
RT: Emerson, Timberlake, Ladd, Lawrence, Hayes

SCORING
Touchdowns: Thomas 3, Baker, Derrick, Pricer, Dodd, Pellow, Sandefer, Day
Conversions: Pricer 3, Brown, Dodd, Sherrod
Officials: W. Pierce Astle (Emporia State), John Waldorf (Missouri), Ben Beckerman (Iowa), Ferry Rosenberger (Morningside)

Kansas State:	0	0	0	0 = 0
Oklahoma:	13	20	14	19 = 66

OKLAHOMA 45   TEXAS 0

OU		TU
24	First Downs	14
8–10	Passes Completed	9–27
133	Passing Yards	114
360	Rushing Yards	74
502	Total Yards	188
5–36	Pass Interceptions	1–0
2–55	Punting	6–23.8
4 of 9	Fumbles Lost	2 of 3
5–65	Penalties	2–16

INDIVIDUAL STATISTICS
Rushing

McDonald 16–140, Thomas 13–153, Baker 9–27, Morris 3–26, Pricer 5–14, Harris 12–10, Holland 2–7, O'Neal 4–6, Derrick 3–5, Brown 1–3, Dodd 1–2, Sandefer 1–2, Rolle 1–2

Passing

Harris 2–2–0 = 61, Baker 3–2–0 = 18, McDonald 1–1–0 = 27, Dodd 1–1–0 = 16, Derrick 1–2–0, Sandefer 1–1–0 = 5, Sherrod 1–0–1 = 0

Receiving

McDonald 2–61, Bell 1–27, Sandefer 1–16, Derrick 1–11, O'Neal 1–7, Baker 1–6, Dodd 1–5

SOONERS WHO PLAYED (44)

LE: Stiller, Long, Coyle, B. Harris
RE: Bell, Timberlake, Rector, Hood
LT: Gray, Searcy, Ballard, Fitch
QB: J. Harris, J. O'Neal, Holland, Sherrod
LG: Oujesky, Jennings, Powell, Broyles
LH: McDonald, Baker, Sandefer, Pellow
C: Tubbs, Harrison, Scott, Lynn Burris
RH: Thomas, Derrick, Dodd, Day

RG: Krisher, D. Jennings, Gwinn, Shilling
FB: Pricer, Morris, Brown, Rolle
RT: Emerson, Ladd, Lawrence, Corbitt

SCORING

Touchdowns: McDonald 3, Thomas 3, Day
Conversions: Harris, Pricer 2
Officials: Cliff Ogden (Wichita), Charles Trigg (SMU), Marcus Rosky (Duke),
Cliffore Domingue (Texas A&M), Herm Rohrig (Nebraska)

Texas:	0	0	0	0 = 0
Oklahoma:	6	13	13	13 = 45

OKLAHOMA 34   KANSAS 12

OU		KU
24	First Downs	14
3–7	Passes Completed	2–10
39 ·	Passing Yards	36
363	Rushing Yards	170
402	Total Yards	206
2–8	Pass Interceptions	0–0
4–35	Punting	7–38
2 of 3	Fumbles Lost	1 of 3
14–130	Penalties	11–75

INDIVIDUAL STATISTICS
Rushing

McDonald 16–91, Thomas 12–71, Derrick 8–56, Morris 7–44, Harris 10–43,
Baker 5–29, Pricer 4–24, J. O'Neal 4–10, Sandefer 1–4, Holland 4–(–5)

Passing

McDonald 1–1–0 = 23, Baker 2–1–0 = 10, J. O'Neal 3–1–0 = 7, Harris 1–0–0
= 0

Receiving

Stiller 1–23, Timberlake 1–10, Baker 1–7

SOONERS WHO PLAYED (35)

LE: Stiller, Long, Coyle, B. Harris
RE: Bell, Timberlake, Rector
LT: Ballard, Searcy, Fitch
QB: J. Harris, J. O'Neal, Holland
LG: Oujesky, Powell, Jennings
LH: McDonald, Baker, Sandefer
C: Tubbs, Harrison, Scott
RH: Thomas, Derrick, Dodd
RG: Krisher, D. Jennings, Gwinn
FB: Pricer, Morris, Brown, Rolle
RT: Emerson, Ladd, Lawrence

SCORING

Touchdowns: McDonald 2, Thomas, Timberlake, Baker
Conversions: J. Harris 2, Baker 2
Officials: Bob Finley (SMU), M. G. Volz (Nebraska), Earl Schlupp (Colorado),
Alex George (Notre Dame)

Oklahoma:	7	20	7	0 = 34
Kansas:	6	0	0	6 = 12

OKLAHOMA 40   NOTRE DAME 0

OU		ND
12	First Downs	16
4–5	Passes Completed	11–19
88	Passing Yards	99
147	Rushing Yards	119
235	Total Yards	218
4–99	Pass Interceptions	0–0
5–42.6	Punting	5–23
2	Fumbles Lost	2
50 yds.	Penalties	20 yds.

INDIVIDUAL STATISTICS
Rushing
Thomas 11–69, McDonald 12–52, Jim Harris 7–23, Holland 3–12, Pricer 2–9, Morris 1–1, Derrick 1–1, Jay O'Neal 1–1, Dodd 2–(–6), Baker 3–(–15)

Passing
Jim Harris 3–3–0 = 39, McDonald 2–1–0 = 49

Receiving
Thomas 2–57, McDonald 1–17, Bell 1–14

SOONERS WHO PLAYED (40)
LE: Stiller, Long, Coyle, B. Harris
RE: Bell, Timberlake, Rector, Hood
LT: Gray, Searcy, Ballard
QB: J. Harris, J. O'Neal, Holland
LG: Oujesky, S. Jennings, Powell
LH: McDonald, Baker, Pellow, Sandefer
C: Tubbs, Harrison, Scott
RH: Thomas, Dodd, Derrick, Day
RG: Krisher, D. Jennings, Shilling
FB: Pricer, Morris, Brown, Rolle
RT: Emerson, Ladd, Gwinn, Lawrence

SCORING
Touchdowns: Thomas 2, McDonald, Jim Harris, Bell, J. O'Neal
Conversions: Dodd, Jim Harris 3
Officials: Rollie Barnum, John Waldorf (Missouri), Herm Rohrig (Nebraska), Archie Morrow

Oklahoma:	13	13	7	7 = 40
Notre Dame:	0	0	0	0 = 0

OKLAHOMA 27　　　　COLORADO 19

OU		CU
23	First Downs	12
6–12	Passes Completed	1–4
86	Passing Yards	8
348	Rushing Yards	242
434	Total Yards	250
0–0	Pass Interceptions	2–0
4–30	Punting	9–41
3	Fumbles Lost	1
93 yds.	Penalties	94 yds.

INDIVIDUAL STATISTICS
Rushing
Thomas 15–93, McDonald 15–73, Pricer 10–42, Dodd 8–39, Baker 9–33, Jay O'Neal 8–31, Jim Harris 7–25, Morris 2–12

Passing
Jim Harris 8–5–1 = 80, McDonald 2–1–1 = 6, Thomas 1–1–0 = 0, Dodd 1–0–0 = 0

Receiving
Thomas 3–27, McDonald 2–45, Pricer 1–14

SOONERS WHO PLAYED (23)
LE: Stiller, Coyle
RE: Bell, Timberlake
LT: Gray, Searcy, Ballard
QB: J. Harris, J. O'Neal
LG: Oujesky, S. Jennings
LH: McDonald, Baker
C: Tubbs, Harrison
RH: Thomas
RG: Krisher, D. Jennings

FB: Pricer, Morris
RT: Emerson, Ladd

SCORING

Touchdowns: McDonald 2, Thomas 2
Conversions: Jim Harris 3
Officials: Mike Oberhelman (Kansas State), John Waldorf (Missouri), Buzz
Rosky (Duke), Herman Rohrig (Nebraska)

| Oklahoma: | 6 | 0 | 14 | 7 = 27 |
| Colorado: | 7 | 12 | 0 | 0 = 19 |

OKLAHOMA 44   IOWA STATE 0

OU		IS
21	First Downs	4
6–9	Passes Completed	1–4
104	Passing Yards	11
339	Rushing Yards	84
443	Total Yards	95
1–78	Pass Interceptions	0–0
1–35	Punting	10–29.8
4	Fumbles Lost	2
75 yds.	Penalties	76 yds.

INDIVIDUAL STATISTICS
Rushing

McDonald 10–97, Thomas 1–49, Derrick 5–42, Harris 9–32, Dodd 6–28,
Pricer 4–18, Sherrod 3–18, Sandefer 3–15, Holland 3–15, Pellow 2–11, Baker
1–9, Morris 1–4, Rolle 1–3

Passing

Jim Harris 6–4–0 = 77, Baker 1–1–0 = 15, Sherrod 2–1–0 = 12

Receiving

Stiller 2–30, Thomas 1–36, Timberlake 1–15, McDonald 1–11, Derrick 1–12

SOONERS WHO PLAYED (36)

LE: Stiller, Long, Coyle
RE: Bell, Timberlake, Rector
LT: Gray, Searcy, Ballard
QB: J. Harris, J. O'Neal, Sherrod, Holland
LG: Oujesky, S. Jennings, Powell
LH: McDonald, Baker, Sandefer
C: Tubbs, Harrison, Lynn Burris
RH: Thomas, Dodd, Carpenter
RG: Krisher, D. Jennings, Gwinn
FB: Pricer, Morris, Brown, Rolle
RT: Emerson, Ladd, Lawrence

SCORING

Touchdowns: McDonald 2, Thomas 2, Dodd, Stiller, Tubbs
Conversions: Pricer 2
Officials: Mike Oberhelman (Kansas State), Dick Sklar (Kansas), Earl Schlupp (Colorado), Alex George (Notre Dame)

Oklahoma:	13	19	6	6 = 44
Iowa State:	0	0	0	0 = 0

OKLAHOMA 36   MISSOURI 14

OU		MU
20	First Downs	20
17	Rushing	13
3	Passing	7
5–14	Passes Completed	12–29
138	Passing Yards	122
464	Rushing Yards	201
602	Total Yards	323
4–54	Pass Interceptions	1–0
2–47	Punting	3–27.7
5 of 7	Fumbles Lost	3 of 7
8–80	Penalties	2–20

INDIVIDUAL STATISTICS
Rushing
McDonald 11–136, Jim Harris 5–50, Thomas 7–49, Baker 6–41, Pricer 5–31, Dodd 3–30, Pellow 3–27, Day 2–25, Sandefer 3–24, Brown 2–20, J. O'Neal 2–(–8)

Passing
Jim Harris 5–3–0 = 88, McDonald 4–2–0 = 50, Dodd 1–0–0 = 0, Sherrod 1–0–0 = 0, Holland 1–0–0 = 0, B. O'Neal 1–0–0 = 0, Crossland 1–0–0 = 0

Receiving
Stiller 3–88, Thomas 2–50

SOONERS WHO PLAYED (57)
LE: Stiller, Long, Coyle, B. Harris, Martin, Buck
RE: Bell, Timberlake, Rector, Hood, Bowman
LT: Gray, Searcy, Ballard, D. Nelson
QB: J. Harris, J. O'Neal, Sherrod, Holland, Crossland
LG: Oujesky, S. Jennings, Powell, Broyles, Johnson
LH: McDonald, Baker, Sandefer, Pellow, Lyle Burris
C: Tubbs, Harrison, Lynn Burris, Scott, Talbott
RH: Thomas, Dodd, Derrick, Day, B. O'Neal
RG: Krisher, D. Jennings, Gwinn, Shilling
FB: Pricer, Brown, Rolle, Depue, Evans
RT: Emerson, Ladd, Lawrence, Corbitt, Hays

SCORING
Touchdowns: McDonald 2, Thomas 2, Dodd, Stiller, Sandefer, Sherrod, Baker, Pellow
Conversions: Harris 3, Dodd 2, O'Neal, Rolle
Officials: Cliff Ogden (Wichita), Clarence Kellog (St. Mary's), John Lloyd, Herm Rohrig (Nebraska)

Missouri:	0	0	0	14 = 14
Oklahoma:	7	27	19	14 = 67

OKLAHOMA 54   NEBRASKA 6

OU		NU
24	First Downs	14
21	Rushing	11
3	Passing	3
6–12	Passes Completed	7–24
150	Passing Yards	80
506	Rushing Yards	172
656	Total Yards	196
2–11	Pass Interceptions	0–0
2–32	Punting	9–30–3
3–4	Fumbles Lost	2–4
8–80	Penalties	6–36

INDIVIDUAL STATISTICS
Rushing
Thomas 8–100, McDonald 11–91, Harris 11–76, Brown 2–56, Dodd 3–40, Pricer 3–28, Rolle 3–22, Sandefer 7–21, Sherrod 3–21, J. O'Neal 4–14, Depue 3–13, Holland 2–7, Baker 1–5, Derrick 4–5, Pellow 3–3, Lyle Burris 2–5, Day 1–3, Crossland 2–(–5)

Passing
Harris 6–2–0 = 71, Sherrod 1–1–0 = 31, Baker 2–2–0 = 30, Dodd 1–1–0 = 18

Receiving
McDonald 2–77, Thomas 1–25, Long 1–18, Timberlake 1–18, Dodd 1–12

SOONERS WHO PLAYED (56)
LE: Stiller, Long, Coyle, B. Harris, Martin, Buck
RE: Bell, Timberlake, Rector, Hood, Bowman
LT: Gray, Searcy, Ballard, Fitch, Nelson
QB: J. Harris, J. O'Neal, Sherrod, Holland, Crossland
LG: Oujesky, S. Jennings, Powell, Broyles, Johnson
LH: McDonald, Baker, Sandefer, Pellow, Lyle Burris
C: Tubbs, Harrison, Lynn Burris, Scott, Talbott

RH: Thomas, Dodd, Derrick, Day, B. O'Neal

RG: Krisher, D. Jennings, Gwinn, Shilling

FB: Pricer, Brown, Rolle, Depue, Evans

RT: Emerson, Ladd, Lawrence, Corbitt, Hays

SCORING

Touchdowns: McDonald 2, Dodd 2, Harris 2, Brown, Sherrod

Conversions: Harris 2, Dodd 2, J. O'Neal, Ballard

Officials: Cliff Ogden (Wichita), Bud Knox (Des Moines), Ben Beckerman (Iowa), Alex George (Notre Dame)

Nebraska:	0	6	0	0 = 6
Oklahoma:	14	20	13	7 = 54

OKLAHOMA 53   OKLAHOMA A&M 0

OU		A&M
33	First Downs	6
7–14	Passes Completed	1–7
89	Passing Yards	18
520	Rushing Yards	72
609	Total Yards	90
2–47	Pass Interceptions	1–10
2–47	Punting	10–36
4–6	Fumbles Lost	1–1
6–52	Penalties	3–21

INDIVIDUAL STATISTICS

Rushing

Thomas 15–23, McDonald 13–75, Pricer 7–70, Harris 11–67, Baker 9–46, Derrick 5–36, Brown 4–34, Pellow 3–21, Rolle 3–15, Dodd 4–14, J. O'Neal 4–8, Sherrod 3–7, Gray 1–2

Passing

Harris 3–1 = 27, Baker 3–2 = 25, O'Neal 1–1 = 19, McDonald 1–1 = 8, Sherrod 2–1 = 6, Holland 1–1 = 4, Dodd 2–0 = 0, Thomas 1–0 = 0

Receiving

Dodd 3–44, Thomas 1–8, McDonald 1–27, Coyle 1–6, Pellow 1–4

SOONERS WHO PLAYED (42)

LE: Stiller, Long, Coyle, B. Harris
RE: Bell, Timberlake, Rector, Hood
LT: Gray, Searcy, Ballard, Holland
QB: J. Harris, J. O'Neal, Sherrod
LG: Oujesky, S. Jennings, Powell, Broyles, Pellow
LH: McDonald, Baker, Sandefer
C: Tubbs, Harrison, Lynn Burris, Scott, Day
RH: Thomas, Dodd, Derrick
RG: Krisher, D. Jennings, Gwinn
FB: Pricer, Brown, Rolle, Depue
RT: Emerson, Ladd, Lawrence

SCORING

Touchdowns: Thomas 2, Baker 2, Pricer, J. O'Neal, McDonald, Gray
Conversions: Harris 2, Dodd 2, Baker
Officials: Harold Matthews (Hardin Simmons), M. G. Volz (Nebraska), Earl Janson (Illinois), Ben Beckerman (Iowa), Alex George (Notre Dame)

Oklahoma:	12	21	13	7 = 53
Oklahoma A&M:	0	0	0	0 = 0

BUD WILKINSON'S COACHING RECORD AT THE UNIVERSITY OF OKLAHOMA

145 wins, 29 loses, 4 ties, .826 %, Three National Championships

1947

24	Detroit	20
26	Texas A&M	14
14	Texas	34
13	Kansas	13
7	Texas Christian	20
27	Iowa State	9
27	Kansas State	13
21	Missouri	12
14	Nebraska	13
21	Oklahoma A&M	13

1948

17	Santa Clara	20
42	Texas A&M	14
20	Texas	14
42	Kansas State	0
21	Texas Christian	18
33	Iowa State	6
41	Missouri	7
60	Kansas	7
19	Oklahoma A&M	15
SUGAR BOWL		
14	North Carolina	6

1949

46	Boston College	0
33	Texas A&M	3
20	Texas	14
48	Kansas	26
48	Nebraska	0
34	Iowa State	0
39	Kansas State	0
28	Santa Clara	21
41	Oklahoma A&M	0
SUGAR BOWL		
35	LSU	0

1950 National Champions

28	Boston College	0
34	Texas A&M	28
14	Texas	13
58	Kansas State	0
20	Iowa State	7
27	Colorado	18
33	Kansas	13
41	Missouri	7
49	Nebraska	35
41	Oklahoma A&M	14
SUGAR BOWL		
7	Kentucky	13

1951

49	William and Mary	7
7	Texas A&M	14
7	Texas	9
33	Kansas	21
33	Colorado	14
33	Kansas State	0
34	Missouri	20
35	Iowa State	6
27	Nebraska	6
41	Oklahoma A&M	6

1952

21	Colorado	21
49	Pittsburg	20
49	Texas	20
42	Kansas	20
49	Kansas State	6
41	Iowa State	0
21	Notre Dame	27
34	Nebraska	13
54	Oklahoma A&M	7

1953

21	Notre Dame	29
7	Pittsburg	7
19	Texas	14
45	Kansas	0
27	Colorado	20
34	Kansas State	0
14	Missouri	7
30	Nebraska	7
42	Oklahoma A&M	7
ORANGE BOWL		
7	Maryland	0

1954

27	California	13
21	Texas Christian	16
14	Texas	7
65	Kansas	0
21	Kansas State	0
13	Colorado	6
40	Iowa State	0
34	Missouri	13
55	Nebraska	7
14	Oklahoma A&M	0

1955 National Champions

13	North Carolina	6
26	Pittsburg	14
20	Texas	0
44	Kansas	6
56	Colorado	21
40	Kansas State	7
20	Missouri	0
52	Iowa State	0
41	Nebraska	0
53	Oklahoma A&M	0

ORANGE BOWL

20	Maryland	6

1956 National Champions

36	North Carolina	0
66	Kansas State	0
45	Texas	0
34	Kansas	12
40	Notre Dame	0
27	Colorado	19
44	Iowa State	0
67	Missouri	14
54	Nebraska	6
53	Oklahoma A&M	0

1957

26	Pittsburg	0
40	Iowa State	14
21	Texas	7
47	Kansas	0
14	Colorado	22
13	Kansas State	0
39	Missouri	14
0	Notre Dame	7
0	Notre Dame	7
53	Oklahoma State	6

ORANGE BOWL

48	Duke	21

1958

47	West Virginia	14
6	Oregon	0
14	Texas	15
43	Kansas	0
40	Kansas State	6
23	Colorado	7
20	Iowa State	0
39	Missouri	0
40	Nebraska	7
7	Oklahoma State	0

ORANGE BOWL

21	Syracuse	6

1959

13	Northwestern	45
42	Colorado	12
12	Texas	19
23	Missouri	0
7	Kansas	6
21	Nebraska	25
36	Kansas State	0
28	Army	20
35	Iowa State	12
17	Oklahoma State	7

1961

6	Notre Dame	19
15	Iowa State	21
7	Texas	28
0	Kansas	10
14	Colorado	22
17	Kansas State	6
7	Missouri	0
14	Army	8
21	Nebraska	14
21	Oklahoma State	13

1960

3	Northwestern	19
15	Pittsburg	14
0	Texas	24
13	Kansas	13
49	Kansas State	7
0	Colorado	7
6	Iowa State	10
19	Missouri	41
14	Nebraska	17
17	Oklahoma State	6

1962

7	Syracuse	3
7	Notre Dame	13
6	Texas	9
13	Kansas	7
47	Kansas State	0
62	Colorado	0
41	Iowa State	0
13	Missouri	0
34	Nebraska	6
37	Oklahoma State	6
ORANGE BOWL		
0	Alabama	17

1963

31	Clemson	14
17	Southern Cal.	12
7	Texas	28
21	Kansas	18
34	Kansas State	9
35	Colorado	0
24	Iowa State	14
13	Missouri	3
20	Nebraska	29
34	Oklahoma State	10

INDEX

Mitchell, Bobby, 140, 236
Mitchell, Dale, 74
Mix, Hal, 143
Montana, Joe, 47
Moore, Archie, 196
Moore, Lenny, 121
Morris, Bob, 96
Morris, Dennit, 96–97
Morrow, Bobby, 196
Munoz, Anthony, 93
Murphy, Jim, 184
Murray State Junior College, 103

Nagurski, Bronco, Jr., 99
National Collegiate Athletic
    Association, 12, 152, 239
National Football League, 85, 93,
    122, 140, 157, 236–37
National Football League Hall of
    Fame, xxviii
Nebraska. *See* University of
    Nebraska
Nelson, Don, 65, 199
Nelson, Lindsey, 112
New Mexico. *See* University of
    New Mexico
New York City, 94, 111, 127,
    161, 180
New York Giants, 122, 143
New York Times, 3
New York Times Magazine, 19
New York Yankees, xxvii, 54, 74,
    75
Newcombe, Don, 36, 54, 75,
    127
Newman, Chuck, 199
Newman, Howard, 25, 26
Neyland, Robert, xxiv, 146
Nichols, John, xix, 243

Noble, Lloyd, 50
Norman, Okla., 53, 72, 76, 92,
    125, 143, 158–59, 187–88,
    192, 215, 212-22; OU games
    in, xvii, xxv, 27, 35–36, 38,
    43, 45, 55, 112, 162, 178,
    182, 245–47; Norman High
    School, xx, xxii, 221; Town
    Tavern, 29; Benton Ladd's
    memories of, 103–5, 108;
    Prentice Gautt's memories of,
    230–31, 234, 240–41
North Carolina. *See* University of
    North Carolina
North Carolina State University,
    38
Northcutt, Ken, 42, 183
Northwestern University, and
    Chez Paris food-poisoning
    incident, 213–32; OU's loss
    to, 235
Notre Dame. *See* University of
    Notre Dame

O'Brien, Perry, 196
O'Neal, Benton, 199. *See also*
    Appendix
O'Neal, Jay, in OU–North
    Carolina game, 41; relation-
    ship with teammates, 46, 166,
    201, 204, 209, 211; in
    OU–Kansas State game, 58;
    in OU–Kansas game, 97; in
    OU–Notre Dame game, 113;
    in OU–Missouri game, 164;
    in OU–Nebraska game, 183;
    in OU–Oklahoma A&M
    game, 198. *See also* Appendix
O Club, 178